Automania

Julian Pettifer and Nigel Turner

Automania

Man and the Motor Car

COLLINS
8 Grafton Street, London W1
1984

William Collins Sons and Co Ltd
London · Glasgow · Sydney · Auckland · Toronto · Johannesburg

This publication is based on the television series Automania
produced by Central Independent Television plc.

CENTRAL

Pettifer, Julian
Automania.
1. Automobiles Social aspects
I. Title II. Turner, Nigel, *19*---
306'.46 HE5613

First published 1984

ISBN 0 00217134 1

Typeset in Monophoto Ehrhardt
by Ace Filmsetting Ltd, Frome
Colour originated by Gilchrist Bros., Leeds
Printed by William Collins Sons & Co. Ltd, Glasgow

Contents

Acknowledgements

Since *Automania* was written while we were making the television series of the same name, we wish to say a special word of thanks to all our colleagues at Central Television, Birmingham for their enthusiastic support, and especially to our three tireless researchers: Deborah Richardson in New York and Jane Mercer and Susan Winter in London. To directors Ashley Bruce, Nigel Warrack and Michael Weigall and production assistants Josephine Chawnor, Bryony Kinnear, Peggy Morris and Julie Stoner we also extend our grateful thanks.

In addition we are deeply indebted to scores of individuals and institutions around the world who were ungrudgingly generous with their time, advice and research material:

In *Asia* J. Y. Chung, S. W. Chon and Stan Lee of the Hyundai Motor Co., South Korea. Akira Hosono of the Toyota Motor Sales Co., Satoshi Kamata, Yasuhiro Kano and Eigi Takanuma, Japan. Aida Mendoza and the Lady Drivers Association, Romeo Ordinario, Francisco Motors, Manila. P. S. Pashricha and A. F. S. Talyarkhan, Bombay. Alan Scott, David Roads and Winnie Pong, Hong Kong. Joginder Tandon, Mike, Ishwar and Harsaran Pandey and the Maruti Car Co., and Romesh Thapar, Delhi.

In *Australia* John Bremner of General Motors Holdens, Pedr Davis, Muriel Dorney, Suzy and Gerald Dunn, Evan Green, Sir Lawrence Hartnett, Brian McKibbin, Eric Montgomery, Tony Packard, John L., George Roberts, Helen Styles, Dr. Gordon Trinca, Bill Tuckey, Peter Wherrett.

In *Brazil* J. Amardeil, Maria Dos Anjos, Moyra Ashford, Agostinhu E. C. Gaspar and Bob Garretty of the Ford Motor Co., Brazil. Lauro Cavalcanti and Dinah Guimaraens, Phillip Gold, Jose Goldenberg, Joao Gurgel, Jose Medeiros, Francisco Onetto.

In *Continental Europe* Marc Charlan, Johannes Christ of Mercedes-Benz, Luigi Colani, Countess Frochot, Jean Panhard, Sergio Pininfarina, Fritz Schlumpf, Eduard Siedler, Werner Webber, Gunther Weischmann.

In Great Britain we made extensive use of the magnificent automobile archives of Peter Blair Richley. To Peter and his wife Joan a special word of appreciation for their help and hospitality. Our thanks also to Roy Axe, Andy Barr and Mark Snowden of Austin-Rover; Col. Eric Barrass, Rolls-Royce Enthusiasts Club; Stephen Bayley, Bill Boddy, David Boole of Jaguar Cars; Barbara Cartland, Victor Gauntlett of Aston Martin Lagonda; William Hancock, Dr James Hemming, Eric Johnson of Mercedes-Benz UK; Sir Godfrey Llewellyn, Brian Palmer, Sir William Lyons, Murray Mackay, Mike McCarthy, Lord Montagu of Beaulieu, David Presland, Ian Robinson, John Tyme, Michael Ware, Gerald Wingrove.

In the United States the Henry Austin Clark Junior collection of automobilia is justly renowned. To Mr Clark and his staff at Glen Cove, Long Island, we are especially indebted. Our thanks also to Scott Bailey, David Bausch, Warren Belasco, Michael Berger, Roger Billings, B. A. Boaz of the National Highway Traffic Safety Administration, Dr Joyce Brothers, Blaine A. Brownell, Jan H. Brunvand, Gordon Buehrig, David Cole, Keith E. Crain, David E. Davis Jr, James Dunn, Elizabeth Elliot, James Flink, Don Friedman, Paul Gikas, Joe Girard, Carol Golin, Bill Harding, Bill Harrison, Walter Hayes of the Ford Motor Co., G. Herman, Kenneth Hey, Ray Holland, Chuck Jordan and the General Motors Corp., Maryann Keller, Ben Kelly of the National Highway Insurance Institute, Beverley Rae Kimes, Philip C. Kwiatowski of the Alfred P. Sloan Museum, Hugh Lesley, David Lewis, Chester Liebs, Candy Lightner, the Low Conspiracy, New Style and New Classics car clubs, San José, California; Leon Mandel, Ray Manning, Keith Marvin, Roy Matthew, Clay McShane, Ruth Metzger, Richard Michaels, Bill Mitchell, Ralph Nader; Harry and Vicky Nelson and Sgt.Larry Brown in Muncie; Jack Nethercutt; Byron Matson and Laurelle LeVine at San Sylmar; Miller Nicholls, David Phillips, John Rae, Charles Sandford, Julian Smith, Peter Smith, Jane and Michael Stern, Dick Teague, C. Gayle Warnock; James Wren and Bernice L. Huffman of the Motor Vehicle Manufacturers Assoc., Detroit; Brock Yates and the late Alice Ramsey.

10 H.P.
Arth. Thiele

40 H.P.
Arth. Thiele

60 H.P.
Arth. Thiele

80 H.P.
Arth. Thiele

A Most Exciting Toy

'Glorious, stirring sight!' murmured Toad, never offering to move. 'The poetry of motion, the real way to travel! The only way to travel! Here today – in next week tomorrow! Villages skipped, towns and cities jumped – always somebody else's horizon! O bliss! O poop poop! O my! O my!'

(Toad of Toad Hall on first seeing and falling in love with the motor car –
Kenneth Grahame, *The Wind in the Willows*, 1908)

From the very beginning man's relationship with the motor car was a manic affair. No other inanimate object has in our century inspired such a close and involved relationship with its creator or triggered such an outpouring of love, hate and obsession.

In its first one hundred years of active life it has been described as a menace and a blessing, a blight and a godsend, as a saviour of our countryside and cities and as their curse, as socially divisive and as the greatest social leveller. It has been worshipped and reviled, celebrated and scorned. On the subject of the car no one is neutral because it is arguably the most powerful instrument of social change mankind has ever encountered. In barely a century the motor car has reshaped society in its image and in the process has become both part of man's personality and an expression of it. But what has been the basis of the passionate relationship between mankind and the motor car – that we here call 'automania'?

The car began life as a rich man's toy rather than as a means of transport or as an instrument of social change, although those possibilities were quickly realized. At the root of 'automania' has always been man's incredible enthusiasm for the machine itself, the constant factor which was established in the 1890s and has shown little sign of diminishing.

It is not hard to see why. The coming of the motor car was the fulfilment of one of man's most ancient dreams of the 'horseless carriage', self-propelled and capable of extraordinary speeds. For centuries man had fantasized about the glories of such independent travel. Roger Bacon, the thirteenth-century scientist and philosopher, had written of the day when 'we shall endow chariots with incredible speed, without the aid of any animal'. By the 1890s, the bicycle had given the average man a foretaste of the possibilities of individualized long-distance road transportation, creating a demand that neither the horse nor the railway could satisfy. Thousands of riders had acquired a passion for speedy mechanical road transport, entirely under their own control, which could at least take them a little way towards the horizon. The cycle craze of the 1890s put 10 million Americans on their personal pair of wheels. For the wealthy and intrepid the emergence of the motor car was a great step forward in the furtherance of that ultimate dream. Drivers found they experienced an innate sensory pleasure derived from speed, motion and power under control. 'There are few people who want a slow automobile after having ridden in a moderately fast one', commented an early 'scorcher' in *The Horseless Age*, in March 1902. And if the first vehicles of the 1890s were stuttering, asthmatic runabouts of extreme unreliability that could barely outpace a horse, the larger models that appeared after 1900 gave drivers the opportunity of unprecedented speed and manoeuvrability. Speeding cyclists, known as 'cads on castors', were swiftly replaced by a new highway menace, the 'road hog'. There was an

Early motoring attire seemed as outlandish to contemporary eyes as it now does to ours.
A German view: the greater the horse-power, the more bizarre the garb.

insatiable demand for more and more power, and many of the cars began to feature silencer cut-outs, allowing their speeding owners to enjoy more fully the ear-shattering noise of the engine in full cry. Cars went so fast so quickly. As early as 1907, S. F. Edge was able to celebrate the opening of the Brooklands Circuit by covering 1582 miles in twenty-four hours in his Napier. The phrase 'going like sixty' came to connote the devil-may-care attitude of the early 'scorcher'. Early 'exoticars' such as the 1903 Mercedes 'Sixty' model, heralded as 'the car of the day after tomorrow', could attain 80 m.p.h. in racing trim. John Bolster in *The Upper Crust* relived the emotions of being in control of such a car:

You are a god among men, singing exultantly at the top of your voice, crouching over the wheel to cleave the wind, willing this marvellous machine to go faster, faster, faster . . . and while the dusty macadam seems to have become as narrow as a plank, you are staying alive because your skill and the strength of your arms are alone keeping the wayward monster from dashing itself to pieces against the trees. It is not frightening, because you are drunk with the sheer exhilaration of it!

For pioneer automaniacs driving at speed, as Toad of Toad Hall discovered, was an intoxicating thrill in which too often 'all sense of right and wrong, all fear of obvious consequences, seemed temporarily suspended'. It led, as we shall see, to much of the early hostility to the motorist and mayhem on the roads.

Alfred Harmsworth, press baron and one of Britain's first motorists, knew how to travel in style in 1900. While he enjoyed the fun of the open road in his Panhard Levassor, a support vehicle followed closely behind complete with provisions and serving man.

Abundant auto enthusiasm was also required to withstand the explosions, fires, breakdowns and ridicule. Early drivers travelled hopefully and often did not arrive. 'Personally, I used to become depressed if my car went particularly well', wrote Charles Jarrot, the English racing driver, in 1906, 'because this always preceded some great catastrophe.' In the United States, the state of Tennessee demanded one week's notice before the commencement of a car trip. A typical auto 'tourist kit' in 1906 weighed eighteen pounds and contained thirty-eight wrenches and screwdrivers. The Saks and Company Emergency Motorist Kit included four pounds of meat and two pounds of chocolate. In England, when the eleventh Duke of Bedford made a car journey, he sent a servant in advance to reconnoitre the entire route . . . Anti-motorist legislation on both sides of the Atlantic was frequently ludicrous. Britain's 'Red Flag Act', repealed in 1896, is well known. What is less well known is the Motor Car Act of 1903 which imposed licensing of drivers and vehicles and raised the general speed limit to a heady 20 m.p.h. Amazingly that limit remained in force until 1930. In the United States one bill, stemming from the road locomotive days, demanded that any self-propelled vehicle must come to a complete halt upon approaching any cross-roads. Thereupon, 'The engineer must thoroughly examine the roadway ahead and sound his horn vigorously. Then halloo loudly or ring a gong . . . discharge a Roman candle, Vesuvius bomb or some other explosive device as final warning of his approach.' Frightening horses incurred huge fines. The first motorist to drive up New York's Broadway in his French De Dion Bouton was a gentleman called Philip Hagel. It was an expensive excursion. He had to pay out $48,000 in damages to owners of those horses terrified by their first sighting of a horseless carriage. One law that definitely favoured Old Dobbin demanded that, should a horse refuse to pass a particular car, the driver must then camouflage his vehicle with a cloth painted to look like a landscape . . .

Early enthusiasts, variously known as autocarists, chauffeurs or autoneers, even had difficulty in giving a name to the newfangled novelty. Autowain, self-motor, petrocar, autobat, diamote, autogo, pneumobile and ipsometer were some of the more serious contenders. In 1895 a Chicago newspaper awarded a $500 prize for the best name. The winner was 'motocycle' . . . The *New York Times* in an editorial of January 1899 fulminated against the French term 'automobile' – and even against the car itself:

There is something uncanny about these newfangled vehicles. They are unutterably ugly and never a one of them has been provided with a good or even endurable name. The French, who are usually orthodox in their etymology if nothing else, have evolved 'automobile' which being half Greek and half Latin is so near to indecent that we print it with hesitation . . .

To the world at large the motorist of the 1890s and his vehicle were bizarre objects. Charles Duryea, the American pioneer automobile manufacturer, read the public mind best of all in one of his early promotions. After taking part in the London to Brighton 'Emancipation Run' in November 1896, he returned to the United States to appear with his car in Barnum and Bailey's circus . . . between the Indian elephant act and the ape-man from Borneo.

Man's ardour for his new toy was unquenchable. Rudyard Kipling, an avid pioneer motorist, expressed the view of many when he wrote in April 1904:

Mr. Blast, Mrs. Blast, Billie Blast,
Bessie Blast, the blasted Car, and the whole Blasted Family!!

The pleasures to be gained from early motoring – and the pains, with explosions, breakdowns and accidents. But even between colliding motorists, united in a common enthusiasm, there was always perfect courtesy.

I like motoring because I have suffered for its sake. Any fool can invent anything as any fool can want to buy the invention when it is thoroughly perfected, but the men to reverence, to admire, to write odes and erect statues to, are those Prometheuses and Ixions (Maniacs, *you used to call us*) *who chase the inchoate idea to fixity up and down the King's Highway, with their red right shoulders to the wheel.*

This heroic self-image is an important element in the whole development of the intense relationship between man and the automobile. 'Auto' equals self. Automobiles meant autonomy, freedom from horses and blacksmiths, trains and overcrowded trolleys and trams. Automobiles also meant self-reliance. Each difficulty gave the motorist the chance to demonstrate his reflexes, his skill, his intrepidness . . . From the beginning cars served as an infinitely adaptable canvas for self-expression.

In 1899 the belles of America's summer society at Newport, in perhaps the earliest example of 'customizing' and 'cruising', were lovingly decorating their automobiles with yellow field flowers and green and white clematis, and taking part in midnight motor parades in which 'every vehicle was brilliantly illuminated with countless little glow lights interspersed among the floral wreaths'. Eulogized *The Automobile Magazine*: 'Thus the procession of scintilating vehicles sped swiftly over the dark country roads . . . like a veritable pageant of fairy chariots. A belated stage driver, pulling up his horses on the Post Road, rubbed his eyes in wonder. To him and his snorting steeds it was like a whiff of the century to come!' As cars' speed, mechanical refinement and luxury increased, so did the opportunities for their owners to make personal statements about themselves to the world. Cars became appendages of their masters. Even by 1900, a mere fifteen years after the car's creation, there were 600 makes in France, 60 in the USA, 110 in Great Britain, 80 in Germany and 20 in Italy from which to choose.

Out for a spin in 1906. Sabattier's tongue-in-cheek portrayal of a Parisian family sporting typical motoring fashions of the day.

Owners were making personal statements about themselves through their cars from the very beginning. This 1892 Peugeot, the world's first 'customized car', belonged to the Bey of Tunis.

In 1904 the car was strictly a rich man's toy. At a time when a working man's salary was $600 a year, a powerful touring car could cost as much as $7000. Wealthy participants in the New York to St Louis Tour in the spring of 1904 line up in front of the impressive mansion home of William K. Vanderbilt, one of America's earliest and most avid automobilists.

In Europe, particularly from 1905 onwards, when cars became elegant and also acquired windscreens, wealthy automaniacs were able to indulge their greatest fantasies with all kinds of exotic coachwork, such as the *limousines de voyage* created for them by Paris coachbuilders like Kellner, Rothschild and Labourdette. These featured fully equipped kitchens, silk brocade armchairs that could be converted into beds, and in the case of one wealthy American a built-in flush toilet. Royalty around the world was swift to place its imprimatur on the car. The preferred automobile of kings, emperors and heads of state was also French – the Delauney-Belleville, 'The Car Magnificent', and its most enthusiastic royal customer was the Czar of Russia. British royalty favoured the Coventry Daimler, and it was only later that Rolls-Royce acquired its laurels as the Best Car in the World.

As the newfangled device became more reliable and ever grander, the motorist ceased to be an object of ribaldry and more the member of an envied elite – the new 'cavalry of the highway' – a master race, frightening in appearance, with its own extraordinary garb of caps and goggles, turbans and veils, goatskin coats and, in the United States, parkas lined with wombat fur. For Frenchmen, a whole epoch lives in the phrase *peau de bique* – though not all such coats were made of goatskin. One firm even advertised '*peau de bique* coats made from genuine mink'.

In France Tristan Bernard, as early as 1904, was even drawing satisfaction from breakdowns. Cars, he found, exalted their owners. They established status instantly – as the crowds gathered it was a good time to show off, to draw the admiring glances, to act the part of the grand seigneur, a conquistador in passage . . . In 1903 an Englishman, Hugh Rochfort Maxted, after a motoring tour of the Continent and North Africa, wrote of his French motoring experiences in *Three Men in a Car*: 'Some people contend that country folk show a marked hostility towards automobiles, but our experiences in France refute this statement for we, although foreigners, were always received with every civility and afforded ready assistance everywhere . . . even on the highroad the peasants saluted us as we passed.'

But if the car was conceived in Germany and born in France, America was to be its adoptive home. It was there that the motor car was swiftly 'democratized' and where 'automania' was to make its deepest and most lasting impact. Until 1904 the Americans, out of touch with European technical advances, had continued producing small, horseless buggy-type vehicles of a rather hopeless kind, with single or twin cylinder engines set beneath the seat. In 1904 they switched to producing larger cars of the European type with a four cylinder engine mounted at the front. By 1906 they had overtaken France as the world's largest car producer and by 1907 the car was commonly referred to as a necessity. In 1908 General Motors was formed in Detroit and was destined to become the largest company in the

'To be absorbed in the mechanical details of motor cars . . . to spend one's time on them, to think, talk, read about them to the exclusion of real and vital matters – this is to put oneself on a level with stablemen and jockeys,' wrote Filson Young in 1906. Yet King Edward VII of England and King Alphonse XIII of Spain had been avid promoters of the new conveyance from its earliest days, and by 1915 every royal family in Europe had several.

S.M. ALPHONSE XIII
ROI D'ESPAGNE
au volant de sa 12 HP
4 Cylindres De DION-BOUTON

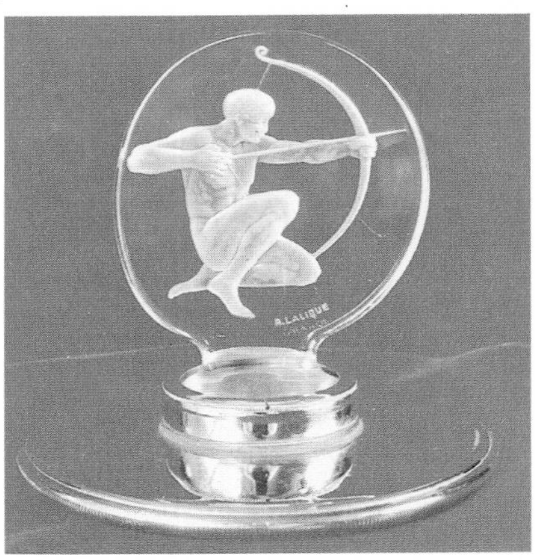

right] Early accessories were many and ingenious. This directional indicator arm fitted to the 1912 Hispano-Suiza Alfonso was illuminated by electric means.

world. In the same year Ford introduced his Model T, 15 million of which were to be made in less than twenty years. By 1920 half of the 8 million cars on American roads were Model Ts.

In the United States automobility was quickly perceived as promoting individualism, as well as mobility. They saw the automobile as a fulfilment of the promise of democracy that every American had an equal chance of success. As James Flink has observed in his *Three Stages of American Automobile Consciousness*: 'The automobile, which tremendously increased the individual's geographic mobility, traditionally closely associated with social mobility in the United States, was certain to be prized by Americans. In our materialistic, migrant society, the motor car was an ideal status symbol.' The early American love affair with the car, was in fact, the confluence of several historically specific situations: namely, a far greater need for individualized car transport in a vast land of scattered communities and poor communications; a higher per capita income and more equal income distribution than Europe; and cars made more affordable by the early adoption of mass production techniques. The automobile was the fullest expression of widespread consumer desires for machines and their perceived benefits.

Nothing expresses the early American euphoria for the car better than the 600 or so songs of Tin Pan Alley devoted to the motoring obsession. Although the passing of the horse was lamented, with the simple 'Whoa Dobbin' and 'I Love My Horse and Wagon But Oh! You Buick Car', the majority of songs if not dealing with the romantic possibilities of the vehicle (which we examine later) were paeans of praise to the new device: 'Hurrah for Henry that Built the Famous Ford' and all its twenty-one verses, and the 'Little Ford Rambled Right Along' which tells us of a car that 'don't need gasoline' and which could be patched up 'with a piece of string, spearmint gum or any old thing'. The Ford, after all, was the product of a thrifty era.

Cars brought people together into friendly association. Motorists pulled each other out of the mud, swapped stories and explored each other's territory, and there developed a camaraderie of the roads, with its own etiquette and jargon. Most Americans were meeting each other for the first time. The 1920s became the common man's age of exploration, the automobile his ship of discovery.

It is a further important feature of 'automania' that from the very beginning owners rapidly established an intimacy with their vehicles, giving them personalities. The typical owner thought of his car as a 'friend' on which he could always rely. In his study of *American Automobiles and Their Buyers* Roger B. White points out that doctors, who were amongst the first non-bluebloods to take to the motor car, 'learned the meanings of various throbs and mechanical motions much as they "took a patient's pulse" and while they worked on them the automobiles became "extensions" of their bodies'.

With a mode of transport as individualistic as the motor car, it was inevitable that man would wish to personalize it, to make it uniquely his own. One of the first car 'customizers' was Lord Montagu of Beaulieu, when he placed a bronze statuette of St Christopher on the dashboard of his 1896 Daimler. Car mascots rapidly caught on and a mammoth car accessory industry grew up devoted to this cause, providing through the years thousands of niceties ranging from acetylene lamps, bulb horns and folding glass windscreens through to mag wheels, hood scoops, steering wheel knobs, go-faster stripes and giant plush dice. For the Model T alone there were an estimated

below] In-car entertainment, 1920s style. The portable 'Superhet' promised music and entertainment wherever you drove. 'With such a set you will be a welcome visitor anywhere,' purchasers were assured.

opposite] Our personalization of the motor car reached its finest flowering with the mascots and hood ornaments that graced some of those Olympian radiators. From top to bottom: the most famous of all, the Silver Lady from a Rolls-Royce. She was designed in 1911 by Charles Sykes, an eminent sculptor, who wanted to depict a girl who 'has selected road travel as her supreme delight and has alighted on the prow of a Rolls-Royce car to travel in the freshness of air and the musical sound of her fluttering draperies'; the devil from a 1912 Léon Bollée; the unmistakable archer from a Pierce-Arrow, in Lalique crystal, and the distinctive flying stork from a Hispano-Suiza.

5000 optional extras and additions. There were even devices to defeat the short-sighted car thief in the form of stuffed Alsatian dogs and inflatable rubber drivers. 'It's so lifelike and terrifying that nobody a foot away can tell it isn't a real live man', promised an ad for Bosco's Collapsible Driver. In car bric-à-brac, however, the Japanese, as in so many things, now lead the world with 'mini-emperor' car chandeliers, 'fizz' space lights 'for being delightful in your private space', tyre manicure sets and in-car fragrances with such fascinating names as 'Grace-Mate', 'Soft 99' and the high-octane sounding 'Racing Spirit'. In the soft furnishings department, car seat covers emblazoned with intriguing – if not baffling – logos proliferate: 'CUTE – I will spend my whole life through loving you'; 'Tampo is Foppery One'; 'Australia Climax: Beautiful Land of the Sea'; and 'Wander Series No 1. We are Grand Dig Mate'. Such inscrutable messages are *de rigueur* for all those anonymous Toyotas, Datsuns and Mazdas.

For status seekers in America and Europe during the 1920s and early 1930s the choice was a less perplexing one. This was the Golden Age of the motor car and its finest flowering as an art form. In this period styling, coachwork and interior appointments reached a pinnacle of excellence in craftsmanship and grandeur of proportion never to be achieved again. In the United States there were Packard, Auburn, Cadillac, Duesenberg; in Europe, Hispano-Suiza, Isotta Fraschini, Bugatti, Rolls-Royce. And for the wealthy the choice was an important one. In *Babbitt*, Sinclair Lewis wrote:

In the city of Zenith, in the barbarous Twentieth Century, a family's motor indicated its social rank as precisely as the grades of the peerage determined the rank of the English family. There was no court to decide whether the second son of a Pierce-Arrow limousine should go into dinner before the first son of a Buick roadster, but of their respective social importance there was no doubt, and where Babbitt as a boy had aspired to the Presidency, his son, Ted, aspired to a Packard Twin Six and an established position in the motored gentry!

Equally in Europe in the 1920s, one could no more appear at a Biarritz or Deauville *concours d'élégance* in last year's Isotta than in last year's fashions. Motor cars enjoyed an artistic life of their own, not only as fashion accessories of the wealthy, but as works of art in their own right. English, Italian and French coachbuilt bodies of rakish line and vivid colour were built to customers' precise specifications, sometimes decked like boats with planking in mahogany or walnut and using dummy rowlocks as doorhandles and ships' ventilators to complete the nautical effect; intricate interiors of lizard and snake skin or silk brocade, and walnut veneers contrasted with satinwood, often with ebony cross-binding. One of the most superlative cars of this period was the 1928 Duesenberg Model J created in homespun Indiana. It cost $18,000 (in Europe more than a Hispano-Suiza or Rolls-Royce) and was capable of 130 m.p.h. in supercharged form. Nothing could equal its sophistication, performance and awesome opulence. In eighteen years barely a thousand cars were made. Clark Gable, Gary Cooper, Mae West and the royal families of Rumania, Spain, Italy and Yugoslavia were customers. Today they fetch prices approaching half a million dollars. Even more exotic was Etorre Bugatti's 12.7 litre Royale of 1929, which he

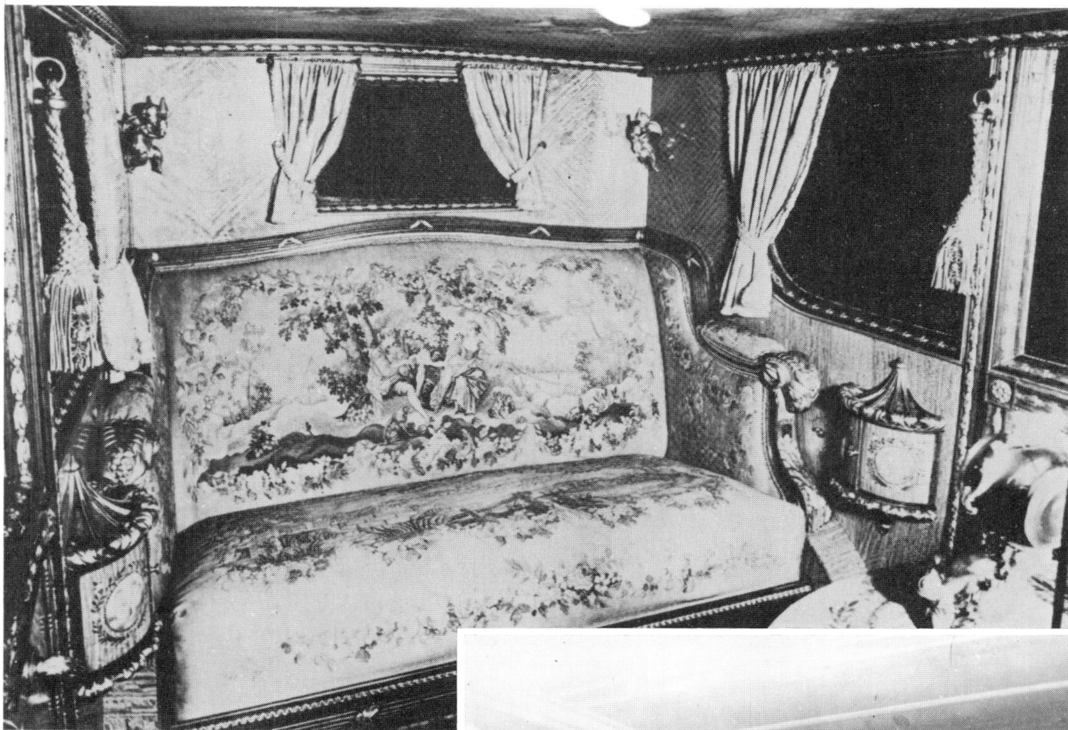

above] The coachbuilder's art reached its apotheosis in the late 1920s. The interior of this 1927 Rolls-Royce Phantom I by Clark of Wolverhampton featured Louis XIV door panels and woodwork, with upholstery in Aubusson petit point.

right] Most early cars bore open coachwork, but the elegant interior of this closed 1912 Lanchester displays all the luxurious trappings that the grand marques inherited direct from the horse-carriage trade.

below] Jean Bugatti, son of Ettore, with his personal Type 41 'Royale' Roadster. He had much of the design genius of his father but was tragically killed in 1939, aged only twenty-seven.

above] The Maharajahs of India commissioned some of the finest motor cars of all. Some have been spirited back into private Western collections. Others soldier on in post-imperial India, occasionally appearing, like the blue and silver Bentley, for a royal wedding in Jaipur.

left] In the 1920s and early 1930s Olympian cars became fashion appendages frequently made to match the elegance of their surroundings. For wealthy automaniacs it was not simply a question of arriving, but *how* you arrived. In Palm Beach, a 1929 Lincoln Sports Phaeton and in London, a 1931 Bentley Tourer.

intended to be the car of kings. Thoroughbred – *pur sang* – was one of Etorre Bugatti's favourite expressions. Only six were built and their value is now beyond calculation. The maharajahs of India were the most dedicated autophilists of all, accumulating vast stables of the finest bespoke cars from Europe and America – cars for tiger hunts, for durbahs, or cars simply to upstage the prince next door. The most startling of all was undoubtedly the massive Lanchester commissioned in London by the Maharajah of Alwar. A replica of the British royal family's coronation coach, complete with gold and ivory fittings, was built on to a massive chassis. There were postillion seats for two footmen and on its doors gold crowns the size of soup plates. It could rumble along at 3 m.p.h. without overheating to allow an escort of Alwar Lancers to trot in procession in front of it – or it could accelerate across the desert roads of Rajasthan at a steady 80 m.p.h.

It is such extravagances of rolling sculpture that continue to fire the imagination and nostalgia of men in love with cars. As today's products have been reduced to the level of mere utilities, the era when man conquered and was conquered by the car takes on even more epic proportions. The father of the first modern car museum, which opened in 1939, was Count Carlo Biscaretti di Ruffia of Turin. There are now over eighty major car collections in Europe, and in Britain alone there are forty car museums and collections open to the public. The grand auction houses of Christie's and Sotheby's deal in all aspects of motoring ephemera and the company of Kruse International in the United States, the world's largest classic car auctioneers,

below] The 'swan' car, created in 1912 in Lowestoft, England – to the special order of an English eccentric living in Calcutta, a Mr R. N. Mathewson. It featured a beak that opened, lifelike hisses produced by compressed air and water from the car's radiator, and eight organ pipes linked to a musical keyboard. Though its Suffolk creators are long gone, the 'swan song' has not yet played for this remarkable vehicle that lives on in India still terrorizing those who dare to cross its path.

offers 10,000 cars a year at thirty different sales. It is the cars with celebrity connections that fetch the highest prices: Hitler's Mercedes-Benz parade car, with a raised floor that gave the Führer six inches' extra height when he stood up to salute, and which was built in such a way that he could keep his hand on a revolver at all times; Greta Garbo's Duesenberg with six built-in safes; Bonnie and Clyde's death car, a Ford V8, complete with original bloodstains and 106 bullet holes; John Lennon's psychedelic Bentley that sold for an astonishing £150,000 . . . However, the Holy Grail for many collectors is the Porsche that actor James Dean was driving when he crashed fatally in September 1955. It was stolen from a train taking it back east and has not been seen since.

left] A startling survivor – the Maharajah of Alwar's magnificent 1924 Lanchester with its bespoke landau coachwork, made in Sparkbrook, Birmingham – and parked today in the palace gardens of Alwar in remote Rajasthan.

below] Hitler, ever conscious of his lack of inches, gaining stature in his favourite Mercedes-Benz parade car in Berlin 1938. These magnificent Mercedes were an essential part of Nazi regalia.

Our fascination with the motor car over the last hundred years has manifested itself in a variety of distinctive ways.

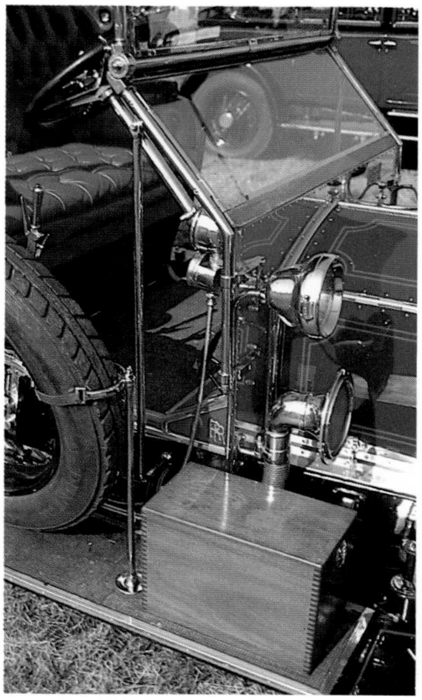

When the cost was incidental and wages were low, the workmanship on the grand marques attained levels of excellence never to be repeated again.

1933 DUESENBERG
20 GRAND

The car culture today consists of an infinite number of sub-cultures, comprising hot-rodders and Lowriders, racers and rallyists, van people and off-road people. At the annual Pebble Beach Concours D'Elegance in California cars are displayed like precious jewels before an enthralled public and wealthy collectors around the world hoard rare cars as they would a Rembrandt or a Matisse. Gunter Artz in Hanover, West Germany, runs a thriving business preserving cherished cars for eternity, either boxed or cocooned in plastic bubbles. For a fee of £1500 his time warp team ensures your slumbering beauty remains rust- and mildew-free until its second coming. One Detroit enthusiast assembled over a thousand cars in a warehouse – and to save on storage space, parked them end up. William Harrah in Reno gathered the world's largest, but most haphazard collection before he died. It totalled 1560 cars. The late William Everett Miller even amassed a staggering *thirty-five tons* of automotive literature, totalling 30,000 books, 50,000 sales brochures and 60,000 car catalogues. But two collections in particular, one in France, the other in the United States, raise man's love affair with the motor car to its most exalted levels. Nestling in the shadowed foothills of the San Gabriel Mountains in California, stands the Merle Norman Tower of Beauty, one man's personal shrine to the automobile. Built by Jack Nethercutt, a cosmetics millionaire (known to his friends as J.B.) it is a stunning 'treasure house of functional fine art' perhaps the ultimate tribute to our love affair with the automobile.

Behind doors of solid bronze stands the Grand Salon – a recreation of the opulent American car showrooms of the early 1920s. Columns of marble from the Congo soar thirty-six feet to a finely painted ceiling decorated with 24-carat gold leaf. Vast chandeliers of hand-cut Bavarian crystal illuminate cars restored to a perfection unequalled, one suspects, even when they were new: Rudolph Valentino's Avion Voisin, with its cobra mascot, a Duesenberg SJ built especially for the 1933–34 Chicago World Fair, Lincolns, Cords, Packards and Pierce-Arrows – America's finest of the late 1920s and early 1930s. There are even baroque oddities, like sad Fatty Arbuckle's McFarlan Knickerbocker Cabriolet. And naturally, a huge Rolls-Royce collection occupies an entire floor of the Tower of Beauty.

Few are privileged to explore this private treasure house of toys, its value set in the millions. To do so is not merely to journey back to the days of the car when perfection was everything and cost secondary, but to feel the very pulse of man's adulation for his extraordinary invention. Every car is 'gassed to go' – in permanent readiness should J.B. wish to take a spin in this 'Duesie' or that Pierce-Arrow. And on one glorious day a year the Tower empties and the entire collection, led by Mr and Mrs Nethercutt, moves in splendid convoy on to Interstate 5 to startle the world for a few hours . . . A splendid picnic with friends follows, then the cars return to their sand and sable tower for another year.

Another collection of extraordinary proportions lies in the textile town of Mulhouse in Alsace. In this French backwater two brothers, textile millionaires Fritz and Hans Schlumpf, set out in the 1950s on a remarkable spending spree during which time they acquired 560 of the world's most precious cars. Of these, 160 were Bugattis – that is, 10 per cent of the remaining models of that entire marque. They then housed them in one of their textile mills, from which they had stripped the machinery. Covering an area of five acres, it was floodlit at night and protected by high barbed wire fences

Star among stars in the Merle Norman collection, the Duesenberg 'Twenty Grand', designed by Gordon Buehrig as a show car for the 1933 World Fair in Chicago. The asking price for the elegant, platinum beauty was $20,000 at a time when a Ford V8 cost a mere $560.

left] 'Ask the Man Who Owns One!' was the confident slogan of Packard in the 1930s, and one can see why. A twelve cylinder 1934 Packard Convertible Sedan, with yellow-orange Dietrich body, is one of the most dazzling cars in the Nethercutt Collection.

left] Fatty Arbuckle's 1923 McFarlan Knickerbocker Cabriolet. A canopy arrangement at the back enabled Fatty to sit in his director's chair, shielded from the rays of the sun, and gave him easy access to the back of the car, well stocked with liquid refreshment.

above] The Grand Salon – millionaire Jack Nethercutt's magnificent recreation of an opulent American car showroom of the early 1920s in Sylmar, California, which houses 125 of the finest and most valuable cars in the world. He set out to collect thirty-two, but confesses that his acquisitive instinct got the better of him.

below] Bugattis stretch as far as the eye can see. Says Fritz Schlumpf: 'I decided to start a big car collection and to dedicate it to the memory of my mother, to turn it into a temple and a sanctuary for her.'

and ex-gendarmes with large Alsatian dogs. One of the massive cost items in their museum were the 900 ornamental wrought-iron lamps that the brothers commissioned in Belgium and which were modelled on those found on Venice's Grand Canal. Aisles as broad as Paris streets and named after members of the Schlumpf family ran as far as the eye could see, dividing the vast collection. Only the bankruptcy of their textile empire brought the brothers' spending spree to a sudden end. They fled to Switzerland. A workers' occupation of their beloved car collection, which up to that time had remained hidden and visited only by carefully selected guests – including several members of Europe's royal families – lasted five years. The French government finally seized the brothers' property, some say unjustly, and all that the Schlumpfs have remaining from their vast collection are two car mascots. The Schlumpf cars are valued at £50 million, yet one suspects it is not the loss of their vast investment that hurts, but the pain of separation from their joy and *raison d'être*.

Of the 160 Bugattis in his collection this is Fritz Schlumpf's favourite and, like a lost child, is the one he misses most of all.

Fritz Schlumpf, distinguished and autocratic and sporting large mutton-chop whiskers, recalls those earliest 'scorchers' when he defines his passion for the Bugatti: 'The sound of its exhaust is like music. When I was driving in the Valley all the children would come running from their houses and line the road to cheer me. I wasn't making the noise on purpose. It's the normal noise of a Bugatti . . . and it's something fantastic . . . music which is intoxicating. It's better than rock and roll!'

Man's love of the motor car knows no national boundaries, and transcends class, cultural and even political barriers. Ever since Lenin rode to power in a Rolls-Royce, the elite of the classless Soviet society have carried on a fierce love affair with powerful cars. The late President Brezhnev was the most avid enthusiast with a private stable of more than a dozen fast and expensive cars that included two Rolls-Royces, a Cadillac, Mercedes-Benz, Citroën Maserati and a 200 m.p.h. Matra Bagheera. He loved to motor around central

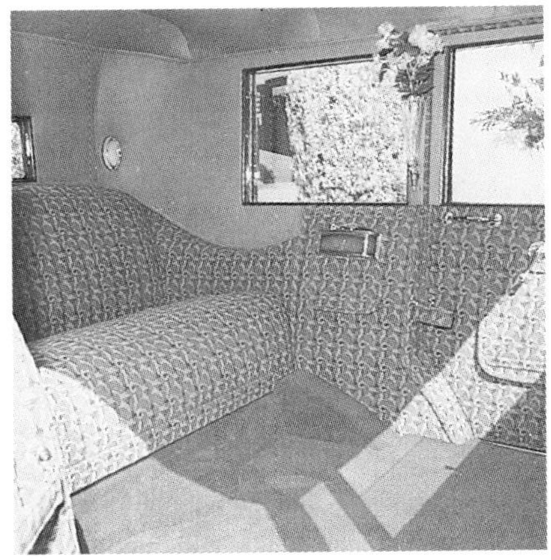

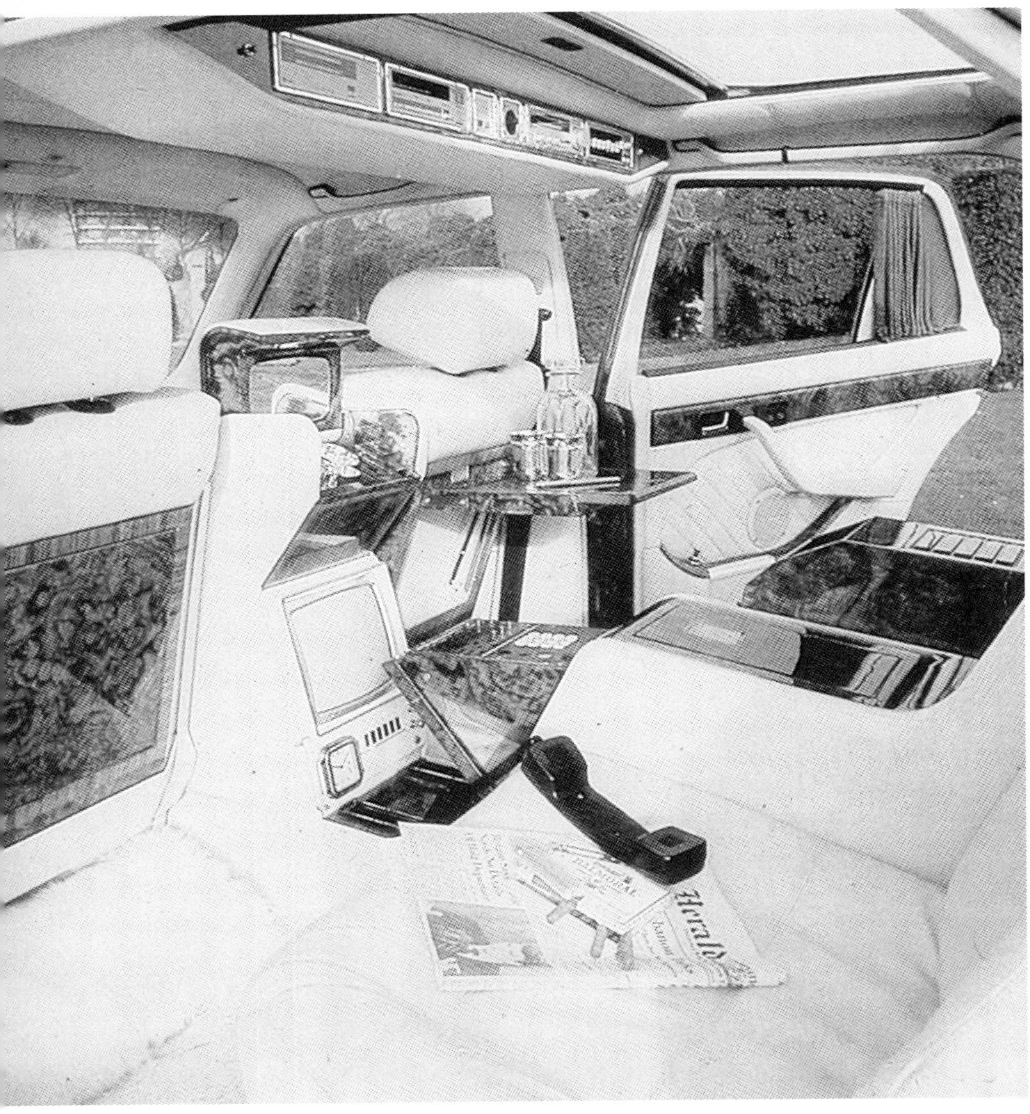

The interiors of cars have always provided the designer full scope for his imagination. Though sixty years apart in time, the flamboyant 1923 McFarlan looks every bit as inviting as the interior of the 1984 Mercedes-Benz, customized by Duchatelet of Belgium, and several degrees more tasteful.

Moscow in his Rolls. 'When I am driving, I relax,' Brezhenev told an interviewer in 1971. 'When I am at the wheel I have the impression that nothing can happen.' His confidence proved ill-founded in one case. When given a Mercedes-Benz during his 1973 state visit to West Germany, he eagerly got behind the wheel and drove off – only to crash into a tree. According to witnesses only his pride was injured. His passion for cars turned into a major diplomatic embarrassment in 1977 during a trip to France, when he was presented with a racing green Matra by President Giscard d'Estaing. 'Blue is my favourite colour,' protested the world's number one Red. Matra had to stop their assembly line hastily in order to respray the presidential gift . . .

At the other end of the social spectrum from the Nethercutts and the Schlumpfs are the Lowriders of California. A typical Lowrider is a working-class Chicano (Mexican–American) male in his early twenties. The first step in pursuit of his automotive dream is to purchase a large second-hand American car. He then sets about transforming it in a way that is wholly peculiar to the Lowrider fraternity. He fits replacement wheels that are brilliantly chromed or even gold-plated and much smaller than standard size. The flawless candy-coloured paintwork in lavender, blues and greens is lovingly embellished with air-brush artwork depicting Aztec or street cruising scenes. Interiors are refurbished with yards of crimson crushed velvet, buttoned to give that bordello look.

However, the essential distinguishing feature of the Lowrider is a set of hydraulics, ex-aircraft parts designed to operate landing gear and wing flaps, but adapted with a little backyard engineering to raise and lower the car's suspension at the flick of a lever. Suddenly a new, strange and somewhat questionable sport is created: car hopping. The Chicanos hold spontaneous contests to find the car that can hop the highest. At night, when these events are held on the California freeways, it is an astounding sight: with the suspension lowered to its limit, titanium skid-pads scrape the road surface releasing a shower of sparks like the glowing tail of a comet. The dedicated Lowrider can be identified not just by his smoke trails but by his sounds. It is not uncommon to find that the rear seats have been removed to accommodate huge speakers that belt out a decibel level of sound that is barely tolerable outside the car, and which inside defies imagination. There is keen rivalry between Lowrider gangs and membership is highly selective. Applicants must bring their cars up to the standards demanded by the group and they must agree to obey stringent and sometimes unexpected sets of rules. Members of 'The Low Conspiracy', one of San Jose's leading gangs, are fined for non-attendance at meetings, for not wearing club shirts and for drinking. Financially and emotionally, the Lowriders pour everything they have into their cars. Says a committee member of the Low Conspiracy: 'Your car brings up a different kind of pride than what you got in yourself [*sic*]. For me it's an extension of my personality. If I were a machine, I would probably look like my car. Put it that way.' Another defines his love affair thus:

I don't get to enjoy the car as much as I might because I'm always inside *it. So sometimes I might just go to the park and place my car across the street, give it a nice pose and just sit back on the grass and admire it, the way the sunshine catches it and how pretty it looks. I'm almost in love with it . . .*

Chromed suspension, psychedelic paintwork 'waxed to the max' and crushed velvet interiors are the colourful hallmarks of the Lowrider. With the aid of aircraft hydraulic systems, 'hoppers' can lift the front ends of their cars six feet off the ground. '*Que carruchitas!*' What cars!

Only in the late 1950s, in what James Flink calls the 'third stage of automobile consciousness', did it first become apparent 'that automobility was no longer an historically progressive force for change in American civilization. Since then the motor car has increasingly been conceived of as a major social problem.' The negative aspects of automobility as the direct consequences of our automania make a depressing litany. An estimated 15–20 million people killed by the car in its first century of existence; environmental pollution; urban sprawl (more than two-thirds of central Los Angeles is given over to the automobile and over 40 per cent of the land mass of Sydney); decay of city centres as the auto mobile head for the suburbs leaving the poor and carless behind; overdependence on the car and the accelerated decline of public transport (despite traffic congestion 90 million Americans travel to and from work by car, two-thirds of them driving alone, while a mere 6 million take public transport); squandering of precious resources . . .

John Tyme, the British lecturer who has spent a great part of his life resisting automania believes 'man-in-motor-car' has not long on planet Earth. In his apocalyptic view he sees man as 'a flawed species and the car is our executioner'. He believes the demands made by the car industry and car ownership in terms of land usage, in terms of chemicals, in terms of energy and the use of 'what politicians know as the strategic metals is such that international conflict can only follow from our commitment to the car'.

Australian conservationist Jack Mundy, puts it another way: 'When you get to the situation where between 1950 and 1980 the world car population jumps from 50 million to 350 million, and in the next decade it will jump to 550 million, I think we've got to say enough's enough. You can't say any longer the car has liberated mankind. In fact, the car has, I suggest, strangled mankind, particularly in our urban areas . . . increasingly in the cities the car will have to be phased out.'

Automania is international and comes in all shapes and forms, from the elongated Royal Marque Personal Limousine for Californian ego-boosters, to the humbler but much loved Austin A30 of one British enthusiast, which has been affectionately named Penelope.

There is little doubt in human terms autophobia is as real as autophilia, and not just amongst trenchant critics of the car. Yet it is a subject that society has barely addressed. Psychiatrist Dr Roy Matthews of Vanderbilt University, in a unique pilot study into the fear of driving in the city of Houston, discovered that large numbers of people in America, the most mobile nation on Earth, are terrified of even going on to the freeways. Pity the poor detective, compelled to drop the hot pursuit when his suspects left the sidestreets and joined the freeway. Or the lady cab driver, who coped with her phobia as long as her passengers were out-of-towners and she could take them her own circuitous routes to their destination. Crisis for her came the day a local Houstonian insisted on the *direct* route to the airport. She fainted at the wheel . . .

For the majority, however, it is difficult to disagree with Lawrence J. White that the motor car has afforded the average man 'control over his immediate environment to a degree not equalled anywhere else in his daily routine – and that automobile transportation may well provide a great many psychological satisfactions that mass transit cannot provide'. And that is the very essence of man's obsessive relationship with the motor car in the first hundred years. From those first faltering journeys in the 1890s the car has stood for so much more than mere transport.

Out of the 4250 makes of car produced between 1896 and 1939 only a handful now remain. Yet in its various forms the car has managed to be a great many things to the greater part of mankind. Man has been conceived and born, made love, lived and died in great numbers in the car. He has given it wings and called it the aerocar, made it go on water and called it the amphicar, and in the case of one Texan lady from San Antonio – irredeemably in love with her Ferrari – even buried in it! As the centrepiece of the affluent society, the car still retains – despite talk of the death of the love affair – the premier place in man's affections and priorities. An international survey of moral values in 1983, conducted by Gallup International in sixteen countries, discovered the worst crime a human being can commit is not genocide, matricide, loot, pillage or even rape, but the taking and driving away of somebody else's car without their permission. It was the only value universally shared amongst the countries surveyed.

James Hemming, the British psychologist, in explaining automania, sees the car both as a symbol for status, wealth, power, potency and virility and as a fantasy object 'to get certain things out of life which we value, such as excitement, fun, adventure, freedom . . . and until we get another equally good object for our fantasies, I think we will stick with the car . . .' That most exciting toy continues to excite – just as it did when it burst upon a startled world one hundred years ago.

The Acceptance of the Car

With the aid of science and art alone, it is possible to make wagons roll in a fixed direction without the help of draught animals, as did the battle-cars of the ancients, with their formidable wheels, armed with scythes and sickles.
(*Roger Bacon*)

As we have said, the idea of a self-propelled vehicle is much more than one hundred years old. Bacon, writing his thirteenth-century treatise on the secret forces of nature, clearly had in mind the contrivances employed by the Persians against Alexander the Great: tremendous cars bristling with weapons that hurtled down the mountains and scythed their way through the advancing Greek army. Similar devices were employed by the wily Swiss mountain folk against the Austrian nobles in the Middle Ages.

But the force of gravity is an unreliable source of motive power (particularly when going up hill!) and the search began for something superior. In the mid seventeenth century, Johann Hantsch of Nuremberg invented a carriage run by clockwork that could be made to attain a speed of three leagues an hour. A few years later Sir Isaac Newton proposed a carriage propelled by steam; but no one positively succeeded in harnessing steam power for another hundred years when a French officer, Nicholas Joseph Cugnot, built his steam wagon for the purpose of transporting cannon. Although this locomotive was exceptionally powerful, its performance caused alarm. It seems to have vibrated so violently that it became uncontrollable; and on its demonstration run it is reported to have run amok and crashed through a wall. More than a hundred years after the steam wagon had been abandoned as a vehicle incapable of improvement, the Count de Valette, president of the Automobile Club of France, pondered on what might have been: 'If the Cugnot carriage had been further perfected . . . we should have had no need for rails and should not have been obliged to invent them.'

This idea, that the industrialized world might have skipped the age of the railways is more than interesting speculation. It tells us a good deal about the mood of the travelling public when the automobile did finally make its appearance. The growth of the railways had made long-distance travel much easier and more comfortable but it had made some shorter journeys more difficult, particularly within the cities. As F. M. C. Thompson pointed out in *Victorian England: The Horse Drawn Society*: 'The mistake is sometimes made of supposing that the railways dealt [the horse] a mortal blow . . . the truth is . . . without carriages and carts the railways would have been like stranded whales . . . for these were the only means of getting people and goods right to the door, of houses, warehouses, markets, and factories, where they wanted to be.' And he concludes: 'the railway age was in fact the greatest age of the horse'. This fact is of prime importance in considering how the car was accepted on the roads of Europe and the United States. It arrived at a time when horse populations were reaching their all-time peak: $3\frac{1}{2}$ million animals in Britain and about 30 million in the USA. Today it is the car that creates traffic chaos and threatens to bring our cities to a standstill; only a short time ago, precisely the same desperate conditions were brought about by the horse.

The car has become such a familiar part of our lives and of our landscape it's easy to forget that the ubiquitous machine is an absolute newcomer, a brash upstart in historical terms. There are those still living today (1984)

Motorist - "Hello, killed anything?"
Sportsman - "No, have you?"

The motorist with his temperamental yet deadly machine became the butt of endless cartoons and music hall jokes. He was either the victim of the car's chronic unreliability or had made a victim of some other unfortunate road user.

who were born before the motor car; and at least one of them is still driving. The Countess Frochot is probably the oldest living motorist. She was born in 1882 and her memories go back to a world untouched by the car, when the roads of her native France were still the sole domain of the horse. The first time she saw a car – 'an extraordinary little machine' – it brought her uncle on a visit:

He was a gentleman of a certain age who had bought a car; he had a chauffeur because he himself understood nothing about the thing and whenever he came to see us – he lived eighteen kilometres [eleven miles] away – he would phone first saying, 'I'm coming. Prepare your horses.' He took this precaution because when the car turned up, it would never start again (for the return journey). Consequently the chauffeur – who was a mechanic too – had to sleep here and repair what had to be repaired. In those days you only went somewhere in a car if you were sure of another way of getting back.

Countess Frochot's recollections point up so much about very early motoring: that the car was a toy of the rich, that it was dreadfully unreliable and that chauffeurs did most of the driving. But above all she reminds us how these first cars impressed simple country folk: 'They thought it was the devil! Everybody hid when a car appeared. Just remember that the hens were being killed, the dogs were being squashed . . . no one knew what to do on the roads when the cars came . . . the horses were terrified and used to bolt. So of course the peasants . . . were all against the car.' And not only the peasants. Hostility to the car was widespread. It was regarded by many as a noisy and dangerous nuisance, a passing fad of the rich that would soon be confined to the scrapyard of history.

Michael Berger made a detailed study of the coming of the automobile to rural America and his findings quite contradict the widely held view that the car was instantly accepted and welcomed throughout the United States. He points out that most of the early automobiles were owned by city dwellers

The destruction of the rural landscape and livestock caused by the early motorist aroused fierce antagonism. Among American farmers it was seen as a reason to oppose road improvement that could only lead to more cars and higher speeds.

THE INVENTION OF THE .9th CENTURY.
THE ABOLITION OF EQUINE SLAVERY.
THE WONDER OF THE AGE.
THE GREATEST MECHANICAL INVENTION
SINCE THE STEAM ENGINE.
GRAND EXPOSITION OF
THE HORSELESS MOTOR CARRIAGE
The first Exhibition in the Provinces at the
PALACE THEATRE,
HAYMARKET NEWCASTLE
FOR SIX NIGHTS ONLY, COMMENCING SEPTEMBER 21st, 1896,
The Self-propelled Vehicle with Explanatory Description of Mechanism.
The Directors of the Palace Theatre have pleasure in announcing that they have secured from the Northern Inventions, Limited, of this City, on behalf of the Anglo-French Motor Carriage Co., Ltd., and will exhibit on the stage of the Palace, the Handsome Motor Carriage which was exhibited, by special request, before the House of Lords and Commons, and ridden in by over 200 Members of both Houses of Parliament in the passing of the "Locomotives on Highways" Bill.
This Autocar has already been awarded several Gold and Silver Medals at Exhibitions held in 1895 and 1896.
DO NOT MISS SEEING THE AUTOCAR AT THE PALACE THEATRE
Which Royalty and Members of Parliament have driven in without the horse.
THE HORSELESS CARRIAGE.
THE MECHANICAL INVENTION OF THE AGE.
INSTRUCTIVE TO MECHANICS.
INTERESTING TO CYCLISTS.
PLEASING TO EVERYBODY.
Printed by F. Devine and Co., Ltd., Newgate Street, Newcastle.

The motor car was regarded as such an exciting novelty that for a short period it was top of the bill at music halls and circuses on both sides of the Atlantic.

above right] It's hard to imagine this driver managing to get his four cylinder Packard through Pennsylvania roads that you would only attempt today with a 4-wheel-drive vehicle. Conditions like this were a boon for some farmers who earned extra money by pulling stuck vehicles out of the mud.

below right] There was a widespread feeling that the law was totally inadequate to deal with the speed-crazed motorist and it was frequently suggested that unless something was done, the non-motoring public would take the law into their own hands.

and that when they ventured into the countryside – in the wake of the cyclist hordes of the 1890s – they were regarded as yet another invasion of 'townies' who had scant regard for farming ways or the laws of trespass. But as the Countess Frochot suggested, it was the slaughter of farm animals that caused the greatest resentment. Berger discovered one study where an investigator in Iowa had counted on one journey '225 dead animals representing 29 (wild and domestic) species'. The investigator concluded that motor vehicles demand 'recognition as one of the important checks upon the natural increase of many forms of life; including of course the human species'.

The car gained its chequered reputation despite the fact that both its appearance and performance were at first far from menacing. The first-generation cars were odd little contraptions, underpowered, unreliable and the butt of endless jokes. When the world's first reliability trial took place in 1894 on a seventy-five-mile stretch of road from Paris to Rouen, 102 'horseless carriages' had been entered with no fewer than twenty different systems of propulsion, including petrol, steam, compressed air and clockwork. One vehicle was claimed by its inventor to derive its power from the weight of its passengers! The first prize in the trial was shared between Panhard and Peugeot whose cars were each powered by 3 or 4 h.p. Daimler engines. The maximum speeds of about 12 m.p.h. and the average speed of 10.5 m.p.h. were well below the speeds cyclists were then able to attain. Only five years later, in the famous 'Thousand Miles Trial' from London to Edinburgh and back, cars of 20 h.p. and more were achieving average speeds of 30 m.p.h. and by 1903 that awesome 60 h.p. Mercedes was on the roads, capable of speeds up to 80 m.p.h.

In just ten years, between 1895 and 1905, the car had been transformed from a staid little egg-beater phut-phutting along at little more than trotting pace, into a snarling monster, eating up the miles at a rate that even leading engineers had thought impossible just a few years earlier. Carl Benz had been of the opinion that 'a car which can attain a speed of more than 60 km per hour [37 m.p.h.] will soon rattle itself to pieces'.

Although carmakers quickly succeeded in making their product almost as powerful and as fast as a modern machine, by today's standards their brakes, suspension and steering were miserably poor, their drivers were largely untrained and the roads they used were designed for farm carts travelling at 4 m.p.h. rather than 40. Inevitably much blood was shed; and since motoring regulations were primitive and only sporadically enforced, victims of the car sometimes took the law into their own hands. According to Michael Berger: 'tacks and glass were strewn over country roads by rural residents who wanted to rid themselves of the danger of motor vehicles. Rope, and sometimes barbed wire, was run from tree to tree across the roads to impede traffic. (The latter action was found to be most expedient at twilight).' Press reports suggest that action sometimes went beyond impeding the vehicles and was directed at the occupants. On both sides of the Atlantic, tales circulated of motorists being horsewhipped, stoned and shot at by testy bucolics and horse owners. One of the more celebrated incidents is worth recalling because it reveals the extraordinary hauteur of the wealthy pioneer motorist. William Kissam Vanderbilt Jr kept a log of his European travels between 1899 and 1908, and if only a few of his fellow motorists behaved as he did it is surprising that lynchings were not a daily occurrence. Here is a sample of Vanderbilt's laconic and lofty literary style: 'on arriving at Fréjus killed two

MUST WE TAKE THE LAW IN OUR OWN HANDS?

dogs that viciously attacked our tyres. With a howling mob behind us, ended up running into a hay wagon. Luckily no damage was done.' Damage to what, one wonders? To the automobile, of course; there was certainly no concern for the hay wagon.

The celebrated incident when Mr Vanderbilt was 'set upon by Italian peasants' made him something of a hero – at least in motoring circles – but even his own version of the affair reflects little credit on him or his party. About forty-five miles from Florence, a six-year-old boy ran in front of his vehicle bringing it to a halt. Then, according to Mr Vanderbilt's account: 'Mrs Vanderbilt and the mechanic jumped down from the car and disappeared in the crowd that had quickly gathered. I stopped the engine, but before I could move, was seized by the mob and pulled from my seat . . . The men around me kicked, punched, pushed and tried to choke me.' After waving his revolver at his assailants, Mr Vanderbilt took refuge in a shop and there hid in a closet until he was rescued by the police. Any temptation for the reader to feel much sympathy for the plight of the Vanderbilt party is modified by the knowledge that the child who ran in front of the vehicle had in fact been knocked down and injured, by the well-established Vanderbilt custom of not stopping after 'incidents' on the road and by the fact that he called his motoring memoirs *A Record of Many Delightful Days Spent in Touring the Continent*.

When the car carrying W. K. Vanderbilt Jr was attacked by Italian peasants following an accident involving a child, Mr Vanderbilt had to be rescued by the police and proudly related that, according to the chief of police: 'it had been the wish of the people to lynch me and that at one time it had been almost necessary to summon the troops from the barracks nearby.'

The Great Motor Race - A Close Finish

The motor car debate was often seen in terms of machine versus horse and races were organized to demonstrate the superiority of the one over the other.

Although the primitive car, with its untrustworthy brakes and unwieldy steering, did present a threat to human life, it was a much greater cause for alarm among horses than among humans. The whole heated debate over the car was frequently seen as 'car versus horse'. To the horse lover the motor vehicle was a gross and unwelcome intruder as the final verse of this ode *To a Horseless Carriage* makes very clear:

Avaunt! thou horridest of modern things!
Vamoose! Unto thy ugly self take wings!
Think not with all thy gaud and glitter coarse
Thou'll e'er supplant that best of friends, the horse.
(*Woman's Home Companion*, 1900)

But to the car enthusiast the horse was a stupid and inefficient animal that steadfastly refused to get used to the car and should therefore be banished from the roads. The arrogance motorists displayed towards horse traffic is abundantly chronicled in their own travellers' tales. In 1897 Henry Sturmey wrote an account, entitled *On an Autocar*, of his journey through parts of Britain where the car had never been seen before, and from his very first hour on the road his vehicle was stampeding the horses. He tells how a horse drawing a market cart panicked on meeting the car on a narrow bridge and broke a shaft. When the driver asked Mr Sturmey to pay compensation, he received a dusty answer: 'I promptly responded that I should do nothing of the kind as the fault was none of mine and forthwith left the party to bewail their fate and to curse motor cars in general and mine in particular.' Not only was Mr Sturmey unconcerned and unrepentant about the mayhem his car was causing, he found it positively hilarious. In what he describes as 'a very amusing incident', he tells how his approach put to flight a tiny donkey carriage 'and we were all very much amused at the frantic efforts of the lady in charge . . . to restrain her restive steed. I confess I could not resist the temptation of an occasional blast upon the trumpet to keep the fun going.'

Not all motorists were like Mr Sturmey and Mr Vanderbilt; not all of them behaved like naughty children with an exciting new toy. They realized that 'the impudence of a few, aggravated the non-motoring public; over-rode their rights and showed a careless disregard for everybody except themselves'. The responsible motoring enthusiast endeavoured to persuade the public that the car could be accommodated peacefully on the roads. Races between horses and cars were arranged to show the superiority of the machine over

Horses stubbornly refused to get used to cars so this was seriously suggested as the solution: the car disguised as the horse. The inventor, Uriah Smith of Battle Creek, Michigan, also recommended this device as a windbreak and as a receptacle for gasolene.

the beast. There was even a serious suggestion that horses should be sent to school. Silvester Baxter, writing in *The Automobile Magazine* in 1899, complains that 'the greatest drawback to a much more rapid introduction of the automobile is the fear of frightening horses and thus causing runaways, smash-ups, serious injuries, and perhaps loss of life. So why not send the horse to school?' The writer goes on to note that driving schools were being established and questions 'why should not this institution also be utilized as a school for the training of horses in paths of familiarity with things that are liable to cause them fright?' Needless to say the horse owners did not see why they should accommodate these arrogant noisy newcomers to the roads and feelings ran high.

Car pollution was a further cause of resentment; in those days not so much because of foul emissions from the engine as because of noise and the dust from beneath the wheels. As C. F. G. Masterman put it in *The Condition of England 1909*:

Wandering machines, travelling with an incredible rate of speed, scramble and smash and shriek along all the rural ways. You can see them on a Sunday afternoon, piled twenty or thirty deep outside the new popular inns, while their occupants regale themselves within. You can see evidence of their activity in the dust-laden hedges of the south country roads, a grey mud colour, with no evidence of green; in the ruined cottage gardens of the south country village.

'To see a lady at the wheel with a gentleman riding beside her was a most unusual event and excited much comment.' In this case the driver was the redoubtable Dorothy Levitt in her De Dion.

In 1901 the Devil Wagon had yet to make its presence felt in God's Country. In Main Street, Blackerell, Oklahoma, there was not a motor vehicle in sight. Ten years later, there would hardly be a horse and cart in sight.

The only country with a reasonable network of metalled roads was France. The rest of the world battled through mud when it rained – and dust when it didn't. The answer to the nuisance of course was to improve the roads, but who was to pay and what kind of roads should be built? Those decisions were yet to be made. In the meantime, so far had sentiment run on both sides of the Atlantic against this destructive vehicle that in the United States Woodrow Wilson wrote, 'Nothing has spread socialistic feeling more than the use of the automobile. Automobilists are a picture of arrogance and wealth, with all its independence and carelessness.' And in Britain, Walter Long, who supported early attempts to regulate the motorist by legislation, wrote of 'an embittered feeling in the general public against all persons who use motors which as a dangerous class feeling is perhaps without parallel in modern time'.

In the cities, apart from frightening the horses, motor vehicles competed savagely with many other road users. At the end of the last century, city streets were not just transportation arteries; they served all kinds of neighbourhood and family uses. As Clay McShane has pointed out, 'push-cart vendors brought their wares to urban housewives . . . surviving lithographs and photos show great herds of children playing in the streets, generally the only open spaces'. City streets were often flanked with stalls selling all manner of produce. Musicians, conjurors and other street entertainers provided the poor with cheap diversion. On to this seething and varied social scene, enter the motor car and exit many other performers! When the car first appeared on cinema screens in the 1890s it was often shown in the role of the bully,

far left and below] The pioneer motorist had to overcome considerable difficulties. The challenge attracted men and women of formidable character and appearance.

left] Dorothy Levitt urged society women to get behind the wheel and wrote a book which argued that they could still be feminine and ladylike while wrestling with the crank handle and the dreaded puncture.

tipping over costers' barrows and fruit stalls; it may have been funny on the screen but it was not nearly so much fun on the streets.

If the car brought pain to the non-motoring public it could be argued convincingly that it brought even greater pain to those hardy souls who ventured out in these primitive machines; it was not an activity for the fastidious or the faint-hearted. Judging from the formidable protective clothing, advertised in the motoring magazines, open cars and unpaved roads provided a wide range of uncomfortable experiences. For men, a heavy coat of leather or linen was standard wear as were stout gauntlets and leggings. To protect the head, ears and eyes the outfitters offered a range of caps, goggles and face masks of bewildering complexity and ugliness. For the woman motorist there was the familiar dilemma; how to be practical and yet retain some measure of fashionable elegance? Countess Frochot believes she never really succeeded: 'we wore such funny clothes. First a hat pinned firmly on your head; and on top of that a veil strongly tied; then a raincoat or a duster. Everywhere you went you created a huge dust cloud. You were turned into a dust statue.' Probably the leading authority on ladies' motoring dress at that time was pioneer motorist and racing driver Dorothy Levitt. In *The Woman and the Car* (1909) she advises the woman driver to aim for neatness and comfort and to avoid flamboyancy: 'Under no circumstances wear lace or "fluffy" adjuncts to your toilette.' One of the most important articles of wear in her mind was the scarf or muffler which worn securely round the throat 'will save you all manner of colds, sore throats and kindred sufferings'. The prudent lady motorist should also carry an overall of butcher blue or brown linen to slip over her clothes for the time when greasy maintenance work had to be done; and a pair of wash leather gloves to help keep hands ladylike. She adds that the woman driver travelling alone should carry a small revolver to defend herself on the highways and byways. But even for the best dressed and most prudently prepared motorist there was suffering in store. Booth Tarkington, writing in the *Saturday Evening Post*, recalled a journey in Belgium in 1903: 'The large wooden wheels had solid rubber tyres, and their passage over an ancient, stone-paved road would have been stimulating to the spinal ganglia if the performance by the engine's two large cylinders had not already attended to that . . .' At journey's end, 'passengers walked into the hotel unaided, but having reached their rooms retired instantly to bed and did not rise again until noon of the next day'. Horseless vehicles, he concluded, 'were intended evidently for people with rubber back bones and no fretful imaginations'.

The pioneer motorist was always prepared for the worst. When Henry Sturmey set out to drive his Daimler from John o'Groats to Land's End, he was accompanied by Ashley, a mechanic from the Daimler Company. This prudent mechanic, according to Mr Sturmey's account of his journey, 'spent the best part of the day previous to starting in getting together a collection of tools for his own use should they be required, likewise taking a supply of asbestos, grease, flour, emery, oil, black lead, lubricating grease etc.'.

Mr Sturmey proudly states that the only other special preparation for the journey was the '"devil" fitted beneath the car. The said "devil" being a heavy rod like a crowbar pointed at the rear . . . which could be let down on a steep incline so that should the car stop it would dig into the ground and prevent the vehicle from running back.'

Despite all these precautions, Mr Sturmey's journal contains frequent references to the Daimler's delicate state of health: 'The motor is still going very poorly and we are making but slow progress . . . it was plain that something was not quite right . . .' But almost as great a hindrance to his progress as mechanical breakdown was the importunate behaviour of and ceaseless questioning from the people he encountered along the route. The far-sighted Mr Sturmey had foreseen this problem 'as I should be traversing much country where an auto-car had never been seen before' and he had prepared a supply of what he called 'Save Trouble Cards' printed as follows:

What is it? It is an autocar.
Some people call it a motorcar.
No, it cannot explode! There is no boiler.
It is worked by a petroleum motor.
The motor is of four horse power.
It can travel at 14 miles per hour.
It can be started in two minutes.
There are eight ways of stopping it so it cannot run away.
It can get up an ordinary hill.

Although cars rapidly became sturdier and more reliable than Mr Sturmey's little Daimler, some of the improvements brought additional difficulties for the motorist. The introduction of pneumatic tyres improved the ride but increased the probability of a breakdown. Until tyres and other components achieved greater reliability, motorists depended heavily on the mechanical skills of their chauffeurs. Hugh Rochfort Maxted, who toured Europe in 1905, offered much advice on choosing 'the right man':

This gentleman [the chauffeur] is a most important part of the engine and he must be a certified mechanic, not merely a greaser. It is also necessary to examine his papers to make sure he has spent some years in a motor factory, and preferably, of course, in the works where your car was built. He must also have good references and a fair record as there are some men who seem to have always had bad luck with their cars . . .

However vexing the mechanical vagaries of the car may have been, the greatest source of trouble was the roads they travelled. In Europe there were at least road systems, more or less well maintained, going back to the days of the Roman Empire. In most other parts of the world, highways were virtually non-existent. In Australia, at the turn of the century, there was approximately one horse for every man, woman and child in the country. The railways did little more than connect the main centres of population; for the rest, people travelled on horseback or by the overland stagecoaches of Cobb & Co. Goods were moved around the outback in carts, sledges and wagons drawn by horses, oxen and camels and even by sheep and goats! Their progress was painfully slow. So bad were the roads that on the important commercial route between Bourke (New South Wales) and Sydney, the bullock teams carrying the valuable wool crop moved at a speed of forty miles per *week*. In other words, if the weather was bad it could take up to four months to make the journey to the coast. In the United States the position was little better; in 1903 less than 10 per cent of the 2.3 million miles of roads were paved. Confronted by conditions such as these and by a well-orchestrated chorus of

When the rains came to the Australian outback, even tall-wheeled carts became hopelessly bogged. These were the conditions faced by the pioneer motorist in his underpowered and unreliable machine.

left] Changing tyres required strenuous physical effort and willing hands. In this case S. F. Edge, the great racing driver and motoring entrepreneur, directs the work on his Napier – making its successful maiden trip – during the Thousand Miles Trial around Britain in 1900.

In the age of the horse, even the grandest city streets ran with muck. In Times Square in 1900, the New York sanitary worker in his white uniform looked altogether more organized than London's ragged army of 'dirt boys'.

opposition from influential quarters, including sections of the Press, the churches and government, it is amazing that the motor car advanced in the confidence of the public as rapidly as it did. Yet, at a time when much of the comment about the 'devil wagon' was far from adulatory, there was also talk of a 'love affair' between man and motor car. It was to be a little time yet before that affair became a serious liaison.

left] Redundant! When the car replaced the horse on London's streets the 'dirt boy' became another victim of the technological revolution.

Even those who were genuinely excited by the possibilities of the car and who supported its development were aware of the social pitfalls it was bound to encounter. Above all, they were concerned by the dangerous antics of rich and foolish persons who treated this important new technology as another sporting pastime to fill their idle hours. *The Automobile Magazine* of October 1899 has a surprisingly sarcastic account of the Automobile Festival at Newport, Rhode Island. There, America's ten wealthiest families showed off 'their much cherished rigs in a blaze of glory'. Photographs show the expensive French imports of the Vanderbilts, the Astors and the Witneys decked out in flowers parading the streets of Newport. First prize for speed went to William K. Vanderbilt for his steam Locomobile. Mr Belmont's 'Kissing Bug Turnout' was disqualified as it turned out to be unsteerable. The wives of the wealthy had taken wholeheartedly to the new motoring sport and it was reported that Mrs Stuyvesant Fish had proved to be such a poor learner that 'though there may be some portions of the well-kept grounds surrounding her house that were not ploughed up by the wild rearing and charging of her automobile, careful scrutiny failed to locate them'. When people like Mrs Stuyvesant Fish were let loose on the public highway – and as there was no driving test there was nothing to stop them – the consequences were often catastrophic. In the early days, the friends of the car were frequently its worst enemies and yet nothing, not even the enthusiastic efforts of very silly people, could halt its progress.

How was this unreliable, dangerous, noisy, dirty and smelly machine able to triumph over its shortcomings? The answer lies not so much in the virtues of the car as in the disadvantages of the horse, particularly in the cities. The principal disadvantage can be stated very briefly: dung. Anyone familiar with London will know that behind all the grander residential streets are the mews: smaller, meaner streets that provided accommodation for horses, coaches, coachmen and grooms. In many of these mews, as many as fifty or sixty horses would have stabled and each one of these animals produced, each day, about 45 lb of dung. It is estimated that by the turn of the century English towns and cities had to dispose of 10 million tons of horse manure every year. As a reminder of those good old days before the car started to pollute our cities, down at London's St Katharine's Dock is a hay barge, just one of scores of such vessels that came up the Thames daily loaded with feed for the horses; other barges departed on the tide with the same stuff after it had been processed by the horse. This never-ending battle with the dung heap was a nightmare for public health officials worldwide. Flies became so bad that those who could afford to abandoned the cities in the summer months. But even in winter it wasn't much fun; in wet weather ladies walked the streets with long skirts raised above their high-buttoned boots to avoid the pools of liquid manure. In London, pedestrians were helped to navigate the sea of horse-droppings by an army of crossing sweepers. Ernest Hancock, who was born in London in 1895, remembers how important these humble public servants were:

as we crossed the Foxley Road, there was the crossing sweeper, and being the youngest I had the honour to hand him a shilling which I thought was a terrible waste of money . . . but the only way you could safely cross any side-road in London, if you had decent clothes on, was to find a crossing sweeper; because on either side it was a damned mess that was only cleared up about once a week.

Mr Hancock's final verdict on his childhood London: 'everywhere was dung'. In these circumstances, those who argued that the general adoption of the automobile would lead to better health conditions were sure of a sympathetic hearing. Medical authorities pointed out that tetanus was spread by horses and that street dust, consisting mainly of dry horse dung, was thought to be responsible for a number of chronic eye and intestinal infections among city children. Armed with this support from the medical establishment, the car was presented by its publicists as the new Elixir of Life. 'When the horse has been eliminated entirely', declared James Rood Doolittle, 'and when sanitary measures are observed to prevent the breeding of flies, it is clearly within the Vision that human life may be extended on the average of five years or more, because the scientists have discovered that flies spread diseases, and fever kills its victims by the tens of thousands.'

Apart from being blamed for all this pestilence, solely on account of his necessary biological functions, poor Dobbin suffered terrible physical distress in his urban setting. As everyone who has read *Black Beauty* will know, the city nag was nothing but a wretched drudge. One hundred years ago, New York City and Brooklyn had a horse population of about 175,000. Many of the poor jades, overworked and ill-treated, simply dropped dead in the streets and were left to rot there. A description of New York's Broadway in *Atlantic Monthly* tells of a street made impassable by 'dead horses and

Another reason to welcome the car! Horse-lovers and humane societies hoped to abolish the brutal equine slavery of the great cities by replacing the draught animal with the horseless carriage.

vehicular entanglements'. In the 1880s, New York City was removing 15,000 dead horses from its streets each year but not before their decomposing carcases had augmented the foul smells and the flies coming from stables and dung heaps.

This equine air pollution was just part of the problem; noise appears to have been an equally intolerable nuisance. With thousands of iron-clad wheels and hooves clattering over cobbled streets it was often impossible to carry on a conversation outdoors. By comparison, the car on its stealthy rubber tyres offered the peace that passeth understanding; in fact, one hundred years ago the car was regarded by many city dwellers as a godsend, *opposite*] There is a widespread assumption that traffic jams in cities were created by the car. Judging from this view of New York's Broadway, the age of the horse was hardly the time of peace and tranquillity it is sometimes made out to be.

a blessing, the only cure for most of the city's ills. It was even argued that cars were safer than horses. In the view of Frank Hugget, expressed in his book *Carriages at Eight*: 'It was, indeed almost as dangerous to walk or to drive in Victorian city streets as it is today. In London, after allowance has been made for the increase in population, almost as many people were seriously injured in road accidents in 1872 as in 1972.' René Bache, writing in the *Saturday Evening Post* in 1900, calculated that in the United States horses were responsible for three-quarters of a million more or less serious mishaps a year. The chief cause of horse accidents, he concluded, 'lies in the fact that this noble animal – beautiful, docile, affectionate; man's faithful friend and patient servant – is born a fool and never gets over it. Its intelligence is overestimated.' To emphasize the dangers of the horse, the writer compared its record with that of other animals: only one accident in 500 was attributed to dogs, one in 800 to cattle and one in 15,000 to the bite of the rat. Safest of all in this league table was the cat: 'Record is obtainable of only one cat mishap to an insured person; but in this case the policy holder kicked at the animal, and, missing it, broke his leg against a sofa. Blood-poisoning set in, and he died.'

By 1910, cars were already well-represented in the traffic flow around Piccadilly Circus. However, the sign on the horse-bus in the bottom left of the picture still advertises the London Riding School with horses and carriages for hire.

When the Detroit Athletic Club opened its new headquarters the members' wives were invited along to inspect the facilities; and of course they came by car. Note that, with only a couple of exceptions, all the vehicles in view are electric.

Overall, there is a mass of evidence to suggest that the man in the street one hundred years ago was ready for the car and expecting a great deal from it. He was expecting it to provide a cure for most of the ills for which the car is now blamed: air pollution, congestion and death on the roads. Cars were judged to be more reliable, safer and cleaner than horse-drawn transport; and they were certainly cheaper to run. The cost advantage afforded by the car was probably first perceived by physicians. They needed transport that was instantly available twenty-four hours a day. Horses took time to harness, feed and groom, which meant that the conscientious doctor needed at least two horses and a groom or stable boy to make sure he could answer emergencies as speedily as possible. One car could do the same job more cheaply and efficiently. Other businessmen quickly followed the trend set by the doctors. The grocers of Australia were advised by their trade paper that to keep their delivery horses healthy they should be fed and watered long before the driver had himself breakfasted. Throughout the rest of the working day the animal needed to be groomed three times, fed three times, rested for an hour, blanketed in inclement weather and shod when necessary. The message was obvious! A motor vehicle can do the work of several horses at a fraction of the cost. A writer for the journal *American City* pointed out that the motor vehicle, which did not suffer from fatigue or adverse weather conditions, did two and a half times as much work as the horse in the same time and caused only a fraction of the street congestion. The conclusion? 'The horse has become unprofitable. He is too costly to buy and too costly to keep.' Once that message started to get across, the contest 'Car versus Horse' became 'no contest'. Dobbin was put out to grass and the carmakers moved in to stay.

The first automobile boom lasted from 1895 to 1908; during that period the manufacture of steam, electric and gasoline powered cars became a glamour industry. Thousands of entrepreneurs moved in on a market that seemed to offer quick and easy profits and, as we have seen, the choice of vehicle confronting the prospective buyer was daunting. During these early years the gasoline engine steadily gained precedence over steam and electric. Strict safety requirements on steam boilers inhibited the development of steam cars, and electric vehicles quickly demonstrated the disadvantage they still exhibit today: an unacceptably short range of operation. Nevertheless, electric cars sold well in the United States for some years. Until American roads were improved, almost all cars kept within the city limits where the short range of the electric car was no great drawback; in addition, in the United States, there were relatively large numbers of women drivers who preferred the electric because it started so effortlessly. Hand cranking a gasoline engine was strenuous, dangerous and, above all, unladylike. Once the self-starter was introduced in 1912 and the roads gradually improved there was no competition for the gasoline engined passenger car; time and again in races and trials (as we shall see in chapter 3) it demonstrated its superiority and reliability over long distances.

The appearance of the Model T Ford is generally regarded as the milestone in the transition of the car from its role as 'toy of the rich' to 'tool of the people'. But even before the rugged little Ford appeared in 1908, the American farmer had already been changing his mind about 'the devil wagon'. According to James Flink, 'between 1905 and 1908 the major market

While W. K. Vanderbilt Jr was laying waste the roads of Europe and getting set upon by Italian peasants, his wife was making more sedate progress in her 1910 Detroit Electric. Electric cars were very popular with American society ladies as they would start without cranking.

for motor vehicles in the United States shifted from the big cities to the country town'. As cars became better and cheaper (as they very quickly did) their practical usefulness, particularly to the farmer, became plainly evident. Furthermore, as a group of potential buyers, farmers were far less intimidated by the challenge of maintaining a car than other social groups. For many years they had been coping successfully with all kinds of agricultural implements, some driven by steam, others by the stationary gas engine on which car engine technology was based. As evidence of their skill, motoring magazines were filled with tales of helpful farmers and blacksmiths who had rescued motorists in distress and who, according to one correspondent, 'could locate the trouble of his machine and repair it as well as an expert mechanic'.

The level roads of the prairie states was another factor favouring farmer ownership of motors; so was government policy. The State governments from Indiana west to the Rocky Mountains actively encouraged car ownership. They reasoned that if the horse could be replaced by machines, then a huge acreage of productive land could be turned over to providing food for people instead of fodder for horses. America's horses at the turn of the century had for thirty years been consuming the annual yield of 100 million acres of farm land which included 40 per cent of the total grain crop.

Government was also worried in that the continuing movement of rural population into the cities would seriously affect food production and it was hoped that the general adoption of the car would make the life of the farmers more attractive and profitable. In Iowa, the state education authorities even provided free winter courses in the theory and use of the gasoline engine. In Europe the position was very different. The average peasant was much poorer, more conservative and more mechanically backward than the American farmer; and for the most part car ownership was confined to the 'country gentleman' class. From very early on patterns of ownership in the USA were generally much more democratic than they were in Europe. This was encouraged and exploited by entrepreneurs like Henry Ford and Ransom Olds with spectacular results. The first American Automobile show was held at Madison Square Gardens in 1901. By 1905 this event had become the leading industrial exhibition in the calendar. On that side of the Atlantic the car was no longer a luxury or a foolish toy; it was regarded as one of life's necessities – which was not yet the case in Japan. The country that has become the world's leading manufacturer of cars and where the car culture is now so dominant played no part whatever in the early history of motoring. In fact, at the same time that engineers in the West were working to develop the internal combustion engine, a Japanese called Izume Yosuke was perfecting a form of transportation that was to dominate the streets of Japan for many years to come: the ricksha. The vehicle was an instant success. In the words of one Japanese: 'Our country has become a busy place to which even foreigners have come to reside. All this is due to the development of the ricksha.' This may seem extravagant praise for a vehicle that employed man as a draught animal; but horses were rare and expensive in nineteenth-century Japan and manpower was plentiful and cheap. It is said that the first horseless – and manless – carriage to appear in Japan was imported from France by the Mitsui family in 1904. By 1909 several women motorists whirled about the street frightening the ricksha pullers; but it was to be another fifty years before Japan truly entered the age of the automobile – and what an entry it was to be!

Today Japan's mighty motor industry grows daily more dominant. Yet in 1911 in Tokyo there were 22,403 rickshas, 12,547 bicycles, 156 horse-drawn carriages and just 82 automobiles. From *Sights and Scenes in Fair Japan*, published 1910.

Pushing Back the Frontiers

The miles, once the tyrants of the road, the oppressors of the travellers, are now humbly subject to the motor car's triumphant empire . . . It flattens out the world, enlarges the horizon, loosens a little the hands of time, sets back a little the barriers of space. And man who created and endowed it, who sits and rides upon it as upon a whirlwind, moving a lever here, turning a wheel there, receives in his person the revenues of the vast kingdom it has conquered . . .
(A. B. Filson Young, *The Joy of the Road*, 1904)

Proponents of the car vigorously sought to popularize it by every possible means, and manufacturers especially vied with each other to demonstrate the superiority of the four-wheeled machine to the four-legged beast . . .

In this promotion it is hard to overestimate the importance of early races and trials; they were undoubtedly a key factor in the motor car's rapid acceptance. James Flink asserts in his study *America Adopts the Automobile 1895–1910* that Americans first started to think about the car as something more than a cute toy when the French mounted a contest which began on 11 June 1895, over a 727-mile course from Paris to Bordeaux and back. The race was, among other things, the first of many demonstrations of the superiority of the internal combustion engine over steam and electric powered cars. (Eight of the finishers had petrol driven cars, against a single steamer.) It was also striking proof of the superiority of French roads. Without their great network of Napoleonic *routes nationales*, France could never have mounted motor car spectaculars like the Paris–Bordeaux race. It was won by Emile Levassor driving a two cylinder Panhard, and as Jean Panhard, scion of the great motor manufacturing family, today explains:

As a technical and indeed a physical performance, it was quite extraordinary because Levassor stayed at the wheel – except it wasn't really a wheel, but a kind of rod – he stayed there more than forty hours non-stop [the longest service stop was only twenty-two minutes] and he won the race with a lead of more than six hours on the runner up. People really believed that a fantastic new opportunity had opened up because the average speed had been 24 km an hour [15 m.p.h.] and no horse could travel at that speed.

Reports of these great achievements in France caused a stir even farther afield than the United States. Australia, too, had been tinkering with the possibilities of a horseless carriage. The Shearer, the Pioneer, the Ziegler and the Thompson were all early experimental Australian-built vehicles; but they were primitive in comparison with the contemporary French and German designs. It was a petrol-driven Benz imported from Germany in 1900 that launched Australia on its path towards total automobility. Like the United States, Australia was a late starter, but once the car had proved its usefulness in conquering the yawning distances it was taken up with astonishing rapidity. As James Flink points out: 'Australia, New Zealand, Canada, English-speaking countries with vast sparsely populated hinterlands, this is where the car was most readily adopted.' Outside the English-speaking world, Argentina was another large early market.

However, the races, of which the Paris–Bordeaux race in 1895 had been the first, came to an abrupt halt in 1903 with the disastrous Paris–Madrid race. Despite safety precautions taken by the organizers, there were ten

The catastrophic Paris–Madrid Race, 1903. Olliver urges on his Serpollet while his mechanic, hand on the bulb horn, peers anxiously through the blinding dust-cloud behind. For those following, the only way to steer was to look at the line of the roadside tree tops – not easy in cars which even then were travelling at speeds of up to 100 m.p.h.

The French road races drew headlines around the world, and from 1895 to the disastrous Race of Death in 1903, did more to promote international interest in the motor car as an effective replacement for the horse than any other events.

below] Those early automaniacs, with their overpowered machines and inadequate brakes, and driving without the benefit of protective clothing or crash helmets, were instrumental in making the motor car a swift and docile form of everyday transport. Here Maurice Fournier and his mechanic Louvel die in a fatal accident at Sarthe in 1911.

fatalities and many injured. The reasons were clear. Cars were now performing well beyond the capabilities of their brakes with speeds of up to 100 m.p.h.; unsurfaced roads which threw up great clouds of dust were inadequate for the high speeds being attained; and enthusiastic spectators, more accustomed to the leisurely days of the horse, crowded on to the country roads, often showing a fatal disregard for their own safety.

One of the 314 starters was carmaker Louis Renault's brother, Marcel. Negotiating a sharp bend south of Poitiers, he was momentarily blinded by a cloud of dust. He careered off the road down an embankment and was killed. The fatalities mounted and the race was dramatically stopped at Bordeaux by order of the French Prime Minister Emile Combes. The cars were not even allowed to return to Paris under their own power, but suffered the double ignominy of being dragged to the nearest railway station by horses and transported back to the capital by train. Newspapers called it the 'race of death' and it effectively marked the end of road-racing in France.

Similar spectacular city-to-city races had been organized by an American living in Paris. James Gordon Bennett was the wealthy son of the owner of the *New York Herald* newspaper (his father had sent Stanley to search for Livingstone in Africa). He instituted his first race in 1900, in part to generate interest in this exciting new sport amongst the folks back home. Countries with national automobile clubs were asked to nominate official teams of no more than three cars, which for the first time were to appear in national racing colours. The winner in the first year was the Frenchman Charron, who gained victory after killing five dogs that threw themselves under his wheels, maddened it seems by the unfamiliar sound of the cars.

Peugeot and Delage battle it out in the Automobile Club of France Grand Prix, held on a new circuit at Amiens in 1913. During the previous ten years racing had moved from the roads to closed circuits.

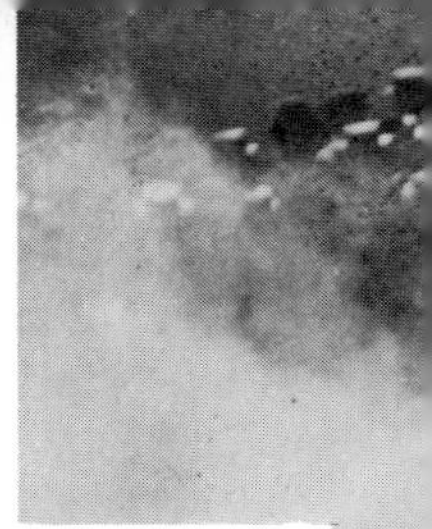

Circuit d'Auvergne. Coupe Gordon Bennett 1905
5. Tournant du GENDARME
L'Hirond

Postcard reminiscences of the last of the Gordon Bennett Cup Races, held in 1905 in France. Over a period of five years these races did much to establish motor racing as an international competitive sport.

Helping to promote the cause of automobilism in the United States are Italians Saratori (driver) and Latrini (mechanic), poised for action in their Fiat on the starting grid of the 1905 Vanderbilt Cup Race. These Long Island events – the inspiration of millionaire pioneer motorist William K. Vanderbilt – generated tremendous interest amongst an American public that had been slow to realize the motor car's potential.

The Indianapolis speedway, August 1909, and the beginning of a 100-mile inaugural race at the track which was billed as the 'greatest racecourse in the world'. In three days of competition on the rough and treacherous dirt track, five people were killed. Nonetheless, closed courses where spectators got a better view swiftly took over from road races.

In the United States, millionaire sportsman William K. Vanderbilt, inspired by his European exploits, instigated the Vanderbilt Cup contests 'to encourage the development of the automobile in this country'. Run on the back roads of Long Island between 1904 and 1910, it became the biggest social event in the automotive calendar. Described by *The Horseless Age* as a 'barbarous exhibition', sometimes over a quarter of a million spectators would line the roadside to gape at the cars as they rocketed by.

But if speed was firing the public's imagination, cross-country expeditions and long-distance journeys were fundamentally even more inspiring to the potential car-owner. As a *Horseless Age* editorial put it in 1900:

The most important man in the automobile industry today is the pioneer user, because as the conscientious operator of a more or less experimental machine he occupies a unique position. He is an authority on the new locomotion among his friends and fellow citizens and is the gatherer of data upon the road . . . for the improvement of his product and the better adaptation of it to meet the general demand.

The indefatigable American motoring pioneer, Charles Glidden, with wife (*second from the right*) and friends, blazing a trail across India in his British Napier on one of his early circumnavigations of the globe. To him the motorcar was mankind's greatest invention and one that should be shared by people throughout the world.

'Down Mexico Way' in 1906. Glidden's Napier, with those interchangeable flanged wheels for running on railroad tracks, took him where roads could not. 'There is a vast difference between a comfortable, quiet, smooth-running automobile and a hot, stuffy, local train,' he later declared.

The car was a tool of exploration. Glidden's Napier, here being punted across a river in Japan, was one of the first cars to be seen in the Far East.

One man in the United States, totally unconnected with the automobile industry, did perhaps more than anyone else to prove to a sceptical world that motoring was here to stay, that its place was in the countryside as well as the city, that it was neither a toy nor a showthing but, above all, a means of safe, economical transportation. Bostonian Charles Glidden became America's foremost automobilist. He had made his money in telephones, at one time controlling one-sixth of the Bell Telephone Company. In 1879 he had managed the first long-distance telephone line in the USA; he had sent the first round-the-world telegram, had plans in 1901 to operate airship travel between New York and Boston and was an experienced balloonist, having made a total of forty-two ascents.

His automobile accomplishments were no less startling. This Phineas Fogg was the first man to go round the world in a motor car, and he did it a total of three times. Starting in 1901, driving a British Napier, he took the better part of eight years. 'Touring at 17 m.p.h. for not more than ten hours a day', he declared 'is enjoyable, lengthens life and is without perils of any kind.' With his equally intrepid wife he travelled 46,528 miles, visiting thirty-nine countries and 12,000 cities. In August 1903 he was the first person to drive a car into the Arctic Circle. Eighteen months later he drove his Napier to the most southerly part of New Zealand then yet reached by a car.

He was indefatigable in his imaginative use of the car as a tool of exploration – where roads could not yet take him, railway tracks often did. Attaching flanged wheels to their Napier, the Gliddens drove almost 7000 miles along railroad tracks, scheduled as a regular train and necessitating the carrying of a guard on board for the entire trip, complete with regulation flags and whistle. In 1906 the Gliddens left Chicago travelling to El Paso, Texas, and there joining the Mexican Central Railroad to Mexico City. Another 'flanged tour' was from Minneapolis to Vancouver, a total of 1976 miles.

The Glidden entourage was a remarkable sight. Not for Mr and Mrs Glidden, however, the wild attire of some of the early automobilists. As they circumnavigated the world they sported the most meticulous fashions of the times. Glidden appears in his photographs as the veritable Victorian gentleman – rarely without coat, tie, or waistcoat. He also had that Victorian sense of mission. It was the motor car that would push back the frontiers of time and space, that would free man from the dark ages of inefficient transport. To this end he launched two great crusades – one for the building of better roads, the other for better motor cars. He maintained that the first would be overcome with the satisfaction and realization of the latter.

The Glidden Tours promoted good roads. Here a pathfinder car, a Premier, makes its way through Johnstown, Pennsylvania on a trial tour prior to the regular run some weeks later. The citizens of Johnstown had sent a delegation to persuade the Glidden officials to run the 1908 tour through their town. In return the city fathers had promised to improve their roads. The Glidden pathfinder photographer verified that the city was struggling with sand and clay to fulfil that promise.

In areas where roads *were* being improved their benefits were perceived immediately. In answer to a general inquiry sent out by the Chairman of the New Jersey State Board of Agriculture in 1900 as to whether a newly built road had worked an improvement in their conditions, one farmer replied: 'We are very proud of the country road in our neighbourhood so recently put in shape. Even before it was laid by the state, property near it advanced nearly 50 per cent in value.'

In 1904 Glidden was behind the idea of a cross-country reliability run from New York to St Louis conducted by the American Automobile Association. He believed that such tours, with rules and supervision, rather than speed races that he felt had now served their purpose, would help manufacturers improve their models and also help to promote the pleasure, the comfort and the reliability of the automobile to thousands of people. It was the day-to-day arduous abuse given by roads and climate that offered the best test for improving the breed. Most important of all was his belief that

'the motor car is really the father of the good roads movement . . . and in a few years there will be good roads connecting every town of consequence in this broad land'.

The cars covered 1250 miles in two weeks, pausing in Utica while their drivers petitioned the Governor of New York State. They wrote, 'Throughout the civilized world there do not exist roads in such wretched condition.' There was in fact marked divergence between the states in their attitudes to road improvement. Massachusetts and New Jersey were the leaders in the building and maintenance of roads. Many of the states had laws providing for the use of convict labour in improving the highway, and North Carolina had, by the early 1900s, built more miles of road under this system than any other state. But all the states looked to Europe – and especially France – with envy.

The success of this reliability run encouraged Glidden to establish the first of his celebrated Glidden Tours in July 1905. It was a landmark in the development of the automobile and the acceptance of motor transport on the American scene. For eight years the Tour was the premier event in the motorist's calendar and it convinced thousands of Americans, especially in the rural backwaters, of the car's capabilities for the future. It gave many their first exciting glimpse of a motor car: 'To my youthful eyes', wrote the author Bellamy Partridge, 'they had an enchanted appearance, as the Crusaders of old in quest of the Holy Sepulchre must have looked to the Feudal yokelry.'

The first Glidden Tour went from New York to Bretton Woods, New Hampshire, and back. Glidden had hoped to exclude the manufacturers from the competition and to run it for the benefit of the pioneer user and enthusiast, but in this he was outwitted. It was too good an opportunity for the manufacturers to pass up, and they fooled him through the simple expediency of joining the American Automobile Association. This first Glidden Tour, therefore, drew such automobile pioneers as Ransom Eli Olds (Oldsmobile), Percy Pierce (Pierce-Arrow) and Walter White (White Steamer), but, curiously enough, not Charles Glidden himself. He had uncharacteristically failed to ready his car in time, and instead went by train and met the group nightly. The tour lasted eight days and covered 870 miles.

The pioneer Gliddenites met varying receptions. Near Plymouth, a farmer's family had gathered a number of local musicians and as each car passed they saluted it with a bass drum and bugle. In New Hampshire a number of inquisitive farmers held their horses close to the road to get them accustomed to automobiles. A newspaper editorial in the town of Manchester, however, described the tour as 'an outrage that ought to be stopped once and for all . . . The lives and property of a perfectly helpless people have been seriously menaced, the laws have been wilfully disregarded and for no other reason than to afford amusement to a lot of strangers. Take the record of their run from Concord here – eighteen miles in forty minutes. Have they any right to *do* such a thing?'

In Worcester, Massachusetts, six were arrested for speeding. Said the judge, 'If these people want to race, let them go elsewhere. If they want to come to Massachusetts they must behave . . .' He fined them fifteen dollars each, and as the Gliddenites left town every car had its headlamps draped with black crepe. A band was hired for the occasion and led them through the town playing funeral dirges and 'Over the Hills to the Poorhouse'.

Glidden and his committee insisted that the tour was a reliability run and not a race, and 'scorchers' lost points. One of the few accidents befell the only lady driver, Mrs John Cuneo from Long Island, who later in life was to become a successful racing driver. In her White Steamer, with three passengers aboard, she crashed into the rail of a bridge entering Greenwich, Connecticut, but was unhurt. Her car was pulled back from the river bed and she limped on to the next checkpoint. Only four of the thirty-two starters failed to finish and the grand Glidden trophy was awarded to Percy Pierce of the Great Arrow Car Co. of Buffalo (the marque known from 1908 onwards as the Pierce-Arrow). *The Horseless Age* declared, 'It has strengthened our belief in the permanence of the motor car.'

Although the last Glidden Tour was held in 1913, Charles Glidden (who died in 1927) was able to see the results of his proselytizing on the car's behalf. He was able to write, early in 1911:

right] The George N. Pierce Company, former builders of birdcages, went into car production in 1901. From 1909, the date of this model, the cars became known as Pierce-Arrows. This grand marque survived until 1938, when the firm's entire assets were auctioned off for a mere $40,000, a sum much below what this car, originally costing $5000, would sell for today.

below] Mishap on the First Glidden Tour in 1905. Mrs John Cuneo, the only lady driver on the Tour, stands on a bridge in Greenwich, Connecticut, while willing hands haul her White Steamer back onto the road.

1905
The Glidden Trophy was awarded to Percy P. Pierce for running a Pierce Great Arrow 890 miles from New York to Mount Washington and return, outclassing all cars with a score of 996 points out of a possible 1,000. After completing the return trip to New York, the car was run to Buffalo, with no repairs whatever. The Trophy was awarded the Pierce Great Arrow by the committee after a vote of the contestants. The Pierce car fulfilled the spirit as well as the letter of all conditions.
1906
In the Glidden Trophy Tour from Buffalo to Bretton Woods, N. H.: Three Great Arrow Motor Cars were driven for 1,200 miles without repairs or adjustment, arriving in perfect condition and capable of resuming their journey, as they did, to home destinations in Buffalo, Pittsburg and Philadelphia. This record was unapproached by any other car. Percy P. Pierce, as the winner of the tour for 1905, retains the trophy. Another confirmation of our claim—an American car for the American conditions and temperament
THE GEORGE N. PIERCE COMPANY, BUFFALO, N. Y.
1906

The Glidden Tour annually demonstrated the car's potential to an ever less sceptical public. It was used by manufacturers to promote the individual superiority of their products, in this case by the Pierce Company, winner of the magnificent Glidden Trophy for five successive years from 1905.

Our whole mode of life, socially, has been more or less changed by the motor car . . . It has brought God's green fields and pure air seemingly nearer to our hives of industry and made the night and morning journey to business quicker, cheaper and a joy rather than a torment . . . Candidly it is doubtful if the present general exodus to country homes would be in progress but for the automobile and the good roads which it has been instrumental in causing to be built.

Across the world, the car was demonstrating its ability to conquer the elements. Two astonishing transcontinental marathons above all proved how the motor car could negotiate atrocious off-road conditions over long distances.

The most famous race of the Edwardian era was the Peking–Paris race in 1907, organized by the newspaper *Le Matin*. The winner was the pith-helmeted Prince Scipione Borghese in his huge 7.4 litre Itala that covered the 10,000 miles in sixty days, despite the most appalling road conditions and near calamities. A band of coolies accompanied his vehicle through China, carrying it across rivers and dragging it over mountains with mules. The only serious breakdown was in Russia. In the Ural Mountains one of the car's wheels collapsed . . . fortunately not far from the only wheelwright for hundreds of miles. Four of the five starters made it back to the place de la République – even two little de Dion Boutons – and the world was amazed.

above] Mongolian tribesmen assist one of the contestants in the Peking to Paris Race in 1907. The winning Itala covered 10,000 miles in sixty days, and even the two tiny De Dion-Boutons that arrived three weeks later managed the epic journey without any mechanical breakdowns.

above left] An admiring throng in Konisberg surround the victorious Prince Scipione Borghese and his companion Luigi Barzini in the final stages of that race. The Chinese were anxious to see the cars out of Peking as swiftly as possible, believing 'they would cause an upheaval in the popular mind, spread everywhere the fatal germs of Western corruption . . .'

left] The ultimate in long-distance expeditions. The Zust from Italy in Chicago on the New York to Paris race in 1908. It was one of six entries. The race began in Times Square on 12 February and ended in Paris on the night of 30 July. In the Zust Antonio Scarfoglio, poet, writer and son of a Naples newspaper publisher, sits at the wheel. His companions are reserve drivers.

Six months later a race from New York to Paris via the Pacific Ocean and Asia was jointly sponsored by the *New York Times* and *Le Matin*. More than a quarter of a million New Yorkers jammed Times Square to watch the six machines set off westward around the world in a sea of swirling national flags and flying champagne corks. Each contestant carried firearms as well as spare parts, food, shovels, sails and skis. Four cars reached Siberia, but only the German Protos and American Thomas Flyer made it to Paris. After covering 13,341 miles in 169 days, the Thomas arrived in Paris sixteen days ahead of its German rival. George Schuster, the American driver, became an international celebrity. Thomas sales jumped 27 per cent and the company ran behind in deliveries for over a year. By the end of 1908 there were 195,000 cars registered in the United States, over 250 manufacturers, and Henry Ford had just introduced his Model T . . .

It was agreed by all the contestants in the race that the most horrendous part of their journey had not been roadless Japan or the icy, trackless wastes of Siberia, but the winter roads of upstate New York. None the less, attempts to drive across the United States had begun almost as soon as Americans discovered the automobile. Many came to grief in desert country, some expeditions ending in tragedy. In July 1899 a Mr and Mrs John D. Davis set out to drive from New York to San Francisco. Leaving Detroit in mid August, neither the Davises nor their machine were ever seen again.

The victorious Thomas Flyer, the lone American entry, in the early stages of the Great Race. Dramatically depicted by Peter Helck in his painting: '1908 New York–Paris, Safe in the Railroad Siding'.

There were, in fact, a total of thirty-seven transcontinental attempts up to the time of the first successful crossing in mid 1903. This was made by Horatio Nelson Jackson, a 31-year-old doctor from Vermont who accepted a sporting wager of fifty dollars to drive a car successfully across the great continent. He bought a second-hand Winton, hired a mechanic called Sewell Coker and on 23 May 1903, weighed down with camping equipment, a rifle, pistols, picks and shovels and a fishing rod, the intrepid pair set out to cross the Sierra Nevada. Punctures were their greatest and most persistent problem. They ran out of fuel. They bogged down in Idaho mudholes. Block and tackle had to be constantly used in Wyoming to winch the car out of sand dunes and river beds. There were mechanical breakdowns too.

Most fascinating were the roadside reactions to their progress. They encountered isolated settlements where people had never even heard of a car, much less seen one. A Nebraskan farmer and his wife were so terrified at the approach of the chugging Winton that they fled in terror. One young enthusiast rode his horse seventy miles across the prairie to witness the mechanical marvel. 'I have seen lots of pictures of them', he enthused, 'but this is the first real live one I ever saw.'

Motoring pioneers faced all kinds of unlikely hazards. *Le Petit Journal*, the French magazine, enthralled its readers with vivid portrayals of automobilists' adventures out on the wild frontiers including attacks by eagles and even, in California, demented ostriches.

Bud the bulldog, sporting driving goggles, sits proudly in the Winton in which he (and his master Dr Horatio Nelson Jackson) made the first coast-to-coast crossing of the United States by automobile in July 1903.

SAN FRANCISC

left] The second coast-to-coast automobile crossing of the United States. Rolls of heavy canvas were used by Tom Fetch to help his Packard (christened 'Old Pacific') get enough traction over shifting desert sands on his epic journey from San Francisco to New York in 1903.

below left] With leaves and brush packed under the wheels of 'Old Pacific', a fence rail serves as a lever to ease it out of the mud on its historic transcontinental run.

It took them sixty-four days to reach New York and 'coast to coast' by automobile suddenly became the advertising catchword for manufacturers eager to promote their products. In August 1903, a month after Jackson and Coker, a factory-sponsored Packard made the crossing in sixty-one days. A month later a tiny curved-dash Olds managed the westbound trip . . . In 1905, as part of a publicity stunt to prove the strength and reliability of the Olds, two curved-dash runabouts with tiller steering completed the journey in a mere forty-four days. The continent had been joined.

Perhaps the most conclusive and remarkable proof of the taming of America's great open spaces came in 1909 when 22-year-old Alice Ramsey, with three female companions, became the first woman to drive across America. In an era when anything more formidable than a frying pan was considered too much for the gentle sex to handle, her forty-one-day safari from New York to San Francisco stood as a landmark in mankind's rapidly evolving relationship with the motor car.

There was remarkably little preparation for the trip. Alice had less than a year's driving experience with a bright red Maxwell, bought for her by her husband when her horse had bolted – ironically after it had been frightened by a motor car. Her skills as a driver had been noted by Carl Kelsey, an accomplished publicist and the flamboyant sales manager of the Maxwell-Briscoe Car Company.

right] The magnificent Alice Huyler Ramsey, who died in 1983 in her ninety-sixth year. In 1909 she became the first woman ever to drive a car across the United States – from Hell's Gate on the Atlantic to Golden Gate on the Pacific.

Alice Ramsey and chaperones, with a Maxwell support car in pursuit, speed along the highway somewhere between Cheyenne and Laramie. In 1909 the road across America often traversed private cattle ranches where gates had to be opened and closed by travellers.

Even in her ninety-sixth year the late Alice Ramsey still had much of the sparkle and zest that she must have required in abundance on her epic journey seventy-four years prior to our meeting. She drove the entire 4200 miles herself. Indeed, none of her three women passengers (two of them were sisters-in-law) knew how to drive. As Alice explained, her husband had given the expedition his blessing, but insisted they went along as 'chaperones'!

The most difficult part of their journey, she recalled, was crossing the state of Iowa:

We spent thirteen days getting across Iowa's 360 miles of gumbo [the black heavy clay in which horses had been known to drown]. Between Sioux City and Columbus we twice had to pay farmers to pull us out of mudholes. Then the rear axle broke again and a replacement had to be sent from Denver . . . In Wyoming the highway bridge over the Platte River was washed out and I had to bump the Maxwell almost a mile across the Union Pacific railroad trestle there . . . In Utah, we hit a prairie-dog hole in the road with tremendous force. The bolt came out of the tie rod connecting the wheels and the front of the car collapsed.

Also in Wyoming and Utah heavy rains had washed out the road in many places to a depth of ten or twelve feet. It was not an easy matter, as Alice Ramsey recalled, to drop into one of them and climb out again on the other side. In recounting this part of her journey in *Veil, Duster, and Tire Iron* she states:

Roads in Wyoming were scarcely what we would designate as such; they were wagon trails, pure and simple; at times, mere horse trails. Where the conveyances had usually been drawn by a team, there would be just the two definite tracks – or maybe ruts – often grass-grown in between. With no signboards and not too many telegraph poles, it was an easy matter to pick up a side trail and find oneself arrived at the wrong destination.

In 1909, the year of Alice Ramsey's remarkable trip, her sponsors – the Maxwell-Briscoe Company – were trumpeting 'a new epoch in the development of modern transportation'.

In the desert south of Salt Lake City, the road became merely two narrow tracks, curving away through the sagebrush. Suddenly the Maxwell dropped into a hidden prairie-dog hole and the front suspension collapsed. Undaunted, the intrepid Alice made temporary repairs with baling wire and continued her journey west.

'Down Under', the success of the early Australian motoring pioneers in taming the 'tyranny of distance' was in some ways even more dramatic than in the United States. At the turn of the century Australia was a land still being explored. The motor car became not merely a means of speeding communications and ending rural isolation, but a major tool of exploration in its own right.

More than any other event, it was the Dunlop reliability trials of 1905 that convinced Australians that the car was sturdy and trustworthy enough to tackle the Australian outback. In the first trial there were twenty-three starters following a route from Sydney to Melbourne then to Ballarat and back. The second trial with twenty-eight starters covered a much tougher route that included 132 miles of mountain roads. This failed to produce a clear winner, so the six survivors decided to scrap it out on a final leg from Sydney to Melbourne. When it comes to sport, Australians are perhaps the most competitive people on earth and this ding-dong contest caught the nation's imagination. Newspapers carried front page accounts of the cars and their drivers and the hair-raising conditions they encountered. The winning time for the full journey was 49 hours and 12 minutes but, according to the *Daily Telegraph*'s account, 'one of the best performances for the whole trip was that of Sid Day who came right through from Albury to Melbourne with both front springs broken and with them simply tied up with string. The steering rod of his car was also bent and he could only steer to the left. One spring was broken during yesterday's stage and another has been broken for four days.' These stirring reports undoubtedly made a deep impression on Australians, particularly on the farmers who were struggling to move their agricultural produce from the settlements in the hinterland to the markets and ports on the coast; and perhaps on the wives who endured the fearful isolation of the sheep and cattle station. It seemed that the motor vehicle was not just a plaything for the sporting rich but a practical tool which could have far-reaching social and economic consequences. The *Daily Telegraph* said as much in its editorial column: 'The fascinations of speed are almost irresistible once they have been tasted, but what is really wanted for the outback conditions is a car that will be modestly capable of twenty miles an hour with engine and tyres warranted to stand the roughest bush tracks.' And that, with the Model T Ford, is what the Australian bush dwellers eventually got.

One remarkable adventurer, barely remembered in his homeland, did more than anyone else to use the motor car to open up the outback and to blaze most of the new motoring trails the length and breadth of Australia. Francis Birtles, Australia's Greatest Overlander, born in Melbourne in 1881, made a series of eighty-eight extended trips in and around Australia, as well as pioneering the overland route from London to Melbourne in a Bean car. Prior to adopting the car, he had cycled round the coastline of Australia twice and set all kinds of push-bike records, including in 1912 a trip from Freemantle to Sydney via Adelaide and Melbourne in which he averaged over a hundred miles a day for thirty-one days. From late 1912 to 1928 he criss-crossed the continent, first in a single cylinder Brush car, then with Model Ts of which he was particularly fond, and later with British Bean cars. As Peter Wherrett, a fellow Australian who has studied Birtles's life, pointed out to us: 'He sometimes did it for a specific purpose, to prove a motor vehicle or to open up an overland telegraph wire or a railway line or something of that nature. But whatever it was, he was doing it principally for the sake of adventuring . . . he just wanted someone to give him food and lodging and a car to drive.' Birtles had a remarkable ability to go without food and drink for extended periods. He was also famous for his mechanical improvisations. When the crankshaft snapped on one car, hundreds of miles from the nearest homestead, Birtles made temporary repairs by cutting up the frame of his bicycle which he took with him everywhere. Some days later, a drive axle snapped and Birtles solved the problem by pinning the parts together, using pieces cut from a screwdriver. 'There isn't any job you can't do on a car', Birtles maintained, 'so long as you have a box spanner, some fencing wire and a bit of common sense.'

He was a compulsive explorer, relishing, it almost seems, the pain and terrible deprivation which were a feature of nearly all his journeys.

In June 1924 he made the first motor car journey across Australia from Sydney to Darwin and back covering over 6000 miles in his Bean. He was accompanied by Malcolm Ellis, a writer, and J. L. Simpson a mechanic from Bean Cars in England . . . and a dog called Dinkum. The car had already made its influence felt around the edges of the outback. Commented Ellis in his book *The Long Lead*: 'The greatest hardship now in travelling through this land is (in the words of Francis Birtles) "suffering the blanky glare from the benzine tins" which careless wayfarers have thrown from their cars.'

J. L. SIMPSON. "DINKUM." M. H. ELLIS. F. BIRTLES.

Francis Birtles, explorer, with M. H. Ellis, writer, Dinkum (Birtles' dog) and J. L. Simpson, an engineer from Bean Cars in England. Together they made the first motor car journey across Australia between Sydney and Darwin in 1924 in a 14 h.p. Bean, nicknamed the Scarlet Runner. The object of the journey was to determine why one hundred years of colonizing effort had left so few marks of progress on the Northern Territory with a population at that time of barely 3000 white inhabitants. It became another of Birtles' great motoring feats.

Birtles's last great journey, a soul-searing drive from London to Melbourne in 1927, again in a Bean, took him eight months and was the first and last complete overland trip between England and Australia. His health was ruined. Writing of his epic journeys in *Battle Fronts of Outback* in 1935, he highlighted the role the car played as an instrument of social change in Australia. 'The car has altered the meaning of life for the men and women – and children – of the interior. It has brought them comfort, given them social opportunities, given them better chances in case of sickness and childbirth, and widened their whole mental and physical horizon.' In essence, Birtles using the car pioneered the exploration of outback Australia *quickly*.

'It would have been done, even had it not been for the car and had it not been for people like Birtles, but the car and Birtles made it happen much faster,' maintains Peter Wherrett.

And where Birtles went others followed. In October 1926 the newly married Muriel Dorney left Brisbane with her husband, 'a very good bush man', and an Airedale named Laddie, in a brand new Overland Whippet on a motoring honeymoon. During the next six months they drove right round Australia, being only the second to achieve that feat. The spry Mrs Dorney, now living in the small town of Chinchilla, Queensland, recalls her husband Jack mapping their route: 'Well, Jack went in and got what maps he could, but some places he wanted maps for, they said: "We haven't got any, we'd like *you* to go and make us some!"'

Their progress was predictably slow, sometimes 'seventy-five yards in ten hours'. For the greater part of their journey there were no roads, only tracks left by bullock teams. 'The people who lived in the country in those days used to get their supplies by camel, donkey or bullock teams twice a year,' she explained. The Dorneys had to get petrol strategically placed by such donkey teams well in advance of their departure. As the journey proceeded, mainly in first gear, it became evident that fuel could be a problem. As the car clattered over a particularly rough section, one tin tied to a running board went missing. In deep consternation they sent a local Aboriginal, who had acted as a guide for them for a part of their journey, on a desperate search to find it. He returned, hours later, with the badly battered tin – fortunately still full. The nearest petrol supply was over 200 miles away . . . It took twenty Aborigines, three whites and five donkeys to get the car across the Fitzroy river. Between Katherine and Darwin they had to make ninety crossings of creeks and rivers, all without bridges . . . Their amazing trip received wide publicity and enormous crowds greeted them on their triumphant return to Brisbane in March 1927. They had achieved the apparently impossible; in their journey of nearly 9000 miles the car had not broken down once through mechanical failure and they had suffered only four punctures.

It was a lesson not lost on the Australian public. The wide open spaces, as in America, could be theirs too – and it was the car that would make it all possible.

Pretty and spry – Muriel Dorney today in the same model of Overland Whippet in which she and her husband made their extraordinary journey around Australia almost sixty years ago.

The press called it 'the world's most strenuous honeymoon'. Muriel Dorney and her husband Jack arrived in Brisbane in March 1927, after their pioneering 10,000 mile journey around Australia in an Overland Whippet.

[B]risbane G.P.O., Saturday, March 26,
at Midday!

The Overland Whippet

Honeymooners Around Australia

The Only American Light Car to Encircle Australia

Mr. & Mrs. Jack Dorney welcomed at Perth, W.A., after the most strenuous part of their trip

The Two Queenslanders who have proved the Whippet to be a Continent Conqueror, able to stand up to Australian conditions at their worst

10,000 Miles in the one Guaranteed Stock Model Whippet without any mechanical trouble whatever **10,000 Miles**

Sole Queensland Distributors:

E. G. EAGER & SON LIMITED

City Sales: Horsham House, Adelaide St. PHONE 6120 Head Office: Newstead, Brisbane

This was Nantasket Beach, Mass. on the Fourth of July holiday in the early 1920s. By the end of that decade the number of Americans setting off on holiday by car had reached 45 million. But in the process a blight was spread on the land. Paradise was turned into a parking lot.

Car Crazy

'What worse can a craze for horseless transport do than to massacre the innocents?'

'It can make a change in the life of the people,' he said . . . 'It will obliterate the accepted distances that are part of our daily lives. It will alter our daily relations to time, and that is to say it will alter our lives. Perhaps everybody doesn't comprehend how profoundly we are affected by such a change; but what alters our lives alters our thoughts; what alters our thoughts alters our characters; what alters our characters alters our ideals; and what alters our ideals alters our morals. Within only two or three years, every one of you will have yielded to the horseless craze and be a boastful owner of a metal demon . . . Restfulness will have entirely disappeared from your lives; the quiet of the world is ending for ever.'

That prediction Booth Tarkington remembered hearing in Paris around the turn of the century. By the time he wrote it down for the *Saturday Evening Post* in 1928, much of that prophecy had come to pass; at least in the United States. The rest of the world has followed – or is following – hard behind. The note of regret for the passing of an age of tranquillity we can regard with some scepticism. As we have seen, life with the horse was far from idyllic; but the forecast of revolutionary change in society has been wholly realized.

In 1910, in the United States, there was one passenger car registered for every forty-four households; by 1930 it was one for every 1.3 households. Levels of ownership rose in Europe too, but sluggishly by comparison. It was not until 1966 that Britain reached the level of car ownership that had been reached in the United States by the time the Depression set in. Holland edged up to that same level by 1970. Or to put the comparison in even sharper focus: in 1929, the United States manufactured 5.3 million cars, ten times the total for the rest of the world put together. By 1940 Detroit could boast that since the turn of the century there had been a 4000-fold increase in the number of vehicles registered; from 8000 in 1900 to 32 million in 1940.

The speed with which the automotive revolution transformed the United States is explained by a unique set of circumstances; the more obvious were the fast-growing population, the burgeoning economy and the soaring living standards that made it a much larger potential market than any single European country. But this alone does not explain what happened; nor do the activities of men of undoubted commercial genius like Henry Ford, Ransom Olds and Walter Chrysler. The car took over because Americans wanted it to. An editorial comment expresses that wish in wholly uncompromising terms. The writer first remarks that in the fiscal year ending June 1915, 660,000 passenger automobiles were sold in the United States for considerably more than half a billion dollars, bringing the total registration of automobiles in the country to just above 2 million. Far from drawing satisfaction from these impressive figures, the editorial concluded: 'The main point is that, with 20 million families and only 2 million automobiles, we have got our national job one-tenth done. When every family has an automobile we can take some credit to ourselves.'

This was by no means an extravagant or an eccentric point of view; some motoring enthusiasts went much farther. In 1916, James Rood Doolittle in his book *The Romance of the Automobile Industry* stated:

The only improvement in road transportation since Moses and the most important influence on civilization of all time [*our emphasis*], *has flowered and fruited on American soil. The real story of the automobile is, more wonderful than the fanciful tale of Aladdin's Lamp. It is more romantic than* Romeo and Juliet. *It is more important than the history of anything else in the world, because it deals with the latest and by far the greatest phase of the art of transportation . . . The mission of the automobiles is to increase personal efficiency; to make happier the lot of people who have led isolated lives in the country and congested lives in cities; to serve as an equalizer and a balance. Elegant in lines, powerful in action, wide in service, economical in operation . . . the silent always-ready servant . . . has accomplished vaster works for mankind's betterment than anything that has gone before.*

Even if the mood of the American public was the palest possible reflection of what was expressed in that purple passage, it would still have been car crazy. In such a state of mind the nation was prepared to make considerable sacrifices to own cars and to make sweeping changes in order to accommodate them. It follows that the rate of social change wrought by the car was proportionally much more rapid and far-reaching in North America than elsewhere. It was also wonderfully well described and documented. One detailed account of what was happening in small-town America (and what has happened since in many small towns elsewhere) is found in a study of Muncie, Indiana, undertaken by sociologists Robert and Helen Lynd. Their research – contained in two bulky volumes, *Middletown – A Study in American Culture* and *Middletown in Transition* – was undertaken in the mid 1920s and mid 1930s, precisely when the automobile was reaching its maximum impact. Judging from the Lynds' findings, the car was having a profound effect on everything from child-rearing and religious observances to the inevitable transformation of the use of leisure. The first revelation is the discovery of just how quickly car ownership became the norm in what was, and still is, a predominantly working-class – or as the Americans would say 'blue-collar' – community.

For this farming family in Nebraska, the purchase of the new car – probably their first – was an event of enormous significance, to be celebrated with Sunday-best clothes and commemorated by the travelling photographer.

The first real automobile appeared in Middletown (the Lynds' name for Muncie) in 1900. According to the Lynds, by 1923 'ownership of the automobile has now reached the point of being an accepted essential of normal living' – even more essential, so the Lynds discovered, than personal hygiene. Of twenty-six car-owning homes sampled, twenty-one were found to lack bathtubs. It seems that country dwellers had the same priorities. When a farmer's wife was asked why they had purchased a car at a time when her home lacked indoor plumbing, she replied tartly: 'because you can't ride to town in a bathtub'. The Lynds discovered that what the wise old prophet of Paris had foreseen had indeed come to pass: the 'horseless craze' had become universal and the world was indeed 'inhabited by a new kind of people': people who suddenly started to question or to abandon such familiar and unquestioned dicta as 'Rain or shine I never miss a Sunday morning at church'; 'A high-school boy does not need much spending money'; 'I don't need exercise, walking to the office keeps me fit'; 'Take a vacation? Never. I've not missed a day's work in twenty years'; 'We've never purchased anything we couldn't pay for right away'; 'Parents always ought to know where their children are' – the list is endless. Thrift was one of the first of the established folk virtues to take a severe battering. Credit

The motor car provided country women with their first opportunity for independent mobility. The farmer's wife could now drive to town to purchase and sell produce. She was no longer so heavily dependent on homegrown and homemade foodstuffs and this meant changes in the family diet and in the whole pattern of retailing.

Is it envy we see in the eyes of those seated on the porch, gazing at their relatives in the new 1910 Empire Runabout? This picture is almost a parable of the times. As leisure time was steadily taken over by the car, the traditional games and conversation on the porch would soon be insufficient to occupy the summer evening.

buying made its appearance very early in the car's history; it was the only way that most working people could finance such a costly acquisition. The Lynds found that Muncie had a local company that sprang up solely to finance automobile purchases. According to its manager, 'A working man earning thirty-five dollars a week and buying a car frequently aims to use one week's wages each month in paying for a car.' If the vehicle was extensively used or needed repairs, more than a quarter of the family income would be consumed and inevitably expenditure on other things was affected. According to the *Chicago Evening Post* of 28 December 1923, 'retail clothiers are unanimous in blaming the automobile for the admitted slump in the retail clothing trade', and the Lynds' findings suggest that the automobile may well have had something to do with it. 'We'd rather do without clothes than give up the car,' said one mother of nine children. 'We don't have no fancy clothes when we have the car to pay for', said another, 'the car is the only pleasure we have.'

Not only working-class families made sacrifices to own their cars. The Lynds interviewed middle-class ladies who spoke of giving up their Country Club memberships and other pastimes. 'We don't spend anything on recreation except for the car . . . We save everything we can and put the money into the car.' Surprisingly, some of these families put emphasis on the car because they felt it kept their families together. Others confirmed what one would expect: that the tendency of the automobile was to unravel the texture of family life. They regretted the passing of the 1890s when

Driving out for a picnic seems to have had an enduring attraction for the motorist – perhaps sustained by the belief that fresh air stimulated the appetite or, in the words of the AAA guide, 'incited the jaded appetite into most unexpected relish of the plainest food and plenty of it'.

'people brought chairs and cushions out of the house and sat on the lawns all evenings. The younger couples . . . would join in the informal singing, or listen when somebody strummed a mandolin or guitar.' For the young in the 1920s that was not a satisfactory way to spend an evening: 'What on earth do you want me to do? Just sit around all evening?' was the reaction of a high-school girl whose father attempted to dissuade her from taking an evening drive with a boy-friend. The same conflict was felt when the draw of the open road began to thin the congregations of Muncie's forty-two churches. In 1923, one of the town's leading ministers denounced what he called 'automobilitis – the thing those people have who go off motoring on Sunday instead of going to church'. But his words seem to have gone unheeded because when the Lynds returned ten years later they found that church attendances had fallen still further because, according to one professional man, 'people drive more and are always out on the road. There are better roads now, and people can go more places at longer distances by starting before morning church and coming home too late for the evening service . . .'

In the mind of the fundamentalist faithful, there could be no doubt that the motor car was doing the devil's business. 'Can you think of any temptation we have today that Jesus didn't have?' asked the Sunday school teacher. The boy's answer was immediate. 'Speed!' The desire of youth to get behind the wheel was a national phenomenon and it was not too far beyond the dreams of many. 'The fact that serviceable second-hand cars can be bought for 75 dollars and up, the simplicity of installment payment, "the fact that everyone has one" all unite to make ownership of a car relatively easy, even for boys.' And the consequences of this, according to the Muncie newspaper, was that boys who have cars 'step on the gas' and those who haven't cars sometimes steal them: 'the desire of youth to step on the gas when it has no machine of its own is considered responsible for the theft of the greater part of the 154 automobiles stolen from Middletown during the past year, 1923.'

If the word 'auto' was writ large across the life of Muncie in the mid twenties, this was even more apparent in the mid thirties. When the Lynds returned to make their second survey, they found that despite six years of Depression, however badly off families had become, they had hung on to their cars above all else. Although car sales declined drastically, car ownership did not. Old vehicles were repaired and kept on the roads come what may. 'Car ownership [in Middletown] was one of the most Depression-proof elements of the city's life . . . far less vulnerable, apparently, than marriage, divorces, new babies, clothing, jewelry . . .' Although sales of all other commodities fell by up to 85 per cent between 1929 and 1933, sales of motor fuel

The Model T! The car that has exhausted all the superlatives. If we accept that the car has been the most important engine of social change of the twentieth century, then the Tin Lizzie was that engine's most important component.

The 'Okies' seeking a new life in their ramshackle cars were immortalized by John Steinbeck in *The Grapes of Wrath*. This nomad family, pictured near Garden City, had an elaborate built-in travelling kitchen.

declined by only 4 per cent, suggesting little curtailment in mileage travelled. Moreover, the Lynds were struck 'by the fact that filling stations have become in ten years one of the most prominent physical landmarks of the city'. Parking had also begun to be a real problem: 'a traffic officer goes about marking the tires of cars parked on weekdays in the business section to enforce parking ordinances'. Even in 1925 they were concerned about children playing in the streets; by 1935 the newspaper was saying that 'children under 8 should not be permitted to play on the sidewalks'!

The Lynds were fascinated to find with what tenacity the working man had clung to his automobile. They concluded that for the business class, personal transportation was a habit, 'a comfortable, convenient, pleasant addition to the paraphernalia of living'; while it represented far more than this to the working class – for them, 'it symbolizes living, having a good time, the thing that keeps you working . . . Car ownership stands to them for a large share of the "American dream"; they cling to it as they cling to self-respect, and it was not unusual to see a family drive up to the relief commissary in 1935 to stand in line for its four- or five-dollar weekly food dole.' No effort was made by those distributing relief to discourage car ownership – which sometimes offered the only chance of employment – and yet the middle class were outraged and regarded it as a scandal that 'some people on relief still manage to operate their cars'. While some workers did lose their cars in the Depression, 'the local sentiment, as heard over and over again, is that "People give up everything in the world but their cars." '

Once country folk recovered from their initial hostility to motorists, they began to exploit them commercially. This farmer appears to have unloaded a heap of produce on his visitors.

617
139-766

Bryant Park, 42nd Street in New York City. By 1919, the horse-drawn traffic jams of the turn of the century had become almost completely motorized.

While the towns and cities were adapting to the horseless age, even more fundamental changes were being felt down on the farm. We have already noticed that after a brief spell of hostility the car was welcomed in rural areas and that it was seen as a possible means of making country life more attractive and thus stemming the population flow into the cities. But in some quarters the mission of the car was seen as even more profoundly important; nothing less than saving the countryside from genetic degeneracy. During the Spanish American War (in 1898) it had been noticed that conscripts from country areas compared unfavourably in physical and mental performance with city-bred troops, despite the natural disadvantages of city life. Studies made in 1910 and 1911 suggested a reason for this state of affairs. Investigations in isolated areas that lacked rail or boat transportation and, needless to say, good roads, revealed one outstanding fact; 'that everybody was related to everybody else, there were whole counties where it seemed as if a half-dozen families represented a majority of the population. In certain townships there were as many as twenty families bearing the same surname.' Inbreeding in remoter country areas was certainly not confined to the United States – until very recently its consequences could be seen in many parts of the United Kingdom – but only in the United States was the car seen as the remedy: 'And then along came the automobile. Finally it reached even the remote spots. Good roads are part of the car and they soon followed. The farmer's boy found that he could court the lady of his choice, even if she lived fifty miles away. He can select his mate from the whole wide world.'

Apart from performing the eugenic miracle, the car, it was claimed, had succeeded in keeping the bright boys down on the farm: 'the real reason for the markedly changed attitude of the young farmer toward the farm might be found in his deep-bosomed mate, wooed and won through the automobile, singing over her housework, and tending his growing brood of healthy children'. This dewy-eyed vision of rustic bliss sounds more like early Hollywood than sound social observation but there is evidence that the car did help to make country life a little less brutish than it had been, especially for women. Once it became apparent that motoring was not just a pastime for the wealthy, the task of improving the execrable roads became more appealing. Just how bad they still were in 1919 is vividly described by Emily Post in her account of a journey across the United States.

Our wheels, even with chains on, had no more hold than revolving cakes of soap might have on slanting wet marble . . . progress became hideously like that of a fly crawling through yellow fly paper, as though it were a question of time how soon we would be brought to an exhausted end and sink into it for ever. At the end of two hours more we had gone ten miles . . .

If that was typical of Iowa country roads in winter time, then it was clearly in the interests of farming folk to do something about them, particularly because at the very season when farm work was light and social activities feasible, the highways were impassable.

Politicians quickly appreciated that there were votes to be won by improving roads and throughout the 1920s, one by one, the state governments began to collect fuel tax to help pay for the roads. Still, these moneys were largely used to surface the main highways: country byways were often left to local voluntary efforts. On 'good road days' whole communities would turn out with horses and tools and set to work filling in the potholes. The

long-standing tradition of communal 'barn-raising' had prepared the way for this kind of event – which seems to have been as much an excuse for a party as anything else. According to one account: 'ladies of the community were out in force to serve the meals. Each evening . . . amusements consisted of music and a variety of entertainments; also some very prominent speakers to preach the gospel of good roads.'

Although Europeans did not go overboard for the car in the inter-war years as people did in the United States the popularity of motoring grew steadily. Attitudes towards car ownership had been changed by World War I when many more people, including women, first had the opportunity to drive. After the war, when industry got back onto a peacetime footing, it began to produce much more reliable and much cheaper cars. Nevertheless, motoring in Britain remained a predominantly middle-class pursuit. In the decade from the mid twenties, the average weekly adult male wage was about £3, which made the acquisition of even a second-hand car almost impossible. For the working classes, credit was hard to come by, and in any case credit buying had not developed as it had in the United States. It was significant that the Hire Purchase Bill of 1938, an excellent measure which sought to protect credit customers from unscrupulous repossession, set the upper limit of the value of goods protected by the Act at £50, which excluded motor cars.

left] When motorists set out to discover 'beautiful England', their welcome was not always as warm as this romantic picture might suggest. Motoring writers grumbled constantly about unfriendly farmers and sleazy roadside inns and compared them unflatteringly with the superb amenities enjoyed elsewhere. *Plus ça change . . .*

below left and right] In the 1920s, as motoring in the United States became increasingly democratic, in England and France it was still portrayed as the pastime of the privileged few.

The car carried services to the people as well as carrying people to the services. Nurses and midwives were among health auxiliaries to become motorized.

Many of the social consequences that mass ownership achieved in the United States were reached on the other side of the Atlantic by other means. Country bus services and rural deliveries helped to improve the quality of life in the villages. Mobile libraries and clinics, school buses and charabancs brought educational opportunities, health care and leisure activities to those who could not yet afford personal transportation.

Elsewhere in the world where settlers had suffered the tyranny of distance and isolation and where they could afford to invest in motor vehicles and better roads, the automobile revolution resembled the American experience. In the Australian outback some of the sheep and cattle stations were so cut off that it was not unusual for a family to go from one year until the next without exchanging words with a single stranger. Travellers often remarked that in the remotest areas the inhabitants – particularly the menfolk – were strangely shy and awkward, so unaccustomed were they to social contact with outsiders. Henry Lawson in his story 'Past Caring' told of the constant struggle of the settler against debt, drought, flood and loneliness: 'I think that most men who have been alone in the bush for any length of time – and married couples too – were more or less mad . . . it's only afterwards and looking back, that you see how queer you got.'

The utter isolation placed a terrible strain on women too, cut off as they were from shops, medical care, schools and entertainment. Frequently they were even denied the company of their own children: those who could afford to, sent them away to boarding schools on the coast. In her account of her epic car journey around Australia, Muriel Dorney makes frequent references to the loneliness of life in the outback: to the pressing hospitality of the station managers and their wives who would go to almost any lengths to delay the departure of their unexpected guests – likewise with chance encounters on the road. In one of the remoter cattle stations in the Northern Territories, Mrs Dorney encountered a settler who vowed she was the first white woman he had seen in twenty years.

The coming of the car was not the instant solution to the transportation problems of the outback. As we have pointed out, it was not that Australian roads were bad; in many parts of that inhospitable land they were non-existent. Where it could take you ten hours to cover seventy-five yards in a car (as it did the Dorneys), you would clearly be better off using some other form of transport and, to begin with, there was considerable doubt about the ability of the car to cope with outback conditions. Bourke, New South Wales, is about 500 miles inland from Sydney. A hundred years ago it was an important centre for the wool trade and at any one time there would be a thousand or more working bullocks in town. Camels also played an important part and from 1880 to 1920 they were a familiar sight. When Lindsay Green came to Bourke in 1915, he recalls there were two cars in town 'a Buick and an Overland'. He added to their number by purchasing a Model T Ford. Using this vehicle he hoped to get the mail contract; but the Post Office demanded that he provide horses as well as the motor vehicle because they considered that in the wet season 'there were still many places where only the horse could go'.

George Roberts grew up in Queensland where his father was the first Ford dealer in a small country town. He recalls that for many years the car co-existed with horse-drawn transport and that one of the reasons for the success of the Model T was that it had the same width of track as a horse and cart. Most other cars, he points out, had narrower tracks which meant you were driving 'with one wheel up the hill and the other down in the gulley – most uncomfortable'. Finding one's way was also a headache: road signs were almost non-existent and, according to Mr Roberts, the best plan was to follow the discarded petrol tins. Fuel was sold in four-gallon cans which fitted on to the car's running board; 'when you filled your car in the bush the tin was thrown away so the track became defined by the petrol tins on either side of the track'.

At a time when driving conditions were as bad and as hazardous as they were almost everywhere, it has been suggested that the hardship itself was one of the attractions of early motoring.

Warren James Bellasco believes that the first great wave of popular enthusiasm for the car in the United States was rooted in a nostalgic return to the simpler times before the age of the railways when (supposedly) travel was filled with a sense of emancipation and adventure, free from the shackles of timetables and iron tracks. Filled with the desire to escape the pressures of industrial society, to explore independently off the beaten track, to recapture a sense of free-wheeling mobility, motorists took to the roads in ever increasing numbers. 'Autocamping' as the new fad was called, soon became pandemic. Those who had never taken holidays before took to the roads, living outdoors, discovering ways to cook, clean and look after themselves far from modern conveniences and familiar surroundings. In Muncie, according to the Lynds, even working-class families were getting the 'vacation habit'. As the practice of giving workers holidays with pay began slowly to take hold, 'the automobile is putting short trips within the reach of some for whom such vacations are still "not in the dictionary"'.

One woman, proudly recounting her first ever away-from-home trip, recalled that 'the women slept in the cars, the men on boards between the two running boards'. It sounds fiendishly uncomfortable but, to begin with, that seems to have been part of the attraction of autocamping, part of the important contrast with the stuffy, comfortable, predictable experience of travelling by train. In *Touring Topics*, 1926, we read: 'Those who want to travel without effort and without interest or excitement, should travel by train. Those who enjoy the open spaces and the strenuous life will find touring a delightful thing.' Delightful perhaps; but it was also at worst dangerous and at best an arduous, grubby and exhausting ordeal. In *Motor Campcraft* of 1923 the advice is 'make sure your automobile is fit to fight a long hard battle'. Henry Ford himself was an autocamping pioneer and it seems that even with him the experience was not exactly sybaritic. According to one of his travelling companions, 'We cheerfully endure wet, cold, smoke, mosquitoes, blackflies and sleepless nights just to touch naked reality once more. Discomfort is, after all, what the camper out is unconsciously seeking.'

right] Sightseeing in America's National Parks was enhanced when tourists could cover the vast areas by car. In 1920 128,000 cars entered the National Parks; twenty years later, the figure reached 2 million annually.

below] According to the *Illustrated London News* of May 1933, 'This year it would seem that many folk are going to take their holidays gypsy fashion, in caravans. Motor owners are now better catered for in these trailers . . . and women's requirements have been specially catered for.' Judging from the photographs of the period, it was still considered improper to suggest that the sexes should share such cramped quarters.

Needless to say, to deal with all the difficulties the motorist would encounter along the road and in the campsite there was, on offer, an extraordinary array of mechanical aids and accessories. 'Quick start in cold weather guaranteed' was a claim made for dozens of devices; then there were all those side curtains, 'gypsy wings' and wind deflectors to cut down draughts. At a time when fuel and oil gauges, electric headlights and speedometers were regarded as 'extras' the car owner was offered scores of different brands to choose from. 'Out in one minute, though in hub deep', says the advertisement for the Auto Chain Pull which 'makes it absolutely certain you will not be stalled in mud or sand'. Among the extraordinary and ingenious new range of camping equipment on sale was a patented washing machine – a metal tank that was designed to be filled with water and soiled clothing and strapped to the running board. In theory it employed the 'natural motion of the automobile over the roads to agitate and clean the laundry'.

Judging from the correspondence in the touring magazines, much of the pleasure of motoring came from a sense of shared adversity and the camaraderie of the road. There are numerous accounts of convivial evenings with strangers, of sing-songs over the camp fire and of the kindness of good Samaritans on the highways. But it should also be said that the car permitted its passengers to be much more selective about chance meetings with

Good clean vacation fun in the fresh air at the end of the glorious open road. With rod, axe and gun, barbecue and cooler (stocked with soft drinks only) the American nuclear family here discovers paradise 1949-style in the Nash family sedan.

strangers than did the train; and this is almost certainly another major reason for its enormous popularity. The breezy and co-operative companionship of fellow motorists was vastly preferred to the tactile and unwelcome intimacy of a stuffy railway carriage.

So rapidly did the motoring holiday catch on that what had started as a spontaneous effort of a few mavericks to break away from the more conventional and structured holiday soon became the accepted norm. In 1929, in the USA alone, 45 million Americans jumped in their cars and drove off somewhere for a few weeks' recreation. No longer did they camp along the roadside or in a farmer's field. As their numbers increased, municipal autocamps began to make their appearance. At first these were free of charge but as the services they provided grew more sophisticated and as the need to keep out 'undesirables' became evident – particularly during the Depression – most municipalities charged a modest user's fee. As soon as the free camps disappeared, the door was open for competition from private enterprise which offered more and more attractive camping facilities and, eventually, tourist cabins or cottages. This was the beginning of what is now known worldwide as the *motel*. The first motels were very unlike the Holiday Inns or the Travelodges that are now slowly making their standardized, reliable and tediously predictable presence felt along the highways of the world. Their distant ancestors, the tourist cabins or courts, offered little more than shelter from the elements. These were superseded by more pretentious structures with a greater range of services. But until the 1950s the average motel was a modest establishment with ten to fifteen rooms, frequently run by a married couple who performed the functions of receptionist, cashier, porter and chambermaid. They rarely, if ever, provided food; that service was left to a whole range of roadside eating houses. Just as the family-run motels gave way to the multinational chain, so the small family diners were largely supplanted by McDonalds, Burger King and all those other names that mean 'heartburn' to motorists the world over.

In the twenties, motorists in Europe commented enviously on the lavish provisions made for touring in the United States and compared it unfavourably with the state of things at home. Writing in the *Sphere* in 1925, R. P. Hearne described the generous parking and free camp sites in the American National Parks and deplored the fact that in the UK there was such a lack of good camping sites. He also commented most unfavourably on British roadside eating. 'An unappetizing cold lunch in a frowsy little hotel in this country is so costly and such poor value that more and more people seek to avoid the expense.' Even more objectionable, in his view, were those 'swagger' road houses where prices were even higher and cooking very little better. It sounds like a story that is all too familiar to today's motorist.

But perhaps it was unfair in the 1920s to compare driving conditions in the United States with Britain – or indeed with anywhere else. There was less inclination and economic incentive to provide for cars and motorists because fewer people owned cars and fewer people believed everything and anything should be done to accommodate the car, whatever the cost. The typical difference between Europe and America in their early appreciation of the car was perhaps demonstrated in a remark that Herbert Asquith made in 1907 when the question of taxing automobiles came before the British Parliament. He said that the tax on the motor car would be 'almost an ideal tax because it is a luxury which is apt to degenerate into a nuisance'.

left] This bird's eye view of the Rose Bowl, Los Angeles, in 1949 underlines just how far Americans have been prepared to go to accommodate the car. Seeing this, a visitor from outer space might be forgiven for believing that it is the car that has inherited the earth and that man is here to serve it.

As we have seen, in 1915 American opinion was demanding one car for every American family. Ten years later the motoring correspondent for the *Illustrated London News* was quite clear that 'if we ultimately get to the average of one car for every ten families, it will be about as much as we have accommodation for'. He concluded that it was quite undesirable that Britain should ever have the level of ownership already achieved in the United States. He was writing at a time when there were only 475,000 private motor cars registered in the British Isles. In Europe at large, because of this more modest rate of growth, the transition to the age of the motor car was achieved without the damage suffered by the environment in the United States. There, the explosive increase in car numbers triggered a building boom along the nation's highways. We have already remarked that on their second visit to Muncie in the mid thirties, the Lynds were astonished by the proliferation of filling stations that had become 'the most prominent physical landmark in the city'. This was a national – indeed an international – phenomenon. In the years immediately following World War I, motor fuel was still sold in chemists' and hardware stores; but during the twenties, as the oil companies grew daily in wealth and power, the number of filling stations climbed until it seemed there was one on every street corner. Indeed, it is not at all unusual today to find four brands of fuel competing for business on the same crossroads.

If the vendor of motor fuel was the first to colonize the roadside he was the first of many. From the twenties onward, the ribbon development of roadside business transformed the appearance of America; and according to the relative strength or weakness of their car cultures and of their planning laws, other nations have tagged along behind. These universal roadside settlements aimed first to serve the car directly: filling stations, garages, body shops, car washes, showrooms, second-hand dealerships and junk-

right] A Californian drive-in, June 1939. They had begun six years previously when Richard Hollingshead opened the first outdoor cinema in Camden, New Jersey, to appease smokers and others who wanted to be able to eat and talk during a movie. Well-wheeled teenagers quickly discovered that the local drive-in (known in Australia as a 'fingerbowl') was a cheap place to avoid parental scrutiny. By 1958 there were over four thousand in the United States, but now there are barely half that number, the majority killed off by high land prices and changing habits of courtship.

yards proliferated. Next, in satisfying the needs of the motorist for food, accommodation and amusement there was the rapid rise of the motel and the drive-in; not just the drive-in restaurant but the drive-in cinema, liquor store, bank, dry cleaner's – in fact, all the services that had been available to man-the-biped became available to the new species of man-on-four-wheels. California, which of course went fastest and furthest, even provided the drive-in church and the drive-in funeral home where the motorist could say his prayers or view the mortal remains without ever leaving the security of his car.

above] The motel has now become such an established institution that it is hard to believe that its lineage is far from respectable. From scruffy auto camps described as 'an assortment of dime dance hotels, beer joints, disorderly houses and criminal hangouts', motels have developed into world-wide chains with household names that epitomise middle-class values.

right above] At the Totem Pole drive-in the clients were promised 'heap good food'. The idea of the motorist as wandering nomad died hard but this style of drive-in, where the order was telephoned from the parking lot, was short-lived.

By the 1950s, the American dream of 'autopia' had become a reality. The sprawling suburbs with a car in every driveway met mounting criticism and voices calling for a more balanced approach to transportation began to be heard.

Coast to Coast
BUSINESS
INDIANA
3
BUSINESS
INDIANA
67
CHARLES ST
LICENSEE OF
McDonald's
SPEEDEE SERVICE SYSTEM
HAMBURGERS
OVER 40 BILLION SOLD
Salad Bar
Nye's

SELF SERVE
TRAM STOP
AUTO-ELECTRICAL SALES
DEREK'S STANDARD
40·5
CENTS PER LITRE
FOOD
MOTOR OIL 4 LITRES $4.99
AUTO AIR CONDITIONING
HOLDEN & COMMODORE SPECIALISTS
$8
SPECIALISTS IN JAPANESE & VW • BMC CARS ALL MAJOR & MINOR REPAIRS
JOG-213
ILM-000

What made this roadside development such a powerful influence on the visual environment was the need of the entrepreneurs to make their presence known to customers in fast-moving cars. The landscape became utterly swamped with gaudy structures and large and garish signs. The best that can be said about this style of roadside architecture is that it is occasionally amusing. In California, there emerged in the twenties what has been termed Direct Programatic Architecture; the structure was itself the sign of what it was selling. Thus in Los Angeles you could buy shoes inside a shoe, ice-cream inside a cone, coffee inside a coffee pot and even, in San Francisco, take music lessons inside a giant accordion. Somehow, this kind of silliness is not out of place in southern California and at least, as David Gibhard points out in the delightful book, *California Crazy*, 'it was evidence of a non-serious view of not only architecture, but symbolism and salesmanship as well'.

If the Lynds could return to Muncie today they would find that the appearance of the town has been utterly changed – largely for the worse – at the dictate of the car. Every approach road is flanked with tawdry commercial development: mile upon mile of those fast-food outlets, motels, car accessory shops and dealerships decked out with plastic bunting. The town centre demonstrates every symptom of car blight. Whole blocks have been razed to provide parking space; the buildings that remain are almost entirely offices. All the residents have departed to the outer suburbs and the retail establishments have followed them to the suburban shopping malls. The only inhabited part of central Muncie today is on the wrong side of the tracks where the poor – and largely black – families reside in peeling houses surrounded by rusting and mainly moribund cars.

What has happened to Muncie has happened to a greater or lesser extent to most cities in North America and nowhere more dramatically than in the motor capital of the world, Detroit. In 1982, the city centre's last great departmental store, Hudsons, closed its doors for the last time. Shoppers could no longer be tempted into an area where vandalism and crime are rampant and where convenient car parking is limited. The owners of the store contributed to its downfall; they had built huge shopping centres surrounded by car parks in outlying parts of Detroit. These new shopping malls quickly became the focus of new suburbs. So the city centre that was built on the wealth created by the car has now been destroyed by the car.

The first man to detect this trend and to exploit its commercial possibilities was a young developer called Jesse Nichols. He purchased some unpromising swamp land in the outskirts of Kansas City and in 1920 announced his plans for the Country Club Plaza, the first major shopping area to be constructed to cater for people who would be arriving by automobile rather than by electric trolley car. Filling stations, garages and parking spaces were to be included. According to Jesse Nichols's son Miller: '[my father's] detractors said, "Jesse's kinda gone nuts with all this car idea" '. The Country Club Plaza opened in 1922 and quickly became a great commercial success; and it succeeded just as Jesse Nichols imagined it would: it attracted a community to grow around it. Today, according to Miller Nichols, there are between five and six thousand family units living within walking distance of the plaza and many thousands more within a few minutes by car.

Though the car hastened the outward growth and inner decay of American cities, it was a process that had started before the age of the automobile.

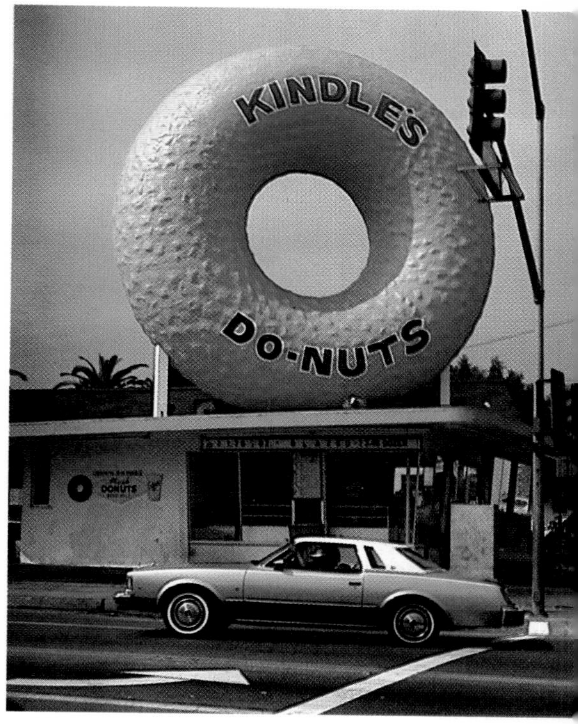

To catch the eye of the speeding motorist, roadside businesses have tried to outdo each other in erecting ever more gaudy, garish and gimmicky signs and structures.

By the end of the nineteenth century, following successive waves of immigration, cities had become increasingly congested and many of the social ills of the time were blamed on the squalid slum conditions that prevailed. One solution that suggested itself to planners was to encourage movement to outlying areas. This was achieved at first by improved suburban railways and electric trams and trolley cars. With the coming of the automobile, what had been a modest flow of population became a flood. The belief that you could build 'Autopia' in the green and leafy suburbs was enthusiastically touted by Henry Ford. 'We shall solve the city problem', he wrote, 'by leaving the city'; and what he meant was 'by leaving the city by car'. Very quickly, what is now termed 'suburban sprawl' assumed massive dimensions, seen at its spectacular worst in the building boom in Los Angeles County. Anyone who has flown over that conurbation today will agree with Mark S. Foster that 'no pre-twentieth-century technological advance has ever wielded so much potential for shaping the urban landscape as did the automobile'. Lewis Mumford, in his outstanding work *The City in History*, after reminding us that 'two-thirds of central Los Angeles are occupied by streets, freeways, parking facilities, garages', turns his attention to the suburbs: 'a multitude of uniform, unidentifiable houses, lined up inflexibly at uniform distances, on uniform roads . . . a low-grade, uniform environment from which escape is impossible. What has happened to the suburban exodus in the United States now threatens through the same mechanical instrumentalities [the car], to take place, at an equally accelerating rate everywhere else – unless the most vigorous counter measures are taken.'

Despite Lewis Mumford's warning, car-created urban sprawl is now almost a worldwide phenomenon.

In 1914 there were 37,000 motor vehicles on Australia's roads; by 1939 there were 820,000. With a population of 6½ million, that gave Australia one of the world's highest rates of car ownership and consequently one of the most drastically car-altered landscapes. The city of Sydney once nestled around its spectacular harbour; but it became a megalopolis stretching from the Pacific almost fifty miles inland to the foothills of the Blue Mountains. Everywhere, the newly expanded cities bear the imprint of the car culture and they bear it so strongly that it has given a dreary sameness to suburbs thousands of miles apart. Driving along the Paramatta Road to Sydney's western suburbs, you could so easily be anywhere in the American sunbelt; even the hamburgers have the same names. Now European roadsides are falling victim to this visual uniformity. With Holiday Inns, McDonalds, Burger Kings, Travelodge and the rest spreading their tentacles, roadside communities are taking on distinctly transatlantic looks.

The car and its attendant services not only became the dominant part of the landscape and blurred the cultural identity of cities, they also closed the gap between city and countryside. This meant that country folk became 'citified' and that many of the traditional rural values and institutions began to wither away. These may be regarded as benefits; but the overall tendency of technology to homogenize all that it touches is far from comforting. 'The motorist' has always been regarded as a distinct social group and there is evidence that car ownership, in itself, implies the adoption of a certain set of values. If the car has contributed to the 'embourgeoisement' of us all, what will happen when we all have cars? That, in another context, was a question asked by Lewis Mumford. His answer is far from comforting.

as long as motor cars were few in number, he who had one was king; he could go where he pleased and halt where he pleased . . . The sense of freedom and power remain a fact today only in low-density areas, in the (rapidly diminishing) open country; the popularity of this method of escape has ruined the promise it once held . . . In using the car to flee from the metropolis, the motorist finds that he has merely transferred congestion to the highway and thereby doubled it. When he reaches his destination in a distant suburb, he finds that the countryside he sought has disappeared; beyond him, thanks to the motorway, lies only another suburb, just as dull as his own.

Spaghetti Junction
No technological advance in this century has done more to change the urban landscape, or developed such an appetite for land resources as the motor car. In the vastness of the United States this may not cause too much concern; but this is an English landscape near Birmingham.

The Car and the Developing World

Just over 40 per cent of the world's cars are in the United States, close to one-third in western Europe, 7 per cent in Japan and another 7 per cent in Canada, Oceania and South Africa. This means that 83 per cent of the world's people own a mere 12 per cent of its automobiles.
(Worldwatch Institute, Washington.
The Future of the Automobile in an Oil-Short World)

To own a car is hopelessly beyond the dreams of almost the whole of mankind. And yet it is still the most coveted of objects. In China you could try to deceive your friends with a photograph taken in a car made of paint and canvas. In Africa, you could build your own and deck it out in tribal war paint.

While a handful of the world's most developed countries were tearing down their social structures and their cities to accommodate the car, many others continued on their way almost untouched by the automobile revolution. For the teeming millions of the Asian land mass, the emergence of the motor car was – and still is – largely irrelevant to their transportation needs.

In China, there are 18,000 people for every car on the road; in the United States the number of persons per car is 1.9. In other words, China has progressed as far along the road to automobility by the 1980s as the United States had travelled by 1900. In most of continental Asia today, and in much of Africa and Central and South America, the likelihood of owning a car must seem as remote to the average man as it was beyond the dreams of the farm labourer in nineteenth-century Europe. Some 7 per cent of the world's population own private cars and only a tiny proportion of that minority of mankind lives in the Third World. In most countries car ownership is still what it always has been: the ultimate symbol of wealth and privilege.

The first cars encountered by the people of India belonged either to their colonial masters or to their hereditary rulers. The rajahs and maharajahs and nizams and their princely offspring purchased between them perhaps the costliest and most exotic array of custom-built automobiles ever assembled, until the oil-rich Arabs started out on their spending spree in the 1970s.

Lord Montagu believes that the very first United States car export, in the shape of an Olds Steamer, went to India in 1893. Between then and the total ban on imports that was imposed after Independence, India's princes went about as far as it is possible to go in transforming a mere machine into a symbol of power and a demonstration of shameless prodigality. Some of their buying was plainly eccentric: Jam Sahib of Nawangar acquired forty-two Lanchesters; while the Maharajah Holker of Indore had his SJ Duesenberg, his Hispano-Suiza and his Phantom III Rolls-Royce all fitted with identical bodies from the coachbuilders Gurney Nutting. The ruler of Rajkot's Rolls-Royce Phantom III Torpedo Cabriolet had twelve forward-facing headlights, probably for night hunting. Shooting brakes, designed for tiger hunting, were carried on all kinds of large and powerful chassis: Maybach-Zepplins, Cadillacs, Minervas and Isotta Fraschinis – the cream of the carmakers' craft was artfully adapted, at whatever cost, to suit the smallest whim of the most whimsical of princes. These unique and splendid vehicles were joined in the heat and the dust of India's roads by the humbler vehicles of the British administrators. The Viceroy always had a Napier while the district officers, the tax collectors and the political agents drove Humbers.

But what the British may have lacked in mechanical magnificence they certainly made up for in imperial self-confidence. In 1913, Charles Watney and Mrs Herbert Lloyd published *India for the Motorist. The Guide for the*

opposite above] The 'Tren-Car' trailer, designed by Labourdette, crossing a river in darkest Africa. The car belonged to the Governor of French West Africa.

opposite below] This is alleged to be the first car in Tanganyika but the model must surely be too late (1920s) to deserve that honour. Judging by the size of the work-force, it seems that the vehicle is about to be lifted bodily across the water.

Between the wars, the Indian royalty and nobility accumulated collections of cars the like of which we shall never see again. These are just a few of the opulent vehicles that passed through the hands of H.H. Jam Sahib of Nawangar. Only six of the forty-two Lanchesters he purchased are on display.

Tourist and Resident. From its pages it appears that those haughty turn-of-the-century attitudes that quickly vanished from European roads were still alive and well in the colonies. According to the Guide:

The native is a poor driver and easily loses his head. Save in the cities, all animals often shy badly at motor cars. Draught oxen . . . will often plunge wildly and swing a cart before a car in the twinkling of an eye. It is common for such carts to plunge off the road into an adjacent field as the car approaches and no motorist need be perturbed by this. Usually a prudent native stops, dismounts and draws well to the side as the car goes by. Everything gives way to the motor car in India, particularly if driven by a white Sahib [*our emphasis*].

Of the two authors of the guide, Mrs Lloyd seems to be the more intolerant of other road users; but then it's said that the memsahibs always were more status-conscious than the men.

above right] India may have banned car imports but there are still those who can afford to drive in luxury. On the streets of Bombay these symbols of wealth and privilege stand out as starkly as did the gleaming limousines of the princes.

Language phrase books always provide a fascinating insight into travellers' attitudes and especially the difficulties they expect to encounter. *India for the Motorist*, in its brief selection of Urdu phrases, includes:

I want a horse, 2 horses, 3 horses,
an ox, 2 oxen, 3 oxen,
4, 5, 6, 7, 8, 9, 10 coolies.

To push the motor car
To pull the motor car
Over the river.

In India in those days, the greatest drawback, even on the main roads, was the absence of bridges. Time after time cars had to be laboriously ferried over rivers or drawn across fords, which made progress desperately slow. However, motorists were advised that 'native assistance is readily available and as a rule, very cheap'. Clearly, the nearest most Indians came to a motor car was lending a shoulder to its wheel or leaping for cover as it thundered past; it had as much relevance to their own transportation needs as the space shuttle has to ours. Things have not changed all that much today.

OUR ONLY GOAL
TO BUILD A STRONG SELF-CONFIDENT SELF-RELIANT & INDEPENDENT INDIA
OUR ONLY GOAL
TO BUILD A STRONG SELF-CONFIDENT SELF-RELIANT & INDEPENDENT INDIA
HERN RAILWAY

Of India's 700 million people, perhaps 15 per cent have actually ridden in a car. Most people have probably never travelled more than ten miles from their village by any means at all, and many have never seen a town or even been able to afford a bus ride. Half of India's villages are still not accessible by all-weather roads and in these areas the bullock cart and the bicycle predominate. Today there are 23 million bicycles and 17 million bullock carts on India's roads and a little over a million cars; but to drive in Bombay you would never believe it.

What cars there are in India are concentrated in the cities and particularly in the major ports. Bombay, Madras and Calcutta have played an important part in the nation's car industry. In the beginning, when fully assembled vehicles were imported, the ports were the point of disembarkation and distribution. Later, Ford and General Motors had assembly plants in Bombay, Calcutta and Madras; and over the years, as technical know-how and skilled labour developed, it seemed logical to establish the indigenous industry in those same cities.

At one level, the story of India's own car industry can be told just by standing on any street corner and watching the traffic go by. It is hardly a spectacle to capture the imagination of the car buff. After Independence, the government decided that the car was not 'appropriate technology' for India, that it should be given very low priority, that imports should cease and that home production should be limited to very few models.

Hindustan Motors was permitted to buy from Britain the machine tools to produce the old Morris Oxford; and Premier Motors purchased from Fiat the machinery to make the old Millecento Fiat. Thirty years later these two vehicles, called in India the Hindustan Ambassador and the Premier Padmini, are still being manufactured in Calcutta and Bombay. Recently, however, the Indian government made an announcement that may signal a profound change of policy towards the car. An agreement has been made with the Japanese Suzuki Corporation to manufacture a small, modern car. Behind this announcement lies a long and murky story.

The Indian government has expended huge sums to give the centre of Delhi the expansive roads and flyovers that are thought to befit a capital city. At present they appear to be a needless extravagance.

below left] According to one view, India would do far better to modernize its fleet of 17 million bullock carts than to invest hugely in new car factories and infrastructure.

below] To those used to the bland modernity of the Western car scene, India offers constant surprises. Vehicles are kept on the road far beyond their natural lifespan. This decrepit old Austin is waiting to be coaxed back to life by some resourceful pavement mechanic.

below right] The venerable Ambassador started life as the old Morris Oxford. After giving thirty years of honourable service, it is shortly to be replaced by something more up-to-date – but not necessarily better suited to India's motoring needs.

The repair and maintenance of cars is a colourful and noisy part of India's street life. With a box of tools and a few feet of pavement, these improvised garages are prepared to attempt anything, from changing the plugs to stripping down the engine.

The Suzuki car is to be produced in the huge Maruti factory outside Delhi which was at the centre of one of the biggest scandals in recent Indian history. The story is important because the Maruti débâcle prevented any real development of the Indian car industry for almost twenty years. Sanjay Gandhi, Mrs Indira Ghandi's son who was killed in an air crash in 1980, was a devoted car enthusiast; he was also blessed with a mother who was willing and able to indulge his automania. If it was Mrs Gandhi's first mistake to buy the infant Sanjay a pedal car, her next may have been to permit him to go to Rolls-Royce as an apprentice rather than go to university. After two years with Rolls-Royce Sanjay announced that he had no more to learn and returned to India where he proclaimed his ambition to build a 'people's car' to be called the 'Maruti' or 'son of the Wind God'. His partner in this enterprise was Arjan Das, a backstreet mechanic who had once repaired a burst tyre for Sanjay. Between them, they had more than enough enthusiasm but perhaps inadequate know-how for the task they set themselves. There was the additional obstacle that after much heart searching the Indian government had repeatedly rejected the whole idea of 'a people's car', on the grounds that in a country as poor as India, public transport must have a higher priority. However, when a doting mother wishes to indulge a favourite son, it seems that policy can quickly change. In 1968, despite charges of nepotism by the parliamentary opposition, Sanjay was licensed to produce more cars than the entire Indian car industry put together and he was given enough political muscle to raise the money to do it. To provide a site for the Maruti factory, 1500 farmers were turned off their land near Delhi; banks were 'encouraged' to provide loans and a vast new industrial complex began to take shape. A prototype car was unveiled in 1972 and production was promised for 1973; similar promises were made every year for the next five years. No doubt a few cars were made in the eight years before Maruti went bankrupt, but they never ran well enough to get beyond the factory gate. If Maruti was 'son of the Wind God', it was a wind that blew no one much good. The farmers lost their land, the workers lost their jobs, the investors lost their money and India lost its chance to create its own modern car industry.

But that was not the end of the story. After Sanjay was killed, Mrs Gandhi nationalized Maruti's assets and announced an abrupt about-turn in India's attitude towards the car.

Suddenly, the modernization of the car industry became a top priority, even if it meant abandoning India's established policy of Indian cars for the Indian people. All the rhetoric about an indigenous car industry was forgotten and the government invited proposals from foreign collaborators to find a partner for Maruti; finally Suzuki clinched the deal. It is intended that the new joint venture Maruti will produce 100,000 small Suzuki-designed vehicles by 1989, and already the Maruti factory has been cleared of weeds and new machinery from Japan has been installed. There are many critics of Mrs Gandhi who regard the whole project with grave misgivings. They argue that the established policy was the right one: that although it was easy to scoff at the old Ambassadors and the Premiers, these were the right kinds of car for India. They point out that what India needs are family cars that are simple, spacious, sturdy and slow. They feel that the new Suzuki will be too small for India's families, too complicated for her backstreet mechanics and too fast for her congested roads.

Faded American dreams in a Bombay back street . . . down but not totally out. The average life of motor vehicles is more than twenty-five years.

Not even the most daunting mechanical problem will defeat this resourceful Indian pavement mechanic and his nonchalant assistant.

left] In countries where cars are expected to go on and on the market for spares flourishes. All India's larger cities have labyrinthine spare-parts bazaars where you can buy almost any bit for any model. And if they haven't got it, they'll make it.

Romesh Thapur, a widely respected figure in India's public life, goes even further. He believes that in countries like his, the single man sitting in a car should be regarded as a criminal. 'There are 300 million people who are still dreaming of a square meal every day . . . that's the reality of priorities in our country,' he says.

Those who support the new Maruti initiative hope and believe that India can do as other countries have done: establish a healthy and expanding home car market which will provide the basis for a foray into the lucrative export field. But, before any more Third World countries begin to foster ambitions of working another Japanese miracle and becoming car suppliers to the world, they should take a long hard look at the experience of Brazil in the past thirty years.

In one important respect, the Brazilian experience exactly reverses that of India. Just as the Indian government made a deliberate decision, in the 1950s, to subordinate the role of the car to other means of transportation and to exclude all foreign intervention in the car industry, so Brazil did the opposite. The decision was made to make road transportation the number one economic priority. New roads were to open up the virgin lands of Brazil's north-west, just as the North American West had been opened up by the railways a century earlier. To hasten the process, President Kubitchek invited the multinational car manufacturers to set up shop with the minimum of constraints on their activities. Volkswagen, the first to go into production in 1959, was followed by Ford, General Motors and Fiat. It was the beginning of Brazil's shortlived 'economic miracle'. Within a very few years, the automobile revolution had transformed Brazil's major cities, and set in motion demographic and environmental changes in the countryside that will prove to be of enormous consequence.

São Paulo is the 'Motown' of Brazil; 90 per cent of the nation's motor industry – which is now the world's eighth largest – is concentrated in and around the city. First-time visitors arriving in São Paulo by air are astonished by its appearance of wealth and progress. Around its fringes are the sprawling car factories, the smoking chimneys and the broad highways choked with traffic. In the city centre the glittering blocks of highrise offices are intersected by raised urban highways, reminiscent of the Los Angeles freeways, packed with colourful Fords, Fiats and Volkswagens. Yet beneath the dazzle, São Paulo is a Third World city and it demonstrates all the difficulties such cities are facing in attempting to come to terms with the car. Throughout the Third World, it is apparent that even where levels of car ownership are relatively low, all the chronic transport problems of the developed world are making themselves felt; and it is equally apparent that nothing whatever has been learned from the mistakes made by the United States and Europe decades ago; on the contrary, it is in the cities like Bombay, Lagos, Mexico City and São Paulo that the very worst examples of car blight are now found. Due to their rapid growth these cities are quite incapable of providing the most basic necessities for their exploding populations, let alone building the costly infrastructure, the new roads, car parks and traffic control systems that even a low vehicle-owning private sector demands. United Nations experts predict that, if present trends continue, São Paulo could have almost 26 million inhabitants by the turn of the century. If such a thing should come to pass and if São Paulo retained the same level of car ownership it has today, (at 20 per cent, Brazil's highest), the consequences for the quality of life do not bear contemplating. Even with today's car density, congestion is severe, road casualties high (particularly among pedestrians) and smog regularly reaches the official danger level.

Paradoxically, what may have prevented the worst scenario of urban horror from ever being realized in São Paulo was the very event that struck the severest blow to its economy: the world energy crisis of the early 1970s. By 1973, São Paulo was still using a road system planned for a city of one million and was on the edge of total traffic breakdown. When OPEC struck, it suddenly became crystal clear that a transport system that gave priority to the private car at the expense of public transport was madness.

For Brazil, a nation with little oil of its own, which had nevertheless used the car industry to spearhead its industrial development and which had opted overwhelmingly for road transportation to open up its vast resources, the oil crisis was an economic catastrophe from which its economy has still to recover. In those circumstances, one of the major objectives was to cut oil imports; and to achieve that end, Brazil has gone to the limit to develop an alternative to gasoline. It has been known for years that alcohol is an excellent replacement fuel and that mixing it with petrol, even in small proportions, improves a vehicle's performance. Another more radical possibility was to use pure hydrated alcohol which required modification of the engine and finding a solution to corrosion problems. Faced with these options, the Brazilian government went for both. Today it is impossible to find a filling station that sells pure petrol. All normal cars run on a petrol/alcohol mixture and since 1980 an increasing number of specially designed cars run on pure hydrated alcohol. Half a million of Brazil's fleet of 8 million cars are running on a product that formerly went down the throats of their owners in the form of *cachaza*, the local white rum. Although it would not be advisable to consume it straight from the pump, Brazilians are now driving on drink: the fuel is ethyl alcohol, ethanol, produced from sugar cane in much the same way as rum. Ethanol already replaces 25 per cent of all petrol used and it is hoped that figure will rise to 50 per cent by 1985.

All filling stations in Brazil must now offer gasoline *and* alcohol. To encourage the purchase of alcohol cars, the sale of gasoline is restricted at weekends while alcohol is freely available.

It can be argued that for the car-owner the alcohol programme has been a great success; it can also be argued that for almost everyone else it has been an unparalleled disaster. Certainly the balance of payments has benefited; but the wealthy sugar barons have benefited much more. More than 6 million acres of the best agricultural land are now devoted to feeding cars; and because each alcohol distillery needs about 15,000 acres of land to be viable, production has fallen entirely into the hands of large plantation owners. In São Paulo State, where much of the alcohol is produced, smallholders have been forced to leave their land and become casual day labourers. In the Amazon, enormous tracts of forest are being razed to grow cassava, also used to produce alcohol. Apart from the destruction of forest, it is reported that rivers are being polluted by the 'vinhoto', a slop which is left after the distillation is complete, and as a consequence some of the rivers in the state of São Paulo have become stinking sewers.

Even within the automobile industry, there is fierce criticism of the scale of the alcohol programme. Dr João Gurgel, who is a small, independent car manufacturer, considers it a disaster 'because the best land is utilized to feed the car and not the people'. He points out that the growing of sugar cane for alcohol is heavily subsidized by the government, while the cost of unsubsidized food is constantly rising: 'Already 45 per cent of a worker's wages are spent on food, much of which has to be imported.' That is perhaps the final irony: to help the balance of payments, alcohol is produced on land that could be used to grow much needed food, food that consequently has to be purchased abroad, thus damaging the balance of payments. It may be that Brazil's PROALCOOL scheme makes little economic sense; it certainly presents a moral dilemma.

Even if there was no moral, political, social or ecological problem, there is still a fundamental question that remains unanswered. It is known that modern agricultural methods, more often than not, have a negative energy balance: more energy goes into the inputs – tractor fuels and fertilizer, manufacture of agricultural machinery and the whole technical infrastructure – than is captured by photosynthesis in the field. When the aim is to produce not food but energy, it really makes little sense to put more into the process than you get out of it. In the final chapter we consider some of the work currently being done on alternative energy sources for cars. The Brazilian experience suggests that finding it in the fields is perhaps not the best answer.

In their relationship with the car neither Brazil nor India is typical. Most Third World countries have not made it a matter of policy either to reject or to embrace the car; in most cases, they have treated it as the ultimate imported luxury and taxed it accordingly. Then, within the restraints imposed by heavy import duties, governments have allowed market forces to operate and have learned to cope, more or less successfully, with the level of car ownership their citizens have been able to afford. In exceptional cases, like Hong Kong and Singapore, that level has been very high and, as we shall see in chapter 10, has prompted extreme measures in an attempt to regulate further growth. In more typical cases, though the total number of cars on the roads may be quite high, they are not, most of them, in private use: they are part of the public transportation system.

With a population of 9 million and 425,000 vehicles of all kinds, Bombay has 35,000 taxis, which must be among the highest proportion of taxis in

The recycling of cars and bits of cars is very big business. These tyres from affluent Japan were shipped to Hong Kong and are about to be carried across the border into China where they will have a second lease of life, probably as footwear.

any city anywhere. Those who knew Saigon in the 1950s and 1960s will remember the shoals of tiny, shuddering baby Citroën and Renault cabs struggling through the fetid heat and diesel fumes, their doors tied up with string. Taxis and taxi drivers the world over are a social study in themselves and none is richer in cultural consequence than the magnificent Jeepneys of the Philippines. Strictly speaking, the Jeepney is neither a car nor a taxi: it is a public utility vehicle based on the design of the World War II Jeep and hence outside the scope of this book. However, anyone interested in transportation will find its story irresistible. It is no exaggeration to say that the Jeepney has become the most dominant and the most memorable visual image in the city of Manila; without it, life on the streets would be sadly impoverished. Like its less flamboyant cousin, the *Pesaro* of Mexico City, the Jeepney runs on a fixed route, picking up and dropping passengers at will and charging a very modest fare. It arrived in the wake of World War II; General MacArthur and his GIs had departed, leaving behind, amongst their 'war surplus', a number of Willys Jeeps. These simple and sturdy little vehicles were ideally suited for the rugged conditions of a developing country and they were very soon put to work. In Manila, where public transport was almost non-existent and where the population finds it too hot to cycle, the Jeepney was an overnight success. Its mechanical performance was wholly satisfactory, but its appearance was not. It was plain, serviceable, square and painted drab green, and that, for the Filipino male at the wheel, was an intolerable way to look. Over the years the Jeepney has been transformed into something that might inhabit the nightmares of whoever designed the Willys original. It has become a mobile work of folk art, a gaudy and unashamed exercise in Filipino kitsch, a Pop Baroque story-board plastered with saucy slogans and even a statement of religious faith; but above all it is an expression of machismo. One of the more prominent of the symbols it carries, the cavalry charge of chromed horses occupying the bonnet, proclaims its speed and power. Other aggressive motifs commonly include fighting cocks, dragons, daggers and lightning flashes. The writings that adorn its rainbow-hued coachwork on all sides will include, as well as the vehicle's pet name, all kinds of invocations, slogans, advice to other drivers, jokes, jeers, prayers and proverbs; but the commonest epithets declare the amorous exploits or potential of their drivers: Loverboy, Sex Appeal, Romantico, Sexy Sam, Macho Boy, Feather Touch, Great Lover, Easy Hand, Wild Kiss, April Love and Virgin Breaker are just a few that are readily understood.

In the metropolitan area of Manila there are almost half a million motor vehicles; over 200,000 of them are Jeepneys, which makes them the single largest group of vehicles, surpassing private cars by several thousand. The rapid increase in Jeepney numbers and the growing congestion on the streets led to demands that this popular and colourful vehicle be banished to make way for more efficient means of transport. But the Jeepney has faced earlier attempts to ban, prohibit, license or otherwise restrict it, and has survived and flourished. For 50 million Filipinos it has become too much an agent of change and too much a cultural institution to be easily replaced by anything as pedantic as a public bus. It has also come to occupy an important part in the national economy; 400,000 people – drivers, operators and their families – now depend on the Jeepney for their livelihood, and building Jeepneys has become a thriving local industry.

Worldwide, which is the favourite toy? In the developing world, it must be the toy car. However crudely fashioned it may be, from wood, tin cans and bits of wire, it is an object that gives pleasure to countless millions of children, girls and boys.

opposite] Jeepneys, the ultimate expression of Philippino kitsch; or perhaps all kitsch, anywhere. By the standards of Jeepney nomenclature, 'sexy chicks' is only mildly suggestive.

Although Jeepneys are still largely hand-crafted and hand-painted according to traditional designs, modern assembly-line methods are used and a labour force of 1500 turns out 4000 vehicles a year. Just like Big Brother in Detroit, Francisco Motors in Manila has regular model changes and even makes a gesture in the direction of market research: their salesmen throughout the archipelago keep them informed about which colours, motifs and shapes are currently in demand. Just like the General Motors product, the Jeepney also comes in a basic, a deLuxe and a super deLuxe model; but at the top of the range, it's not wire wheels and tinted glass that attract the premium price-tag, it's a bonnet loaded with a dozen chrome horses; on the basic model, you get only two.

In many ways, the Jeepney is an ideal form of public transport; and as the cities of the West become increasingly clogged with private cars, a fleet of economical and flexible 'public cars' might be part of the solution; and if these cars, like the Jeepney, could make zestful cultural whoopee, so much the better. The streets of Rome, Paris and London would be more cheerful places in which to drive. At a time when cars are tending to look the same – functional, aerodynamic, bland, efficient but lacking flair – the Jeepney reminds us that the earliest wheeled vehicles were the garlanded chariots and catafalques of the god-kings; and that travel can still be more than mere transport.

Thankfully there are still a few, a very few, areas of this planet where the motor car has not yet intruded. Some governments, in their wisdom, have designated wilderness areas where entry is strictly controlled and motor vehicles are wholly banned. In a rapidly diminishing number of cases, the terrain remains undisturbed simply because it is too difficult and remote and dangerous to be entered. Parts of Papua New Guinea share this distinction. It is part of the unusual history of Papua New Guinea that in many areas air services came long before roads. Forty years ago there was not even a track that would take motor transport more than thirty miles from the coast. The story of how, in the 1920s and 1930s, the Australian administrators explored the interior and contacted unknown tribes by air is well known. The story of the efforts to build roads in this wild and inhospitable country may be less familiar. It is a terrain where everything stands in the way of the road builder – coastal swamps, great rivers that never keep their course for more than a year or two and, above all, the mountains, a switch-back of steep and jungled ridges rising to a towering central spire dominated by the 15,000-foot peak of Mount William. A further discouragement to the road builder, particularly in the Central Highlands, was the aggressive nature of the inhabitants. For all of the clansmen, warfare was a way of life and for some, cannibalism was not unknown. After World War II, the Australian administration was determined to reduce the dependence on air transport. It may have been motivated by a wish to help the European settlers who had started to farm in the Highlands; but it was also true that roads were bound to benefit everyone in an area where man – or rather woman – was the principal beast of burden. The most spectacular single project in the post-war programme of road building was the 310-mile Highlands Highway, built largely with pick and shovel, by thousands of Papua New Guineans.

What 'the new means of transport' has done to Papua New Guineans has gone far beyond what the Australian engineers or the Highland tribesmen could have imagined. It has certainly allowed the farmer to carry his produce

KING
DOY
REBELDE
939
SARAO
SARAO
BAYAN SPECIAL
SEXY CHICKS
Sarao
DCU·954
PILIPINAS
DOY
ANDREW

to market; and by doing so it has enabled him for the first time to enter the cash economy. The fact that the farmer has chosen to spend much of this new-found wealth on beer, and that alcoholism has become a major social problem, is not something that can be blamed on the roads or the vehicles that travel them. It is nevertheless a consequence of their arrival. In the brief period since the roads came, change has been very rapid. Wherever the bulldozers and graders have carved out a route through the forests, the settlers have followed hard behind. Within two or three years, on both sides of the roads, the trees have been cut down and burned to make new gardens. Now throughout the Highlands they produce cashcrops – coffee and cardamom seeds and cattle – and as this new economic activity demands more land, that means there will be less forest. The loss of habitat is already having serious consequences for some of the rarer birds and animals.

The culture shock delivered by the car in a country like Papua New Guinea is hard to imagine. A people that fifty years ago didn't know the wheel or the meaning of money are turning up at motor showrooms in the Highlands with fistfuls of cash to purchase sophisticated motor vehicles. This phenomenon even has a name: it's now known as the 'coffee flush'. The coffee beans have been harvested and sold and the stocky, bearded Highlanders are flush with money. Apart from beer, their top priority purchase is a car or a pick-up truck. These two acquisitions, both wholly foreign to their traditional culture, do not make a happy combination.

Just how important the motor vehicle has already become in the scale of values in Papua New Guinea is illustrated by a recent report from the famous gathering of the clans held in the Highlands. A pick-up truck was offered as first prize for tribal dancing. When the adjudicators were unwise enough to announce a dead heat, there was only one possible course of action. To avoid conflict between the joint winners, an object so much desired as a motor vehicle had to be equally divided between the two; and it was, right down the middle.

In the developing world, all the more negative aspects of automobility become aggravated by the lack of infrastructure to accommodate the car and by the lack of time for cultural adjustment to it. On the positive side, it has been suggested that in some parts it may have helped to break down racial segregation. Hank Nelson of the Research School of Pacific Studies in Canberra has described what the introduction of the car did to a small, racially segregated society in New Guinea in the 1930s. Rabaul was an isolated community with a clear distinction between New Guineans, Asians and Australians. It was, he says, 'almost a caste society with clear rules of appropriate behaviour for each race and each class'. It seems that black men could drive cars for white men, but they could not drive *in* them when white men were driving: they stood on the running board. What could they do when cars with no running boards appeared? Taxis also caused problems. Could a respectable white woman sit in a taxi with its seat still warm from its proximity to a grass-skirted black backside? The taxi owner in such a small town could not afford to run separate taxis for the different races. Then, just before World War II, black men bought their first motor vehicles. Some indignant whites wrote letters to the *Rabaul Times* suggesting that blacks be prohibited from such displays of wealth; only then, they believed, would things revert to the good old days when the native knew his place. But that was not to be. 'How could the black man, last seen driving through town

A river crossing in S.E. Asia. As diaries and photograph albums attest, it was the dearth of bridges and ferries that proved to be the most irksome aspect of driving in these far-flung parts of the world.

and leaving a cloud of dust on good white folks' verandahs, ever return to being a "boy"?' Almost exactly the same point has been made concerning relations between blacks and whites in America's rural South. It seems that hierarchical societies survive best when basic conditions are static; but the motor car is dynamic, constantly changing in design and in function; and above all, it is a sign of success. Once the black man is riding around in the same car as the white man, then the car itself – or the fact of its ownership – becomes more important than the colour of the driver's skin.

The breakdown in segregation described by Hank Nelson in the 1930s was vastly accelerated by World War II. Just as in World War I, when Europeans and Americans from working-class backgrounds had their first chance to drive, so between 1939 and 1945 many parts of North Africa, the Pacific and South-east Asia, that had scarcely seen vehicles, were suddenly deluged by thousands of them. In some cases, local people were employed by the occupation forces as drivers and trained as mechanics; and, as we have seen in the Philippines, when the armies receded, much of their equipment, including vehicles, remained. Car ownership thus became a little less exclusive, not quite the sole prerogative of the governing class and, according to one view, an influence in creating in Third World countries a new middle class. In Brazil, avers economist Bernardo Kuccinski, 'the fact that the car has become available to a large number of people, not only to an elite, has to some extent democratized Brazil's life'. But another economist, Professor Jose Goldenburg, believes the reverse to be true: 'The automobile industry has helped to create an elite in Brazil. About 20 per cent of the population belongs to that elite. The remaining 80 per cent are outside of it and have no hope whatever of owning private automobiles. So I think it would be much wiser to invest resources in mass transportation.' That, according to Professor Goldenburg, is the lesson other developing nations with ambitions to create their own automobile industry should learn from Brazil.

The Image Makers

'Goodbye the horse' was one of the earliest and most familiar themes in motor car advertising. In one case milady disdainfully gathers up her skirts, about to step into her latest love – a Rauch and Lang electric car – while 'jilted' Dobbin stares mournfully on. In another, a Buick advertisement recreates an imaginary confrontation between horse and automobile in which, inevitably, the latter is the victor and 'the technology and tempo of the entire world are changed forever'.

There is still a country where a cowboy can spread his loop without getting it caught in a fence post – where the mountains tickle the sky and ten million stars just almost scare you.

Give me a horse or a car that has a little of the lighted match and stick of dynamite about it. Give me a little more health than there is in the daily dozen – a little more air than you will find in Atlantic City – and a lot more poetry than I ever found in Browning. I want to go in a Playboy. Then I'll be happy.
(Advertisement for the Playboy Car, Jordan Motor Car Co. Inc., Cleveland, Ohio, 1920)

From the beginning of the century, artists and copywriters were fuelling men's fantasies about the new invention. If the horseless carriage was the fulfilment of all kinds of long-held expectations, the dream merchants were there to exploit it to the full. In fact, nothing has been so responsible for promoting our automania than the image-building efforts of Madison Avenue, which have managed to present the car as all things to all men.

Initially, the exuberant young industry was remarkably restrained in explaining the horseless carriage to a curious public. Advertisements emphasized the reliability, safety and simple advantages of the new conveyance. Ransom E. Olds in 1897 could assure potential customers that his automobiles were 'practically noiseless and impossible to explode'. The International Motor Car Co. of Kilburn, London, in 1899 could advertise a doctor's car that 'will mount the steepest hills with ease, and can travel at a great speed on the level . . . and cannot catch fire'.

Much was made of the superiority of the car over Old Dobbin. Oldsmobile, who quickly became one of America's most successful manufacturers, ran a whole series of advertisements drawing direct comparisons between horse and car. A picture of a horse ravenously munching its way through a mountain of hay and oats was placed alongside a trim curved-dash Olds, parked next to a small petrol can; the text ran: 'The graceful and practical automobile will do the work of six horses at an average cost of thirty-five dollars a year (10,000 miles). Board alone for one horse costs $180 a year, so the economy is very evident. The Oldsmobilist has the satisfaction of knowing his machine is always ready' 'The Passing of the Horse' trumpeted another advertisement of 1901:

The silent horse power of this runabout is measurable, dependable and spontaneous. The horse power generated by supplies of hay and oats is variable, uncertain and unresponsive. There is nothing to watch but the road when you drive. The Oldsmobile is the best thing on wheels. You see them everywhere – doctors, lawyers and morticians find the Oldsmobile the most practical vehicle for business purposes.

A Winton car advertisement of 1905 had the definitive statement on the matter: 'The Winton car is as sensitive as a well-trained horse and ten times as reliable . . . The horse might get scared at the sight of a motor car, but the Winton can't get scared nor get tired.'

Once the horse had finally been sent trotting down the highroads of history, silence, simplicity and strength became the advertising watchwords for the car. 'Fit for a King's pleasure in beauty and luxuriousness, with smooth, still engines, whose loudest sound is a subdued hum', proclaimed advertise-

"JILTED"
for the
RAUCH & LANG ELECTRIC

The day everything changed.
THE HORSE was more than sleek flanks, flaring nostrils and sinewy beauty. It represented a way of life. It was the status quo.
Ah, but the car. It was simply a machine trying to shoulder its way into a lifestyle that was still not completely at ease with machines.
There had to be a confrontation.
The machine had to be put in its place.
And so in some unremembered pasture, on some unremembered day, the people lined up to watch some unremembered horse defend their way of life.
What they saw was history.
It didn't matter that the car had won.
The mere fact that it was there was a victory.
The automobile had arrived. And the technology, and tempo of an entire country—indeed, the entire world—had changed forever.
Buick

ments for the Yale car of 1905. 'The Autocar motor can be run at full speed with a glass of water standing on the hood over the motor, without a drop being spilled', boasted the Autocar Co. of Pennsylvania.

As the car became more refined and luxurious, manufacturers began 'image-building' in earnest. Illustrious clients were used to promote the product. S. F. Edge, one of Britain's most colourful early automobile entrepreneurs and drivers, offered a three-year guarantee with the 1906 Napier (two years previously it had been the world's first production six cylinder car) and the assurance of a lengthy list of distinguished owners, which included Sir Oswald Moseley, banker Pierpoint Morgan and even a prime minister – Arthur Balfour.

right] Promoting the product in America in 1903 – Oldsmobile, Darracq, Haynes-Apperson, Pierce – with the emphasis firmly on reliability and simplicity of operation. Only Oldsmobile are beginning to use catch phrases ('The Best Thing on Wheels'; 'Nothing to Watch but the Road') and to show a touch of lyricism in their prose.

left] The 'nuts and bolts' approach to advertising, exemplified in this 1905 advertisement for the Wayne automobile which gives a technical specification of the kind one suspects was of little interest to most purchasers.

Oldsmobile

"The Best Thing on Wheels."

The real pleasure of automobiling is found in the bright, sunny springtime when welcomes her devotees with an ever changing panorama of beauty.

The simplicity of the Oldsmobile enables its drivers to appreciate to the fullest ex- the delights of a spring outing – there is no complex arrangement of innumerable ical devices—a single lever to start with, and a sensitive, yet absolutely certain ntrol leave "*Nothing to Watch but the Road.*" The Oldsmobile cheerfully mounts hest hill, never tires on the longest drives and is ready for a glorious, exhilarating the open country or a sedate pace on the crowded street.

Price $650.00

There are Oldsmobile agencies in every State and in all the larger cities. us for an illustrated book or call on your local agent.

ls Motor Works, Dept. J. **Detroit, Mich.**

DARRACQ

CARS

HOLD MORE RECORDS THAN ANY OTHER MAKE IN THE WORLD

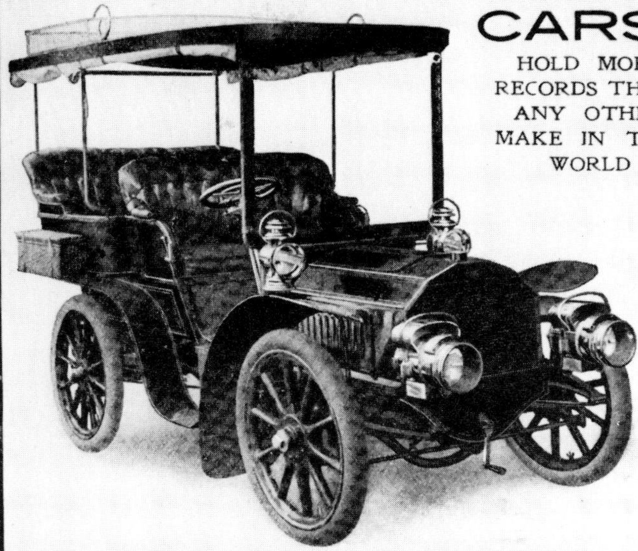

Twenty horse-power 1903 DARRACQ, with top and tonneau detachable.

Noiseless—automatic lubrication—complete throttle control—starts from the seat. 8, 9, 10, 12 and 20 horse-power models.

Weekly importations insure **latest styles** and **immediate delivery.**

See our business delivery wagons. Circulars free.

AMERICAN DARRACQ AUTOMOBILE CO.

Controlled by F. A. LA ROCHE COMPANY

Eastern Agents for the Cleveland Roadster
Branch, 147 West 38th Street

652-664 Hudson Street
NEW YORK

Chicago Branch: 502-504 Wabash Avenue

The only one that always won

ne HAYNES-APPERSON

Every Endurance Contest Held in America, Every Contest or Race Ever ered, More Records Than Any Other Made in the United States, and was he Only Gasolene Car that Ran the Contest from New York to Boston and Back Without Repairs or Adjustments OF ANY KIND

SURREY, 12 H.P., $1800. TOP, AND FRONT HEADLIGHT EXTRA

ecords and Awards all Earned by Stock Machines. The Machine you Buy is the one that Makes the Records

ther maker in the world *can show* such a long record of prizes won by *stock machines.* By and repeated official competitive tests, *no other machine* is anywhere near as *reliable* as the -Apperson.

Get our Catalogue and the "Little Book."

Surrey, $1800—Phaeton, $1500—Runabout, $1200—Tonneau, $2400

irers are urged to visit our factory, where every detail of Haynes-Apperson superiority can be seen lly understood.

HAYNES-APPERSON CO., Kokomo, Ind., U. S. A.

The oldest makers of motor cars in America

nch Store, 381 to 385 Wabash Ave., Chicago. Eastern Representatives: Brooklyn Automo- ., 1239 41-43 Fulton St., Brooklyn, N. Y. New York location to be announced. National bile & M g. Co., Pacific Coast Agents, San Francisco.

The Ideal PHYSICIAN'S Automobile

Made to **RUN ALL** the Time, Under All Conditions of Roads and Weather.

THE ACME of Simplicity and Elegance

Unequaled for Durability and Comfort.

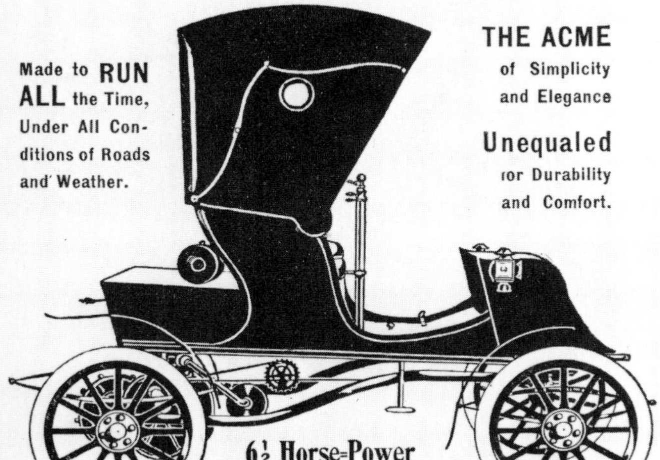

6½ Horse-Power

Pierce Stanhope Motorette.

GEO. N. PIERCE CO. BUFFALO, N.Y.

MANUFACTURERS OF

Pierce Cycles and Arrow Motor Cars

CATALOGUES FREE ON APPLICATION.

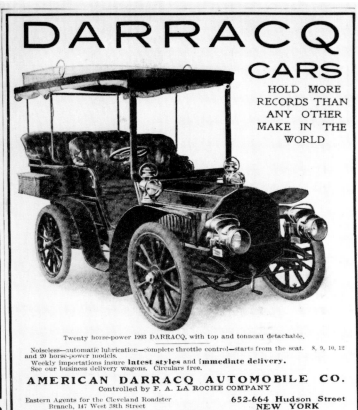

right] Instant imagery in 1934 and an irrefutable slogan. As early as 1905 the Rolls-Royce company had advertised their 30 h.p. model of that year as 'the best car in the world . . .', a reputation which only time has embellished.

ROLLS-ROYCE
The Best Car in the World
ROLLS-ROYCE LTD. 14-15 CONDUIT ST. LONDON. W.I. MAYFAIR 6201

Pierce-Arrow, the make for which there was almost always a permanent waiting list, employed some of America's finest illustrators in its carefully understated advertisements.

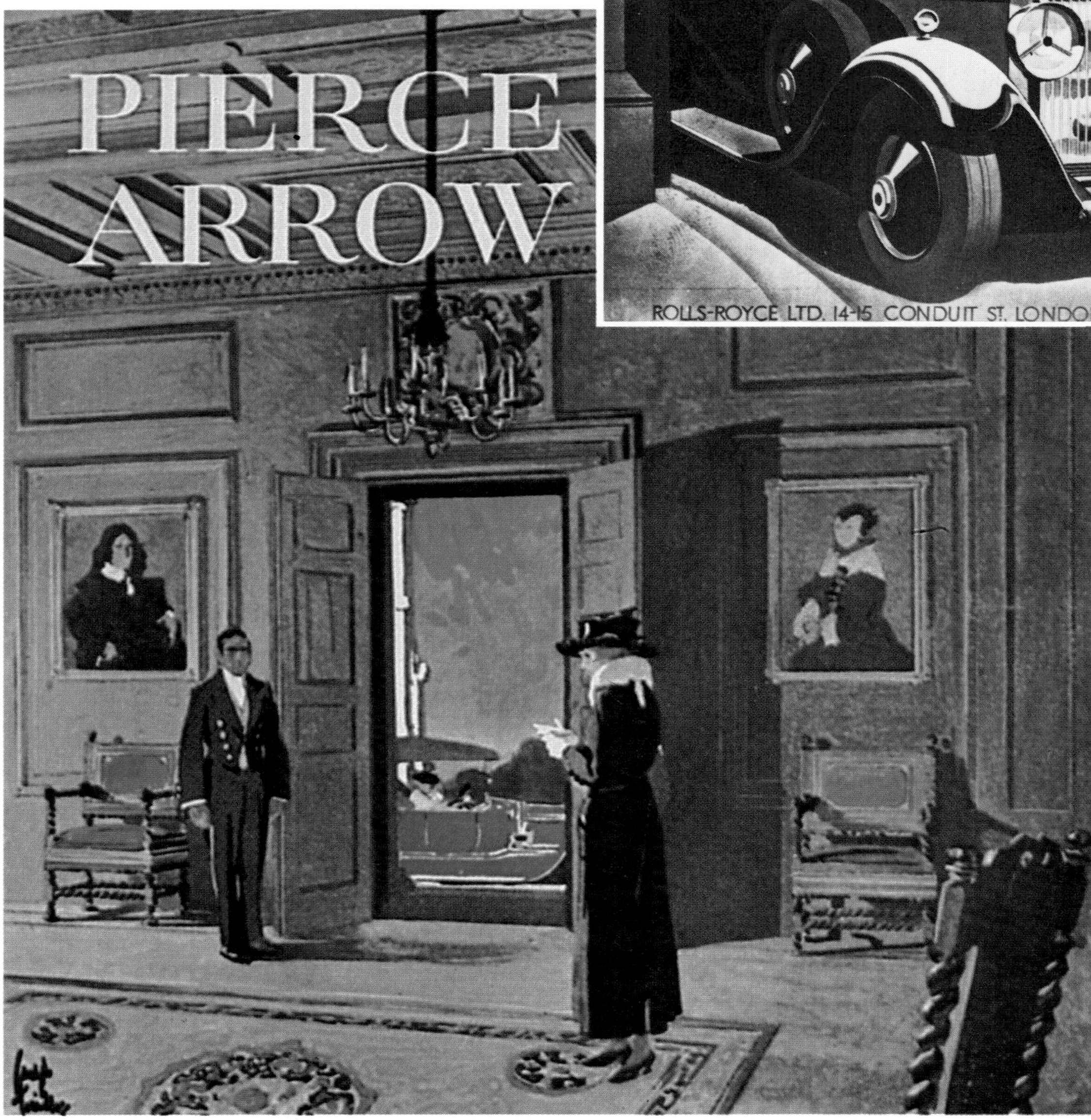

As the reputation and image of particular marques were established, lengthy credentials became superfluous. The words 'The Pierce-Arrow' printed across an opulent social setting, with the car appearing discreetly in the background, were sufficient. Duesenberg, the grandest of all American motor cars, was to extend this kind of image-making to its most subtle limits, by never advertising in colour and not even bothering to depict the car. Patrician figures appeared in commanding roles – the yachtsman at the helm, the woman in hunting regalia – with the simple, telling phrase beneath: 'He [or She] drives a Duesenberg.'

With refinement also came speed and competition success and the image of the car as a symbol of masculine prowess. Early advertisements for Peugeot in France and Wolseley in Britain depicted crouched figures, huddled behind large steering wheels, pressing their mighty machines onwards through clouds of dust beneath glowering skies.

Woman and Machine. The MG Girl was an amalgam of so many of our automobile fantasies: the freedom of the road, the open car, the lure of speed, and the implicit sexual promise offered by the well-bred but thoroughly modern girl raring to go.

left] . . . And not a Duesenberg in sight! Image-building through association taken to its ultimate limits in 1932, by that grandest of American marques.

One man, however, was to revolutionize car advertising copy and change the public's perception of the car for ever. In the United States, Edward S. (Ned) Jordan, manufacturer of the Playboy motor car, pioneered between 1918 and 1926 a totally new style of poetic advertising – aimed particularly at women – which has been described by Tim Howley in *Automobile Quarterly* as 'emotional, rhetorical, illogical, wildly inexplicit, but irresistibly flattering'.

Jordan, a short, pugnacious mid-Westerner, with a penchant for bright ties and white spats, had married money and bought himself into car manufacturing. He complained that automobile advertisements were still talking engineers' language. 'That's all fine and dandy if you're selling locknuts . . . but Eve doesn't give a hoot about locknuts.' He therefore focused on the emotional possibilities of the car and avoided all technical jargon.

In his most famous advertisement, 'Somewhere West of Laramie', the Playboy was touted as the car for 'a bronco-busting, steer-roping girl who knows what I'm talking about'; or for 'A Golden Girl from Somewhere . . . lithe and splendid, touched with a happy craving that will not be denied, she is going to the place where fairy tales come true'.

The Playboy was unremarkable and the company foundered in 1931 leaving Jordan to drink himself into obscurity, but his lyrical copy transformed the marketing of cars with lasting effect. The Jordan car was essentially an advertising and merchandising concept; as Jordan himself said of the Playboy model: 'That was no mundane vehicle of a sordid sphere. That car was an ethereal chariot, imbued with the spirit of young romance and old boxing gloves.'

The classic Jordan ad. that revolutionized advertising copy. 'Somewhere West of Laramie' was written by Ned Jordan in June 1923 while travelling across the Wyoming plains in his private railroad car, en route to San Francisco. Racing alongside the train came a stunningly beautiful horsewoman, causing the diminutive auto magnate to ask a travelling companion where they were. 'Oh, somewhere west of Laramie,' came the yawning reply. The ad. was written in minutes and appeared in the *Saturday Evening Post* a few days later. 'With the right copy you can get a smile out of the Sphinx,' said Jordan.

Somewhere West of Laramie
SOMEWHERE west of Laramie there's a broncho-busting, steer-roping girl who knows what I'm talking about. She can tell what a sassy pony, that's a cross between greased lightning and the place where it hits, can do with eleven hundred pounds of steel and action when he's going high, wide and handsome.
The truth is—the Playboy was built for her.
Built for the lass whose face is brown with the sun when the day is done of revel and romp and race.
She loves the cross of the wild and the tame.
There's a savor of links about that car—of laughter and lilt and light—a hint of old loves—and saddle and quirt. It's a brawny thing—yet a graceful thing for the sweep o' the Avenue.
Step into the Playboy when the hour grows dull with things gone dead and stale.
Then start for the land of real living with the spirit of the lass who rides, lean and rangy, into the red horizon of a Wyoming twilight.
JORDAN
JORDAN
JORDAN MOTOR CAR COMPANY, Inc., Cleveland, Ohio

THIS FREEDOM
FOR a thousand years we Englishmen have fought for our freedom. Our home is our castle; the highway winds unbarred. Every river is musical with memories; every green field, every beacon hill, is rich with the dust of those who fought for " This Freedom."
Have you spied the purple iris blossoming along the river bank? Have you glimpsed a bit of heaven whilst " picnicing " by the scented pinewood? The wind's on the heath, brother; the highway is calling; there's laughter and deep breath and zestful life over there on the hills. Freedom is waiting you at the bang of your front door.
" Is it possible," you ask, " that this freedom can be mine?" Once you ask that question a Jowett is beginning to drive up to your door. For sixteen years the Jowett Car has been bestowing " This Freedom " on grateful folk, at a price you can easily afford. Freedom! at less than you pay for the humdrum, crowded railway train. Read on, and you will ride on —Brother of the Broad High Way!
THIS FREEDOM IS YOURS

Other dream pedlars followed where Jordan had led. In Britain, the small Jowett Car Company in Yorkshire started producing its own distinctive dream copy for its rather spartan cars:

The purr of the Jowett Seven is music to the lover of roads. It sings a symphony of comradeship, this adventurous hill-loving car for two. Listen to its song . . .

Step on the pedal, my master, mountains are molehills today – wheels are wings. Ah! – now you are silent . . . it's now that you hear me and feel the romance in my song. I love to think of you two behind – my master at the wheel, mistress by his side. You two shall ride forever thus, and before the shadows lengthen and the violet deepens on the Hill you shall experience a new understanding of joy.

'Nuts and bolts' advertising was dead, giving way to an approach that stressed the romance of travel, the thrill of car ownership, the communion between man and machine . . . Increasingly it was image that sold cars. As Michael and Jane Stern have pointed out in *Auto Ads*, their study of car advertising in the USA: 'The car buyer was not buying a piece of machinery. He, or she, was buying a new life.'

To provide that 'new life' in the United States was the growing giant of Detroit – General Motors – and its new president Alfred P. Sloan. Whereas GM's founder and former president Billy Durant had been a colourful, impulsive, haphazard entrepreneur, Sloan was in James Flink's words 'the automobile industry's first "gray" man'. A graduate of MIT (Massachusetts Institute of Technology), he was to pioneer a system of management that became a standard for the world. He had viewed with horror Durant's 'master salesman's optimism unchecked by facts' as 'downright disturbing'. He replaced it with Sloanism that stressed tight financial controls, clear lines of authority, precise market forecasting, and committee decision-taking at the top. Above all, he believed the corporation's prime responsibility was to strive for an ever increasing maximization of profits.

By 1925, less than two years after he had become president of General Motors, the first car market in the United States was approaching saturation point and Sloan's solution to this problem was the annual model change which was intended, in his own words, 'to create demand for the new value and, so to speak, create a certain amount of dissatisfaction with past models as compared with the new one'.

Fordism – the concept of the unchanging universal car that only came in black – was replaced by Sloanism in which the quickly obsolescent car changed its style and shape yearly and came in all colours of the rainbow. Planned obsolescence had been invented. As Emma Rothschild in *Paradise Lost* has pointed out, 'Sloan's idea for upgrading consumer preferences was that automobiles should change each year, and should each year become more expensive . . . Cars of the same basic metal parts would be sold with different equipment at different prices.' It was perhaps the most monumental decision taken by Detroit and it became a model for the selling of consumer goods throughout the world.

Status and symbolism became primary reasons for purchasing motor cars, and if it was General Motors in grey Detroit who made this change, it was a man from sunny California who stage-managed it for them.

Brothers Benjamin and Willy Jowett, the Bradford car builders, were responsible for Britain's riposte to the Ned Jordan style of copy. As Michael Worthington-Williams has commented: 'No other manufacturer has managed so successfully to combine straight talk with the lyricism of Laurie Lee and whilst they advertised little, they made every word count.'

Harley Earl came from a family of long-established Hollywood coach-builders who, as the movie industry flourished amongst the orange groves, had turned their hand to producing exotic vehicles for the studios and for stars such as Tom Mix, Jack Pickford and Fatty Arbuckle – a role not unlike that played by George Barris, self-styled 'King of the Kustomizers' in Hollywood today. Dream cars for the dream factory. Through a take-over of the family business by a local Cadillac agent in 1919, the young Harley Earl was introduced to the president of Cadillac, Lawrence Fisher, and offered his first job in Detroit. He created the 1927 LaSalle and caused a sensation. It was the first car built by a major company in which appearance was the principal design goal. With its flowing lines and low profile, Sloan and his grey flannel executives saw in Earl's showy creation a production automobile that was as beautiful and startling as the custom cars of the period. Here was something to excite the imagination of the second generation of automobile consumers, to stimulate static sales, to set the whole industry on a new course of glorious expansion. In June 1927 Sloan announced the creation of a new department at General Motors: the Art and Colour Section, with Harley Earl as its head. In effect, General Motors had hired its first stylist.

'Alfred Sloan did not have an emotional approach to his business: he was not moved by cars,' says Stephen Bayley in *Harley Earl and the Dream Machine*:

Indeed, the most excited he could get in describing them was to say that they were 'the dominant form of basic ground transportation in the United States'. When he created the Art and Colour Section and invited Harley Earl to head it, he was calm and sober, yet, as one employee suggested the moment was rather similar in its cultural implications, if on a much smaller scale, to that day in the fourth century when the Emperor Constantine decided as an act of expedience and on whim to turn the Roman Empire Christian . . . The car was not going to be the same any more.

From 1927 to 1959 Harley Earl, as head of General Motors styling section, was directly responsible for more than 50 million cars and, through the influence of the Detroit product around the world, for many millions more. His most significant innovation, which changed the look of cars for ever, was the introduction of sculptors' modelling clay laid over a wooden frame for the shaping of cars. It led to more fluid and streamlined shapes than could be achieved by 'beating the metal', and it is a practice still followed by car design studios around the world today.

In the United States, where the General led, other manufacturers had to follow. An aging and intransigent Henry Ford had held on to the sadly dated Model T for too long. Constant price reductions – the car had fallen from $850 in 1908 to $290 in 1925 – were to no avail. In the early 1920s Ford had sold half the cars in the country and General Motors a quarter; a decade later their positions had been reversed and Ford was never to regain its preeminence. Under General Motors' influence, with the other manufacturers tagging along, the car in America increasingly became a fantasy symbol for gratification and an expression of power, of youth, of escape, and in the post-war period the very centrepiece of the affluent society. For General Motors the annual model change became enshrined in Harley Earl's 'Motorama' (the first was held in 1949) and featured dream cars of the future alongside current production models. Held at the Waldorf Astoria in New York, and then in major cities around America, Motoramas had all the pageantry and glitter of a Hollywood first night. They were also the means of testing public reaction to future design concepts. Harley Earl had learnt to his cost with his second car at GM, the Buick Silver Anniversary of 1929, that the public reacted unfavourably to designs too far ahead of their times, but if the new idea was displayed as a lavish and unattainable dream car, it became, by the time it went into production not just acceptable, but highly desirable.

There were eight Motoramas between 1949 and 1961 and each one drew as many as 2 million people, who came to stand and stare and dream. Their influence on consumer buying habits, on advertising, on the whole image-making process, was incalculable. As John De Waard comments in his book *Fins and Chrome*, 'the cars of the 50s were like nothing that ever came off the assembly line, before or since. They were the stuff of dreams. And the dream was possible for everyone.'

By exciting the public with a glimpse of tomorrow through his Motorama dream cars, Harley Earl captured the customer of today. For the rest of the world such indigenous design exercises epitomized Americans' narcissistic obsession with gimmickery and external display.

below] Chromed monument to an age of excess. Harley Earl's Le Sabre dream car, which he regularly drove around Detroit, featured a body made from magnesium and aluminium, the world's first 'wrap-around' windscreen and a water sensitive device that automatically raised the convertible top when it rained.

above] Detroit's chief dream-maker in his favourite dream machine, the Le Sabre XP-8, which donated many of its design features to cars of the 1950s. The autocratic Harley Earl of General Motors was the world's leading arbiter of car styling from 1927 to the early 1960s, responsible for some of the industry's greatest innovations and worst excesses.

above left] In 1950s American parlance, a handsome guy was a 'dreamboat', a pretty girl 'dreambait' and the most desirable car a 'dream car'. General Motors managed to combine all three dreamy elements in this promotional photo for its phallic-finned 1959 Cadillac Coupe de Ville.

On the chrome-laden flight deck of Harley Earl's aircraft-inspired 1954 Cadillac. His designs were created as much for the imagination as for the American highway.

'I dream automobiles,' claimed chief dreamer Harley Earl, and from his Body Department Studio poured forth the stylistic clichés of the Golden Fifties: panoramic wraparound windshields, tailfins, 'Dagmar' bumpers (chromed protuberances named after a television starlet of the period), hardtops, polychromed duo and triple coloured paint jobs, and cars that with each year grew longer and longer and lower and lower . . . 'My sense of proportion tells me that oblongs are more attractive than squares', said Harley Earl, 'just as a ranch house is more attractive than a square, three-storey flat roof house and a greyhound is more graceful than an English bulldog.' He and his team pursued their consumer dreams, interpreting their fantasies into chrome and sculptured steel, then feeding it back to them. 'Go all the way and then back off', was Earl's dictum to his styling staff.

While the rest of the world looked on, bemused if not immune, American buyers demanded more and more power, and more and more chrome. V8 engines, which were less economical than a 6 but produced more profit for the manufacturers and more status for their customers, became the standard for the industry. The 1958 Buick established an all-time record; it carried forty-four pounds of chrome trim. In the words of an unrepentant Bill Mitchell, Harley Earl's protégé and successor at General Motors: 'We were putting on chrome with a trowel.' Excess was also reached with the tailfin. By Mr Mitchell's admission, 'We outfinned ourselves . . .'

Detroit's obsession with the fin sprang from a wartime visit of Earl and his team to view one of the most dramatic-looking aircraft of World War II, the twin-tailed Lockheed P38, at Selfridge Air Force Base near Detroit. It inspired their first tailfinned car, the Cadillac of 1948. With the unveiling the following year of Harley Earl's most successful and influential dream car, the Le Sabre XP-8 which incorporated ideas from the first Sabre jet, the F-86, the link between car styling and the aeroplane took a dramatic step forward. Speaking at the 1949 Motorama, Harley Earl was able to say: 'The airplane has developed into being our greatest help in designing automobiles.' If one car fuelled man's fantasies about the automobile as a dream machine, it was the astonishing Le Sabre, for it clearly represented the romance and high-speed, streamlined styling of a fast fighter plane. It was a theme developed by GM and picked up by other influential designers such as Virgil Exner at Chrysler, whose cars were said to feature 'the forward look'. The

tailfin was the first visual novelty that became Detroit's ultimate and most bizarre excess. It ended in each manufacturer struggling to 'outfin' the other.

The memorable war of the fins was fought between 1957 and 1960. Advertisements reflecting (so the agencies believed) consumer demands became obsessed with aircraft imagery. 'It tames a tornado of torque', trumpeted Dodge in 1957. 'It breaks through the vibration barrier. It is swept-wing mastery of motion. It unleashes a hurricane of power.' The 1958 Buick was the Airborne B-58 (after the bomber), featuring 'flight-path dynaflow' and 'air poise suspension which floats you on four columns of air'. Oldsmobile models were called 'Golden Rockets' and 'Starfires'.

It reached a climax in 1959 with the tallest tailfin of all. Earl's Motorama car of that year, the Firebird III, inspired by yet another aircraft, the Douglas Skyray, had no fewer than seven fins and a 'joystick' instead of a steering wheel! The regular production Cadillac had the tallest fins of all, standing forty-two inches off the ground. Chrysler even claimed, rather dubiously,

The tail-fin obsession – Detroit's ultimate design cul-de-sac, which was adopted in more restrained form by almost every manufacturer around the world. We see it here in phallic form and forty-two inches off the ground on the 1959 Cadillac and in shark-fin shape on the 1960 Cadillac.

With tail-fins still growing taller, you were not simply buying a De Soto in 1957 but 'piloting' your personal flying machine with 'torqueflite transmission' and 'flight-sweep styling'.

The Detroit dream life in the 1950s, replete with jet aircraft imagery and rocket ship rides, as portrayed by Philip Castle, Britain's leading airbrush artist, in 'A break in the traffic'.

that their fins provided engineering benefits: 'Based on aerodynamic principles, they make a real contribution to the remarkable stability of these cars on the road.' Even Ford, who had attempted to remain aloof from the tailfin craze, joined the fray in 1957 under the leadership of the head of their styling department, George W. Walker, an ex-dress designer better known as 'the Cellini of Chrome'. He was quoted as saying: 'The ultimate in elegance is to be dressed in a white suit, driving a white Thunderbird with white upholstery, with a white Afghan hound beside you.' Not everyone shared his definition of American chic.

The public began to complain about the extreme discomfort of being half a foot closer to the floor than they had been a decade earlier. Consumer disenchantment with the car as a frivolous and expensive high-fashion item, with gadgetry that quickly went wrong, and with an image that with marketing hype dated even more quickly began to snowball. The Detroit dream came to an end with the notorious Ford Edsel, one of the greatest industrial disasters of the twentieth century. It had been designed by the Ford Motor Company in the mid 1950s and introduced to the market in September 1957, in an attempt to halt the exodus of the *nouveau riches* to more costly marques manufactured by arch rival General Motors. Market research had revealed that when Ford owners wanted to enhance their social status by trading up into the middle-price bracket, some 70 per cent switched to the

ROLEO
RODUCTOS
B.V.D.
DE
19 RUBIS
JOYERIA
Alexander
PERUANA
CD 19

above] Someone, somewhere always loves a loser . . . The Edsel Owners Club boasts a membership of 2000 members, and in deepest Pennsylvania farmer Hugh Lesley, Edsel automaniac, has lovingly collected 132 of them in his appropriately named 'lemon' grove.

above] 'Dramatic Edsel Styling' barely survived three seasons (1958–60) and was the biggest financial flop ever recorded by a make of car. The name has become a synonym for 'loser' and, in a final uncharitable act, the twenty-third edition of Webster's Dictionary made it official.

Oldsmobiles, Buicks and Dodges of GM. The Edsel was heralded as the heir to the accumulated engineering know-how of the past plus the latest wisdom to be gleaned from the latest research techniques in consumer-motivation. The Edsel, so the mountainous publicity ran, was therefore doubly designed for success. It was to be more than the best and newest car in reality; it was to be the embodiment of a dream already existing in the minds of prospective buyers. A special division of the Ford Motor Company had been created for its manufacture and the launch was preceded by an intense and elaborate build-up. Foote, Cone and Belding, the agency that handled the Edsel account, organized a competition among the employees of its New York, London and Chicago offices to find an acceptable name. They came up with 18,000 names, quickly whittled down to 6000, which included ZOOM, ZIP, BENSON, HENRY and DROF (if in doubt, spell it backwards!). Even Marianne Moore, the poetess, was consulted and came up with INTELLIGENT BULLET, UTOPIAN TURTLETOP, MONGOOSE CIVIQUE and BULLET CLOISONNÉ. In a muddled management decision, it was finally and disastrously named EDSEL.

As it turned out, the Edsel was a classic case of the wrong car, for the wrong market, at the wrong time. It was expensive; consumers were looking towards smaller, more compact cars and many hated its looks – especially that distinctive horse-collar grille. Above all it epitomized the many excesses which were repulsing more and more potential car buyers, for the Edsel was longer, more uselessly overpowered, more chrome-laden, more gadget-bedecked, more hung with expensive accessories than any other car in its price class. The Edsel's failure was also the result of a woeful misreading of the consumer psyche. Conventional market research was never used on the Edsel. Instead, Ford employed a type of motivational research called 'imagery studies', based on the premise that a customer can describe what kind of a product will best reflect his image to himself and be most acceptable to him. In their consumer-motivation studies, the Ford Motor Com-

One lemon with another . . . Vice-President Richard Nixon rides in a Ford Edsel convertible during a diplomatic visit to Lima, Peru in 1958. His visit was a failure and the Edsel's first year of production was an industrial catastrophe.

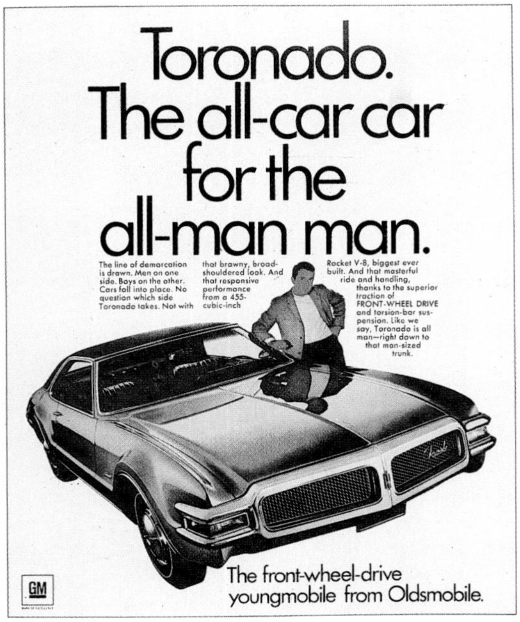

Toronado.
The all-car car
for the
all-man man.
The line of demarcation is drawn. Men on one side. Boys on the other. Cars fall into place. No question which side Toronado takes. Not with that brawny, broad-shouldered look. And that responsive performance from a 455-cubic-inch Rocket V-8, biggest ever built. And that masterful ride and handling, thanks to the superior traction of FRONT-WHEEL DRIVE and torsion-bar suspension. Like we say, Toronado is all man—right down to that man-sized trunk.
The front-wheel-drive youngmobile from Oldsmobile.
GM

In 1973, when John De Lorean, then Vice-President of General Motors, resigned his position, he declared: 'The automobile industry has lost its masculinity.' In 1968, however, full-blooded males were still being wooed by the macho designs of Bill Mitchell, (Harley Earl's design successor at General Motors), one of whose favourite catch-phrases is still 'The shape of things shape man.'

opposite] One of the most brilliantly marketed cars of all time. Reacting to the advance promotion of the 'Mustang Spirit', 4 million Americans went to Ford dealers to look at the new car on the day it was introduced at the New York World's Fair in 1964. They bought half a million of them within six months. Commented Ralph Nader: 'Their immediate involvement with the 'wild Mustang' paralleled in some ways the animism in certain primitive tribes which see inanimate objects, like trees, as possessing animate qualities.' It heralded the age of the 'personal car', with innumerable options available and, with ads like the one above, the promise of excitement and status at low cost. But beneath the snazzy styling and marketing hype the Mustang, in the words of one road test magazine, 'abounded with new and startling engineering features carried over from 1910'. The dominance yet again of stylist over engineer was to prove a further nail in the Detroit coffin.

pany asked no realistic questions at all about prices, cost of upkeep and operation, growing difficulty in parking, irritation at cars too long for garages, etc.

It was a monumental blunder. After costing Ford $250 million to bring it to market, the Edsel lost an estimated $200 million more during the two and a half years it was in production, and a mere 110,000 (minuscule by Detroit standards) were made. 'What the motivation researchers failed to tell their clients . . . is that only the psychotic and the gravely neurotic act out their compensating fantasies,' quipped S. I. Hayakawa, the American semanticist in the spring of 1958. 'The trouble with selling symbolic gratification via such expensive items as the Edsel Hermaphrodite . . . is the competition offered by much cheaper forms of symbolic gratification, such as *Playboy* (50 cents a copy), *Astounding Science Fiction* (35 cents a copy) and television (free).'

Since the Edsel débâcle manufacturers around the world have continued to agonize about the names they give to cars. Americans have generally settled for the openly aggressive (Fury, Marauder, Cougar and Mustang), for birds of prey (Eagle, Skyhawk) and even weapons (Cutlass, Dart, Javelin, Le Sabre). Europeans have played it increasingly safe with numbers (XJ12, 300SL, 320i), while the Japanese have tended to choose the delicate and docile (Bluebird, Sunny, Cherry) or the simply whimsical (Charade and Laurel). The image-making path, however, continues to be full of pitfalls. Many American Indians refused to buy Apache or Cherokee pick-ups on the grounds of traditional tribal hostility, while the Chevrolet Nova translated disastrously in Puerto Rico as 'does not go'. Even venerable Rolls-Royce suffered a near miss in almost naming a recent model the 'Silver Mist'. In German it means dung heap.

Detroit has yet to recover its lead as the world's chief image maker of the automobile business, for although its more restrained products through the 1960s and 1970s have shown a greater regard for the realities of consumer needs, they have increasingly leant heavily on European designs – particularly those of the Italians and Germans, ending up in most cases as rather unhappy compromises which are neither truly American nor truly European.

Beginning in the 1960s the Italian independent design houses in Turin, and particularly that of Pininfarina, became the style leaders of the automotive world. Their influence, of course, had been felt long before then. The Farinas had been coachbuilders since the turn of the century but it was their Cisitalia design of 1946 which was recognized by the New York Museum of Modern Art at a special exhibition in 1951 as being one of the world's greatest automobile designs. The handcrafted creations of Ghia, Bertone, Touring and Michelotti had influenced car styling on both sides of the Atlantic. Pininfarina had consistently applied two great ideals to car design: classical purity and functionalism. Out of Bertone's design studio came Giugiaro, a former portrait painter who had never designed a car before. He founded his own firm, Ital Design, with an emphasis on crisp, uncluttered, aerodynamically clean shapes and his creations have dominated the stark, no-trim design movement that has displaced Detroit as the world's style setter. From his prolific drawing board have come designs for the Japanese, the Americans, the Germans, the Italians and the British.

Functionalism has become the designers' credo, and even in the USA the roles of design and engineering are returning to the more logical relationship

A PRODUCT OF
Ford
MOTOR COMPANY
THE TOTAL PERFORMANCE MUSTANG HARDTOP
Life was just one diaper after another until Sarah got her new Mustang. Somehow Mustang's sensationally sophisticated looks, its standard-equipment luxuries (bucket seats, full carpeting, vinyl interior, chiffon-smooth, floor-mounted transmission) made everyday cares fade far, far into the background. Suddenly there was a new gleam in her husband's eye. (For the car? For Sarah? Both?) Now Sarah knows for sure: Mustangers have more fun!
Best year yet to go Ford
MUSTANG!
MUSTANG!
MUSTANG!

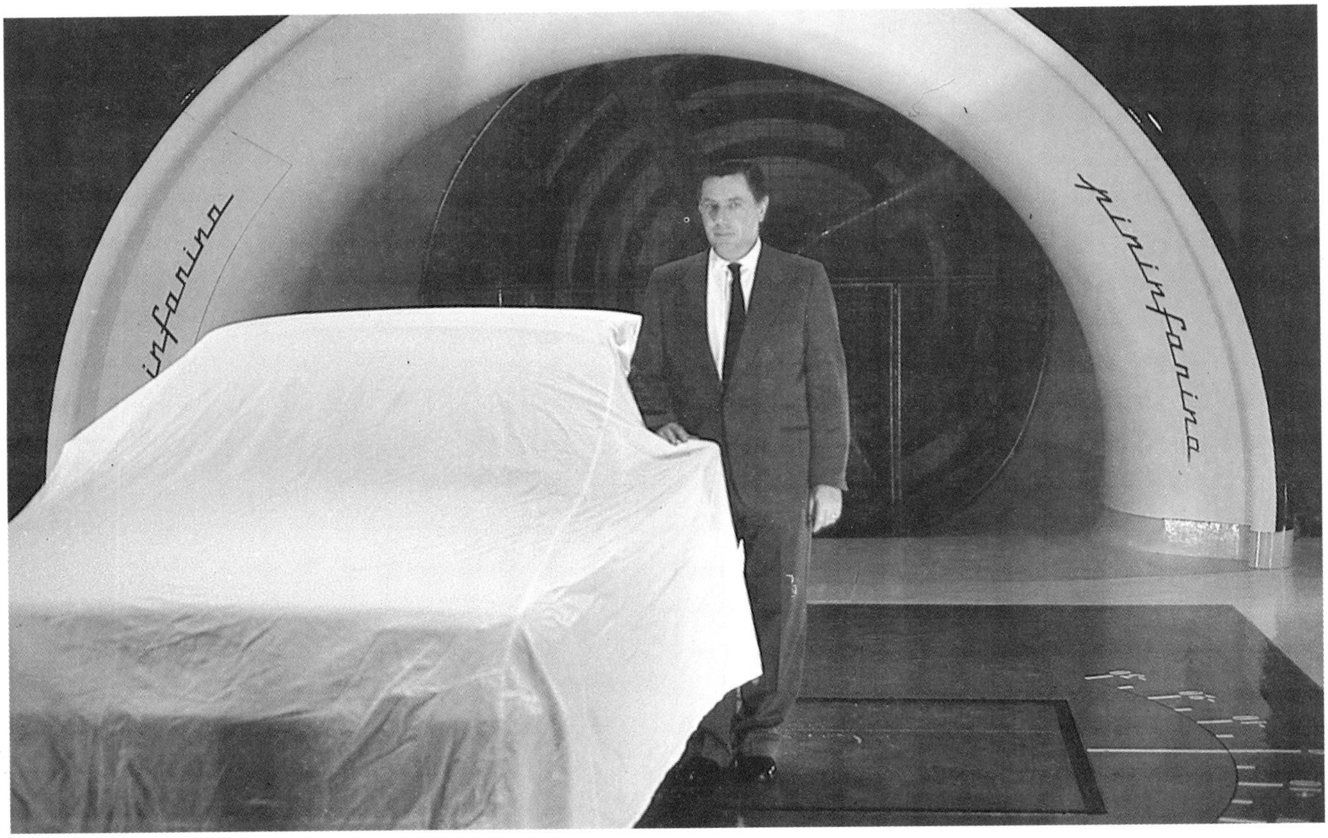

Pininfarina of Turin is one of the world's most influential car styling houses. Sergio Farina, its chief, leans on a secret prototype; behind is one of the wind tunnels in which so many of today's cars gain their shape, form and, some would say, boring uniformity.

A Lamborghini Countach S – considered by many to be the most exotic car made today. Italian styling at its most dazzling, with a 180 m.p.h. performance to match those space-age looks.

they enjoyed before Sloan discovered Harley Earl. 'Dynamic obsolescence' – one of Earl's favourite phrases – proved to be Detroit's ultimate undoing. The stylist's annual cosmetic facelift that gave the *illusion* of improvement and generated high volume car sales, was in the end no substitute for genuine engineering innovation. It has left the men of 'Motown' with a lot of catching up to do on the rest of the car world. Chuck Jordan, vice-president of design at General Motors today heads a design staff of 1300 people. He acknowledges:

We can't do it like we used to do it, with all the chrome hanging on the car. The design is not the mouldings put on the car. The design is the shape of the car and it's our responsibility using aerodynamics to develop new shapes that are appropriate but also distinctive and have personality of their own. When it hits the road it has got to have emotional appeal. You've got to look at that thing and say: 'Wow! I want it, I want it.'

But how do the image makers decide what that emotional appeal is? Jordan is convinced that the public do not know what they want; they know what they like about the cars they see on the street today, but 'they have no imagination and no ability to project themselves four years from now'. That is the designer's job. All manufacturers organize design clinics to get public assessments of their advance designs. Jordan observes: 'The newer the design the less the public tends to accept it . . . however, in four years' time this may be exactly the design to do because in that four-year period of time the public have become accustomed to other influences, have seen other things on the street . . .'

Sergio Farina, son of the great 'Pinin' Farina, believes that 'body design is still fundamentally the best weapon, the most important weapon the motor manufacturer has to attract people to buy'. Bertone, another great designer of the Turin fraternity, believes 'you can't make a scientific guess on people's taste . . . It is our own individual thinking that makes us take the decisions that we do.' Stephen Bayley, head of the Conran Foundation at the Victoria and Albert Museum in London, sums it up best of all:

The best car designers are in some way responsive to public mood, but also anticipate to a degree, so the latest generation of cars, at least the most successful ones, are responding to the designers' perception that the public has a taste for technology, a taste for detail and a taste for cars which look efficient and look responsible, and look as though they have a heavy investment in engineering.

But even as designers, advertisers and consumers discover new levels of maturity as the industry celebrates its hundredth birthday, one cannot help feeling a touch of nostalgia for those individualistic statements that owed nothing to wind tunnels, computer scans and design by committee, but were the creative sweep of one magisterial pen. After all, Sir William Lyons, founder of the Jaguar car company, designed what has been universally acclaimed as 'the most beautiful car of all time' – the inimitable E-type sports car – in two days on the back of an envelope. Even today America's most inspired car designer, Gordon Buehrig, creator in the mid 1930s of the beautiful alligator-shaped Cord 810 and several Duesenbergs, can say of his 'rolling sculpture' of almost half a century ago: 'If I were to do them over again I wouldn't change a thing.'

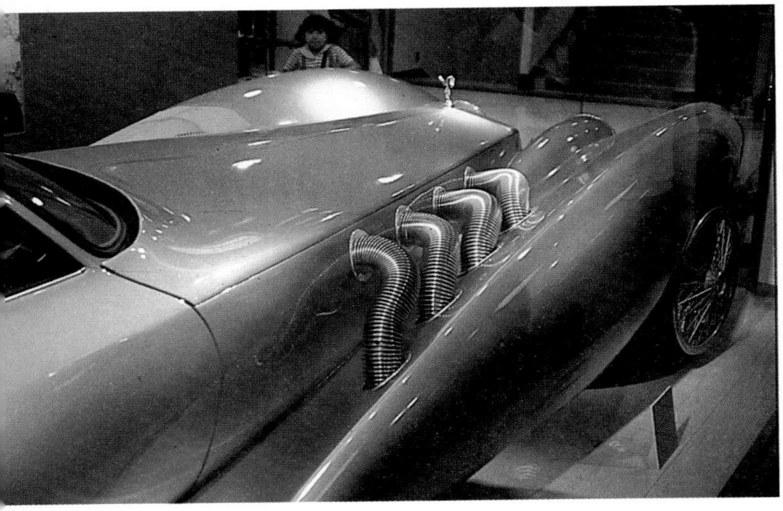

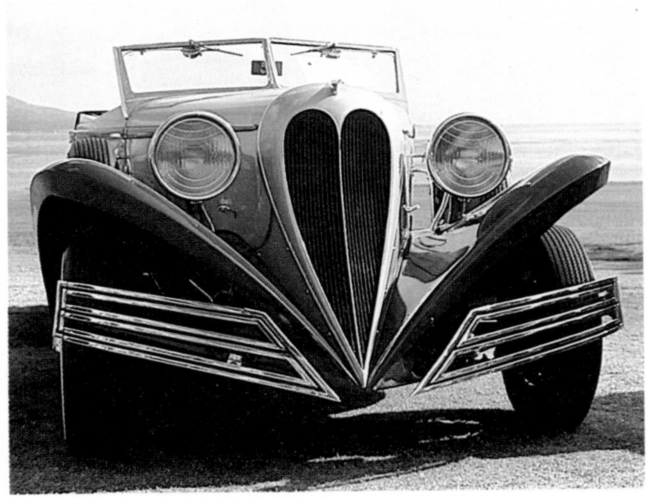

761 494

Some of the more extraordinary, sculptured shapes of car design: a heart-shaped Brewster-bodied Ford at Pebble Beach; Buehrig's revolutionary Cord 810 in its hometown of Auburn, Indiana (*left*); the German designer Luigi Colani's Rolls-Royce roadster on display in Osaka (*top left*); and an ovoid concept car in the Advanced Design Studios of General Motors in Warren, Michigan.

Bill Mitchell, Harley Earl's colourful successor at General Motors also styled some of America's most striking cars – the Toronado, the Corvette Sting Ray and Mako Shark – and is still designing on a freelance basis today. He is a strong advocate for the free-spirited independent designer: 'You've got to believe in yourself and go out there . . . Do you think the fashion designers go up and down the Champs-Élysées asking the women what kind of dresses they want? Why never. You tell them what they want, they don't know what they want. A style should set a style.' Not surprisingly the man who loved tailfins and lots of chrome hates today's fuel-efficient small cars – 'those little cracker-boxes' as he disparagingly calls them:

You've got to have some excitement, you've got to have a car go down the road and you turn your head and say: 'God, what is that?' and you don't have it today. You can't tell one car from another, that's no good . . . and that won't help the sales. Harley Earl used to say: 'If you go by a schoolyard and the kids don't whistle . . . then back to the drawing board . . .'

The Salesman

According to the popular image, an automobile dealer is a flashy dresser . . . probably sports a moustache and spends his days prowling the precincts of his garish, neon-and-chrome dealership in wait for the halt and gullible who make up the ranks of the car-buying public . . . In this view of automobile dealers, they have all migrated from the thieves' market in Tangiers . . . possess the trading skills of a Phoenician, the mathematical genius of a child prodigy, the material lusts of a Vanderbilt, the ethics of a Jay Gould, the conscience of a John Dillinger and the hypnotic powers of a Grigori Rasputin. To cross their threshold is to become a housefly in the parlour of a black widow.
(Brock Yates, *The Decline and Fall of the American Automobile Industry*)

In March 1890 an enterprising but long-forgotten Frenchman called M. Vurpillod committed a most historic act. He went out and bought a motor car, becoming the first person in the world to do so. His purchase was a Peugeot with a Daimler engine made under licence by Panhard and Levassor.

Four years later a Mr Henry Hewetson, a successful London tea merchant, became the first Briton to do the same. 'In the year 1884 I happened to be in Mannheim (Baden), where one of my friends owned a Benz car', he wrote in *A History of Ten Years of Automobilism*:

He showed me the working of it, and then I went to Messrs. Benz & Co. and ordered a two-seater 3 h.p. car which cost me about £80. They explained to me that, although motor cars were being used on the Continent, I should not be allowed on account of English law to run it in England until a special Motor Car Act was passed. This appeared to me so ridiculous that it made me all the more keen to buy the car, and so it was delivered to me about the end of the year 1894 at Catford.

Naturally, as there was no trade-in, he asked for a cash discount and got 20 per cent off!

In the United States George H. Morill Jr of Norwood, Massachusetts became the first man to own a car that he had not constructed himself when, in 1896, he purchased a Duryea motor wagon, one of a total production run of thirteen that year by the Duryea brothers.

Those three pioneer consumers – Vurpillod, Hewetson and Morrill Jr – the world's first paying customers for the 1000 million motor vehicles that have been made since each purchased their machines directly from the manufacturers. In fact, for the prospective motorist of the 1890s in America particularly, there were two methods of purchase before dealer networks were established. Either he collected the car directly from the factory, and having received basic instruction, trusted to good fortune that he and his new toy would manage the journey home. Or he placed his order, with cash up front, and had the car shipped usually in knock-down form in a large wooden crate to the nearest rail-head. Many early American motorists experienced their first taste of the automobile in obscure railway sidings, instruction manuals in hand.

For such pioneers the purchasing of a car at long distance could be a hazardous business. The burgeoning horseless carriage industry inevitably attracted more than its fair share of dreamers, hopefuls, smooth-talking charlatans and fly-by-nights. It was not uncommon for a trio of such rogues

The cycle dealership that turned into a car empire. William Morris trading in Longwall Street, Oxford, in 1912. By 1939 he had manufactured a million cars.

Smart British cycle dealers who were quick to recognize the potential of the motor car were soon selling and servicing them, in this case an 1898 Benz (on the left) and a Panhard.

THE OXFORD GARAGE.
MORRIS
CYCLES & MOTORS REPA
PRATT'S SPIRIT
ES-163
FC 250
FC 278
AD 554
LC 3084
P-2158

CYCLE MAKERS & ENGINEERS
CLOVER BROS,
CYCLES & DOMESTIC MACHINERY REPAIRED.

to arrive in a small country town, bedazzle the local populace with some flimsy machine and talk of a new production facility, and, having taken deposits from the more gullible, to vanish overnight with the token car and their promises unfulfilled.

In the first twenty years of the car in the United States there were almost 5000 different makes, although the majority of these were 'one-offs' or got no further than the blacksmiths' prototype stage. None the less, out of stables and barns and dingy workshops lurched the unlikely creations of hopeful entrepreneurs, built during long nights of trial and error, and destined in most cases for neither fame nor fortune. Some started from scratch, while others had a better basis in engineering or related businesses. Buick, a plumber born in Scotland, had qualifications of sorts. He had made bathtubs. The Dodge brothers had been bicycle makers, the Studebaker family were large-scale manufacturers of horse-drawn wagons. In France, Panhard and Levassor were makers of woodworking machinery. In England, Wolseley had made sheep-shearing equipment; the incomparable Royce (of Rolls-Royce) made the best electric cranes in the world.

Even successful mail order companies like Sears Roebuck in the United States went into car production and sales. Their 1909 catalogue, which claimed a circulation of 5 million people, included the 'Sears Motor Buggy', with tiller steering, a top speed of 25 m.p.h. ('We do not believe that the average man desires to go whirling through the countryside at 30 to 40 m.p.h.', affirmed the sales literature) and a price tag of $395 ('You have nothing to buy when you receive the car but gasoline . . . fill the tank and

One enterprising manufacturer could promise delivery of a new car right to your front door. The Winton Car Company came up with the world's first car transporter in 1899 – which was also required for those inevitable breakdowns.

drive home'). It all sounded so very simple. The car was shipped 'crated or set up, whichever will get the best freight rate. If crated all you have to do is to fasten on the wheels and fenders and the car is ready to run.'

Experience on the whole proved otherwise. With no local dealer to give servicing or sort out technical problems, it was increasingly in rural areas the farm implement dealers who became the distributors and service agents for the new machines. After all, they had the requisite mechanical knowledge and had established relationships with the local community. In the city, it was more likely the bicycle dealer or the more perspicacious horse-drawn carriage maker who handled sales. In Britain, especially, where so many of the early car manufacturers who congregated in Coventry had bicycle-making origins, it was natural that cycle dealers should become the retail outlets for the new product. William Morris in Oxford was such a dealer. He went on to found the Morris motor car empire, inspiration for the MG marque (standing for Morris Garages – and not, as some Americans faithfully believe, GM spelled backwards!) and became Lord Nuffield.

It seems likely the world's first fully fledged car salesman was William E. Metzger, a bicycle dealer in, appropriately enough, Detroit. In 1896 he started showing Waverley Electric cars, but did not make his first sale until the following spring, to a certain Newton Annis, who thereby became the first American retail car customer. He was to be followed by a pharmacist called W. A. Dohany, to whom Metzger sold the first production Olds, a car which in its later curved-dash form was to become America's best seller before the advent of Henry Ford's Model T in 1908, and established Detroit as the centre of the American automobile industry. Mr Metzger was typical of many new car dealers around the world. In the words of the *Automobile*

The Metz (like the Sears Motor Buggy) was sold by mail order and was shipped in knock-down form so the buyer could have the fun of assembling it and at the same time save money. But it took a team of horses to get this fully assembled Metz Racer across a stream to a waiting customer in Massachusetts in 1911.

The Morris Garages
OXFORD

Trade Journal, 'Dozens of those who came into the business in the early days and who prospered, came from the bicycle business and as a consequence understood the fact that they were selling transportation rather than machines, and that service was the fact that made or lost success.'

It was also felt that the salesmen who had graduated from the bicycle business were widely versed in 'road uses and sports' and were therefore in a better position to deal with the well-heeled sporting clientele who thronged into the new showrooms. In 1900, however, the most favoured salesmen of all were Europeans. Almost half the cars in America at that time were in and around New York and imported models such as the Benz, Panhard and Peugeot were especially favoured despite an import duty of 45 per cent. Such salesmen, mostly French, were not only more familiar with the construction of the imported models, with at least four years' greater experience in their actual operation than their American counterparts, but they also brought a greater sophistication to selling that appealed to East Coast 'society' buyers, who looked towards Paris as their cultural home.

'He ought to be pleasant, of clean-cut physical appearance, extreme youth is a handicap', wrote James Rood Doolittle in 1916, describing the ideal car salesman. 'Although academic degrees are quite rare in his fraternity. He does business with men and women of wealth almost exclusively . . . He must be of sufficient mental calibre to influence the opinions and views of the customer without seeming to do so.' Doolittle had observed that the most successful car salesmen were 'fully matured men, mostly heads of family', and it was not uncommon for a first-rate salesman to dispose of $500,000 worth of cars during the course of a year, such an amount of business demanding 'a high degree of energy, industry, diplomacy, enthusiasm, good looks, a good car, and good luck'.

All the family fun of trips to the countryside with winding leafy lanes, roadside picnics, and nature's charms, were promised in this Morris dealer's window display in 1925.

A solicitous salesman stands by as a pensive, pipe-smoking customer signs on the dotted line for a new Bullnose Morris in 1924. After the house, the car is the next largest capital purchase for most people, and choosing it can be a time of considerable anxiety.

In England the selling of cars remained in the hands of 'gentlemen' for many years. Sir Lawrence Hartnett, later to become managing director of General Motors-Holden in Australia, began as a second-hand car dealer in Surrey, buying up the unwanted cars of World War I widows. He recalls:

There was a lovely period, particularly in England and France, where it was just the élite bought cars and you had élite salesmen. They generally had a particular attribute like playing polo, or a good game of bridge. Being of the best family they didn't like to get mixed up in any dirty sort of commerce . . . it was really a personal relationship thing . . . and I think too it was a reasonably honourable profession in those days. There was never a trade-in involved or anything like that. And very little advertising. It wasn't the done thing to advertise too much.

He recalled one particular gentleman salesman, six-foot-two 'Tiny' Maguire at the Vauxhall Car Company, who 'sold probably forty cars over a period of three years . . . to the very best people. He could read off names of earls, dukes, lords and knew them quite well – would go down to Ranleigh with them or Hurlingham.' But as competitiveness grew and the market widened, the 'Tiny' Maguires were replaced.

I found him one day crouched by his desk with a fly swatter and he said, 'That fly thinks that horse on my desk is a real one, you know.' I said, 'Oh, dear, dear, dear . . . I don't think you've got a job, do you?' He said, 'No, I don't think I have.' So we had a very nice understanding and he got a job with Austin . . . He was typical of the type.

Hudson knew how to impress the customer when it came to displaying their cars. Palatial showrooms such as this sprang up all over America and Europe in the 1920s, helping to flatter the plainest cars.

right] Nash in neon, and their Inaugural Sedan in 'Eleanor Blue'. An enterprising dealer makes the most of Roosevelt's presidential inauguration to entice female customers into the showroom with his window display in March 1933. 'Ask the Salesman for a free sample of "Eleanor Blue" – colour of gown worn by Mrs Franklin D. Roosevelt,' states the come-on.

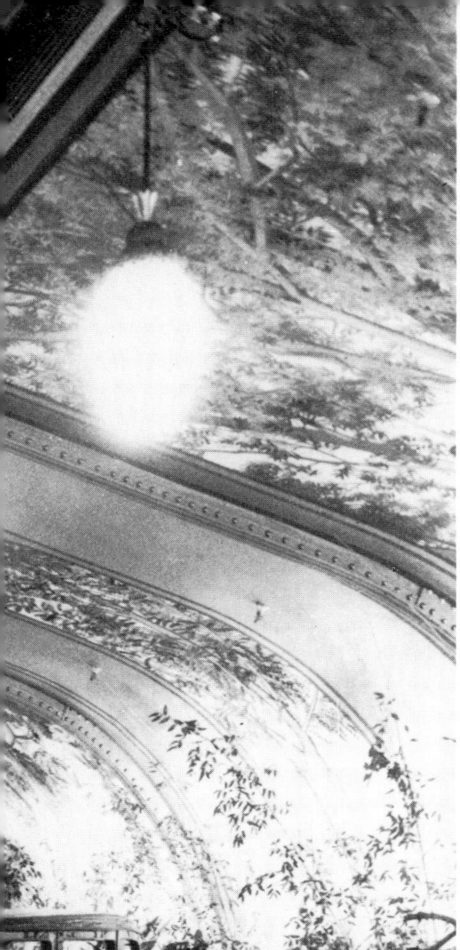

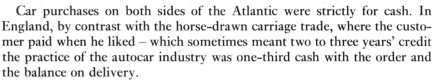

Car purchases on both sides of the Atlantic were strictly for cash. In England, by contrast with the horse-drawn carriage trade, where the customer paid when he liked – which sometimes meant two to three years' credit the practice of the autocar industry was one-third cash with the order and the balance on delivery.

In the United States salesmanship began in earnest in 1902, when a new class of buyer emerged who, in Doolittle's words, 'had made fortunes, or what appeared to be fortunes, in an apparent short space of time ranging from three hours to three months. It was the "hooraw" period of the industry when a considerable amount of selling was consummated to the cadence of popping corks.' John W. Anderson, one of the original investors in the Ford Motor Company, was able to write to his father in 1903: 'Now the demand for automobiles is a perfect craze. Every factory here has its entire output sold and cannot begin to fill orders . . . And it is all spot cash on delivery, and with no guarantee or string attached of any kind.'

With the salesmen came the showrooms. Every American city rapidly developed its 'Gasoline Alley' or 'Auto Row'. In San Francisco a mile-long section of Van Ness Avenue still has the largest concentration of car showrooms in the West. As early as 1911 there were thirty dealers on Van Ness; ten years later the number had doubled. Showroom openings rapidly became gala affairs, broadcast by radio and attended by film stars. Many of the buildings were fantasy palaces, with elaborate display areas rich in leather and mahogany and acres of glistening marble, providing an impressive environment for the salesman and his wares.

For the new dealerships, Saturday was the great selling day. Mondays and Tuesdays were spent, as one veteran salesman recalled, going out to recover the cars that had broken down or crashed in the hands of their enthusiastic new owners. As car sales rocketed (300 sold between 1896 and 1898; 11,000 in 1903 alone) automania moved to the American countryside. Farmers traded in their horses, which were then costing between $200 and $300, for cars which they saw as more economical and increasingly more reliable. It was, as we have seen in chapter 4, the Model T that took the countryside by storm, with an army of dealers and salesmen, like crusading evangelists, spearheading the attack. By 1912 Henry Ford had 3500 dealers across the United States (it was to rise to 17,000 by the end of World War II), and there were more Ford salesmen meeting the public than any other retail organization in America. 'Early to bed and early to rise. Work like hell and advertise', they were exhorted by the *Ford Times* in 1911. They were admonished to keep salesrooms clean, to post 'no tipping' signs, and to separate the showroom from the repairs department to prevent prospective customers seeing mechanical failures. They were also advised that 'The salesman's courtesy is the best antidote for the prospect's crabbiness'! No doubt they were thinking of those irascible yokels that only a short time before had sought the destruction of the motorist from the cities by scattering the roads with nails and erecting cables across the highways at decapitating height!

To promote the versatility of their product, dealers became increasingly involved in stunts, gimmicks and public exhibitions and there developed the 'show-biz' aspect of the selling of the car which reached unprecedented heights of inventiveness in the 1950s and 1960s. The sturdiness and flexibility of the cars were shown in popular dealer-publicity stunts in which they were driven up flights of steps or made to carry prodigious loads. In one demonstration in 1911 the car went up two flights of steps, through a door, and into the hall of a courthouse in Paducah, Kentucky. The same enterprising dealer also carried three hogsheads of tobacco and twenty-six men on one Model T and drove them through the town. At state and county fairs salesmen would drive their cars up slopes built at forty-five degrees to prove their hill-climbing abilities, offer cash prizes to school children for essays extolling the virtues of the Ford car, even in one case paying a weightlifter to stagger through town with a Model T on his back. One Mississippi dealer jubilantly rang the town bell every time he made a sale, thereby turning a quiet country town into a noisy one. Another – hardly mindful of road safety – claimed the Ford handled so easily that a woman could drive with one hand and knit with the other. Ford salesmen were nothing, if not effective. In 1921, of all the cars built in America that year, 61.6 per cent were Model Ts.

In Australia, where the Model T quickly achieved ascendancy, enterprise of a different kind was required of the car dealer. George Roberts describes his trips into the outback to deliver Model Ts to their new owners:

The territory that one had for selling cars in those days could emcompass an area of perhaps two hundred square miles or more, so it was not unusual to deliver a car a hundred, or sometimes even two hundred miles away. The idea of delivering them to the property or to their homes was to teach them how to drive . . . to give them immediate instructions and then find your way home again.

In 1924 the price of the Model T was near its all-time low, and it was this kind of practical advertisement that had been appealing especially to farmers since 1908. Henry Ford and his sales force knew their market well, for even in 1920 40 per cent of America's population still lived down on the farm.

Where a decade before horses had lined the hitching rail in Main Street, Shamrock, Oklahoma, the good ole boys in 1914 surveyed the world from their Model Ts.

Ford
Touring Car
$295
F. O. B. DETROIT
Starter and Demountable Rims $85 Extra
OF all the times of the year when you need a Ford car, that time is NOW!
Wherever you live—in town or country—owning a Ford car helps you to get the most out of life.
Every day without a Ford means lost hours of healthy motoring pleasure.
The Ford gives you unlimited chance to get away into new surroundings every day—a picnic supper or a cool spin in the evening to enjoy the countryside or a visit with friends.
These advantages make for greater enjoyment of life—bring you rest and relaxation at a cost so low that it will surprise you.
By stimulating good health and efficiency, owning a Ford increases your earning power.
Buy your Ford now or start weekly payments on it.

HOTEL
CAFE
NEWS STAND
THE BEST
REGULA
MEA
IN THE CITY
SHAMROCK AUTO LIVEY

27 EXIT

'Heap good fun' for Buffalo Bill's Indians at Grant's Tomb on Riverside Drive in New York – and presumably 'Heap good promotion' for the car dealer who has got them there to help cry his wares.

above left] With Tiny Tim at the wheel, and the Welsh Giant – all $7\frac{1}{2}$ feet of him – standing by, how could anything go wrong for Reo? This half-scale model of their 1906 car toured with the Barnum and Bailey Circus, successfully promoting the sales of the full-size version to audiences across America.

centre left] 'Both have perfect lines,' chorused the audience with approval, when Miss Annette Kellerman ('Diving Venus' of the B. F. Kish Vaudeville Circuit) appeared on stage to promote the 1926 Chandler 'Comrade' Roadster.

below left] Auto polo was one of the early promotions for the Model T. In 1912 on an ordinary football field, two stripped-down Ts with little more than a chassis and protective roll-over bar race after a large ball. Writes Reynold M. Wiks in *Henry Ford and Grass-roots America*: 'A polo player rode on the running board of each car . . . During the game the cars slipped, skidded, danced and bumped about the field. Dealers claimed the Fords were the only car that could play this game, because the planetary transmission allowed the driver to move forward or backward without shifting gears!'

Physical hazards abounded on such trips: the black soil that after rain became a quagmire, and would build up under the mudguards until the wheels on the car would not turn; the prickly pear plant that grew in clumps six or seven feet high and would lacerate the skin with three-inch spines and exude a slime that would cause the car to skid; and of course, the endless, inevitable punctures that necessitated the filling of the tyres with grass to preserve them from further damage. And all endured in order to complete a sale! Delighted owners, with the salesman's help, quickly got the hang of their new machines ('There was virtually no traffic in these areas where they were and they taught themselves to drive on their own property'), although some remained genuinely baffled. One old farmer was found running a Model T in repeated circles round the front of his homestead. When asked why, he explained that he was tiring the car out before putting it back in the stable . . .

It was a feature of outback stations, as George Roberts points out, that such farmers traditionally ran their cars until something major broke. They then either put the car away in a shed or dumped it on some corner of their property, and went out and bought a new one. 'The second-hand market did not grow to any great magnitude until after World War I,' he avers.

"...and the dear man thought he sold me!"
The Hat... Erik's black felt pill box from Bergdorf Goodman
The Jacket... Yvonne Carette designed it herself ...it's short and chunky in black fox
The Car... a Chrysler Royal Touring Sedan
"Of course, John is a lamb . . . but he has to be handled.
"So when he began assembling Chrysler catalogs, I just said, 'Certainly, a home in Newport would be nice, too!'
"And he began to tell me all about Chrysler invading the low-priced field—as if I'd never heard it! Although when I *saw* the 1938 Chrysler Royal, I didn't quite see how such a car could be low-priced!
"Well, we rode in one. And while John kept prattling about horsepower and valves and gasoline mileage, I drank in the beauty and quality . . . the size . . . the room . . . the gorgeous instrument panel . . . the marvelous upholstery.
"I think we both made up our minds when we got to the railroad tracks on Sixth Street. We braced ourselves as usual . . . but that love of a Chrysler just glided over them as if they weren't there at all.
"So John took up weight distribution, and hydraulic shock absorbers and independently sprung front wheels . . . and I just asked him gently if Chrysler engineering wasn't reputed to be the best in the industry. He said it was. So I told him we could probably accept what everybody knew.
"Really, we were both amazed at the low price . . . and the order signing was brisk and pleasant.
"At dinner, John explained the hypoid rear axle . . . and I let him. The dear man had it coming . . . he thought *he* had sold *me!*"
★ ★ ★
☆ NEW 1938 ROYAL . . . 95 horsepower, 119-inch wheelbase. Ten body types.
☆ NEW 1938 IMPERIAL . . . 110 horsepower, 125-inch wheelbase. Six body types.
☆ NEW 1938 CUSTOM IMPERIAL . . . 130 horsepower, 144-inch wheelbase. Three body types.
Tune in on Major Bowes, Columbia Network, every Thursday, 9 to 10:00 P. M., Eastern Standard Time.
Chrysler
ROYAL ... MORE FOR THE MONEY IN THE LOW-PRICED FIELD!
IMPERIAL ... PHENOMENAL PERFORMANCE AT A REMARKABLE PRICE!
BETTER Engineered... BETTER Made!

Showroom window gazing in Germany in 1936. Motoring for the millions, though conceived, had barely arrived, and even for this prosperous-looking couple the purchase of a new car, rather than a secondhand one, would have been unusual.

left] 'John has to be handled,' confides the all-knowing li'l American woman in 1937, especially, it seems, when it comes to car buying. She has presumably been handling poor John ever since, for all contemporary surveys show that in America it is now the woman of the house, not the man, who is chief decision-maker when it comes to choosing the car.

right] Prosperous, middle-class Americans, enjoying the fruits of peace, try a post-war Dodge for size. For salesmen it was the golden era; for every car Detroit produced there were at least a dozen buyers standing in line.

In the United States it came much sooner, and was to transform the relationship between the car salesman and the public. If the image of a car dealer had initially been no better or no worse than the average town merchant, that began to change with the creation of the second-hand car market. Doolittle put that date as 1904. Under the heading of 'The Second-hand Car Problem' he wrote:

It called into being a new class of salesman and added the bargaining element to retail distribution of motor cars. It became the duty of the salesman to buy the used car as low as possible to complete the sale of a new car, and the customer soon learnt the advantages of taking his wares to several markets with the idea of having several salesmen make competitive bids for his old car.

The adversarial element had been introduced. Also into the second-hand car business poured the disenfranchised horse-dealers, the conmen, the entrepreneurs who had neither the respectability nor the creditworthiness to secure a new car retail outlet, but who carried sufficient conviction to deal successfully with an innocent public eager to possess the new transport and the freedoms it gave. The product they sold was of the most miserable kind. The durability of American cars built between 1903 and 1906 was poor, words painful perhaps to those enthusiasts who love and cherish such cars today, but sadly true; their average life expectancy was not much more than 20,000 miles and indeed of the one million or so cars built in the USA prior

From the beginning motor shows were shop windows for the industry, and a source of anticipation and excitement for the consumer. The First National Automobile Show in America in 1900 was held at New York's Madison Square Garden (*left*) and featured test drives for customers along obstacle courses, largely to prove that the darned things worked.

Britain's first professional motor show was held at the Agricultural Hall in Islington, north London, in April of the same year and featured a similar test track.

to 1910, it was calculated that barely 10 per cent survived to that date. Yet it was in such decrepit vehicles – not new ones – that the majority of Americans took to the road and formed their first negative opinions of the profession that in most cases sold them a tarnished dream. It was a view dealers did little to change as the years passed.

For even those 'respectable' new car dealerships that had originally financed and sustained the automakers in the early days became increasingly involved in a frustrating, frequently acrimonious relationship with the manufacturers. It was a disharmony that was passed on to the public. In the slump of 1920, for example, Henry Ford solved his over-production problems by dumping 30,000 cars on his dealers, when they already had 100,000 unsold cars in stock, telling them they could either accept and pay cash for the cars or lose their franchises. Also, through the 1920s the manufacturers began to exert more control over the activities of their dealers, supervising their operations more closely, which meant that under Depression conditions the manufacturers' pressure for volume sales could become an unbearable hardship for the car salesman. A Federal Trade Commission report to Congress in 1939 stated: 'Under threat or fear of cancellation, some dealers have reported they felt compelled to operate their businesses in such a manner that their profits were wiped out and even their investments were largely dissipated . . . All manufacturers utilize this fear to a greater or lesser extent . . . Dealers characterize these effects as pressure; manufacturers as efforts to assist dealers.'

This kind of pressure has frequently turned the car lot into a field of combat. 'The car dealer in America is as close as we come these days, to being a professional gunfighter,' says Leon Mandel. This was certainly true after World War II when the car dealer operated in an absolute sellers' market. Both in Europe and America cars were in painfully short supply and whatever price a dealer asked for a new car, no matter how ludicrous, it would be paid by the car-hungry consumer. Malpractice was rife. Bribes were taken, queues jumped, fictitious charges added, and dealers, while alienating the public, grew extremely wealthy. But while the car dealer was regarded by many as a predator, the majority were also in a forgiving mood: 'The most important reason for Americans' willingness to overlook the auto dealer's post-war sales antics was the automobile itself', writes Art Spinella in *The Master Merchandisers*.

The car, once bought – regardless of the price – was so much part of a person's status . . . And the car was the most obvious and strongest statement about the reason the war was fought in the first place: freedom . . . Being overcharged for an automobile – that symbol of freedom from poverty and war – was of little concern. The automobile was a natural high. And America would pay anything to get it.

As new car deliveries quadrupled to $6\frac{1}{2}$ million in 1950, the American car dealer, his pockets replete with dollars, had every reason to be a high-strutting, if tainted figure. His standing with the public, however, was to plunge to even greater depths in 1955, ending any semblance of respect that remained between customer and dealer. In that year the automakers, following a couple of recessionary years, decided to exceed the bonanza of 1950 and sell 7 million cars in one year. Their method for doing so was relatively simple. Each dealer's quota of cars would be doubled and if he failed to sell them he would either lose his franchise, or face the threat of another factory-sponsored outlet opening up next door. The dealers' formula for survival was the legendary 'System' which began in the south-eastern states amongst Ford retailers and was conjured up by a management firm specializing in sales techniques called Hull Dobbs. They argued that an entirely new kind of customer, the man who could never before afford a car, should be lured into the showroom with blandishments of every kind – a staggering discount, or a holiday in Florida for two, a free television or a mink stole.

'The System' as Leon Mandel in *Driver: The American Four-Wheeled Love Affair* has shown, depended on two devices: 'The first premise of "The System": car buyers were larcenous at heart and therefore if they were offered something to steal, they would come in and steal it.' This meant that cars, often loss leaders, were offered in 'blitz' advertising campaigns at unbelievably low prices. Even if the cars existed (and sometimes they did not), the salesman would never sell it at that price once the customer had been lured into the showroom. 'The second premise was far more sophisticated,' says Mandel. 'It was embraced in the nature of 'The System' itself, a highly developed method of selling a car under any conditions, once the "irresistible" advertising had brought the customer to the door. It said anybody could be sold a car.' In this part of the scenario the unsuspecting purchaser would be trapped in a series of contrived encounters, first with 'the liner', who would write out a sales order on impossibly favourable terms to the purchaser; then 'the appraiser' who would, in effect, hide the customer's car to ensure he had no escape route from the dealership; and finally with the 'TO' (turn-over man), whose office was usually bugged. Here the customer would be weaned, cajoled, bullied away from the liner's impossibly favourable deal into something more realistic (and profitable) to the dealer. Standing in the wings of this frightening confrontation would be the bit part players: 'the stick man', the financial expert (so called because *in extremis* the victim's furniture could be used as collateral!) and the man from the finance company, known variously as 'the happy man' or 'the mouse man' (after 'Mickey Mouse deal').

Just as the styling excesses of Detroit alienated large numbers of consumers, these questionable selling practices, first used on a large scale in 1955, in the words of the editors of *America's Auto Dealer*, 'marked the end of the automobile dealer as a merchant/citizen. From now on, the label merchant/conman was affixed – even for those undeserving of the title.' It is a reputation that has continued to this day, despite the outlawing at state and federal level of the worst abuses of 'The System'. 'Bait and switch' is now illegal. Cars must carry suggested manufacturers' retail prices (under the Automotive Information Disclosure Act in 1958 a list price became mandatory and the dealer could no longer simply charge whatever the market would bear). Truth-in-lending laws require the dealer to sell in a more straightforward way. There is no longer the same model proliferation to confuse the customer.

Yet if the ranks of the slick, silver-tongued hustlers have thinned, the legacy remains. Stepping on to almost any car sales forecourt, and not just in the United States, is for most people an intimidating experience. After all, the car is also the second most expensive purchase an individual makes after his home. Unlike real estate, however, it depreciates rapidly, is often temperamental and can be fiercely expensive to repair and maintain.

Sex, we are told, has been used to sell everything . . . including the motor car. At the 44th International Motor Show at Earls Court in 1959, opened by the Prime Minister, Mr Harold Macmillan, well-bred ladies still wore full-length black velvet gloves to promote the Hillman Minx convertible. Yet a dozen short years later, in the sexy seventies, Miss Jones and Miss Shaw wore nothing at all to draw the Motor Show crowds . . . and what, one wonders, would the first automobilists have made of that?

Australia's 'gasoline alley' is the Paramatta Road, Sydney, where dozens of dealers for mile after mile vie with each other, using every kind of blandishment to lure the customer in. The condition of most of the cars they sell is an eloquent testimony to the Australians' continuing passion for the magic machine.

To lessen the consumers' trauma, Tony Packard, a personable and highly successful General Motors-Holden dealer in Sydney, goes to great pains in the selection of his sales staff. 'The public perception of the car dealer is that he's a charlatan, and *we* are not,' he states. On a plaque on his office wall the ideal Tony Packard-Holden man is described as: 'neat, clean, a conservative dresser, honest, dependable, reliable'. A detailed psychological profile is drawn up of each prospective employee: 'That profile tells us in basic terms what is going on inside the human being, and we know the sort of human being we're looking for is a "people person" . . . somebody who is automatically relaxed with other human beings and goes about relaxing other people. If a person has got that, he'll almost always make a good salesman.'

Also in the selection process he employs astrology: 'Aries is a very good sign, because they're strong leadership people'; interviews wives and girlfriends: 'I try and get in my mind what is happening in their family, whether they're happy, whether they're successful . . .'; even carries out a morning inspection of their dress, to ensure 'that the socks are the same colour as the trousers'. He continues: 'One of the things that I'm really paranoid about in this place is that people don't tell lies. So in our contract of employment we simply have a statement: "I agree that I will not tell lies."'

What have giraffes in Japan got to do with selling cars? Not much, is the answer. But by adopting the American taste for bizarre roadside architecture this Toyota dealer hopes to attract new customers onto his garage forecourt. If all else fails, bring in Paul Newman . . .

American Joe Girard, recognized by the *Guiness Book of Records* as the most successful car salesman of all time (he personally sold 1425 cars and trucks in one year), also believes the truth factor is a vital element in closing a sale. 'The image of car salesmen is that they cheat and lie . . . you can break a promise once, if you break a promise then no one will ever accept another promise from you.' He believes that consumer confidence in the salesman is the basis of successful selling.

TOYOTA
VISTA
ビスタ東名古屋
錦町店
クレスタ
ビスタ
ターセル
サービス
IN
実施中

登場。
の190馬力!
RS-TURBO

Another colourful Sydney car dealer of the extrovert school, John L., writes, produces, directs and appears in his own television commercials, and believes that the image of the car dealer has improved. Furthermore, he thinks it is very often the *customer* who is now the dishonest party, who will turn back the speedometer on his trade-in, or put banana skins or even apples in the differential to quieten a worn transmission. 'A customer feels great if he feels he's sending you down the tube, or sending you broke or that he's getting something for nothing . . . That's our market place and really and truly I don't suppose you can blame them. It's just a case of us living on our wits and them taking advantage of us . . .'

One country where the psychological confrontation in the showroom hardly ever takes place is in Japan. Because land is so scarce, showrooms are small. Even in downtown Tokyo, a leading Toyota dealer will have space for only a few cars, despite the dozens of models in his catalogue. One dealer has a turnover of 15,000 cars a year, but room only to display four at any one time.

Japan's strict vehicle testing laws mean that keeping a car more than three or four years becomes prohibitively expensive. This policy has been good for the salesman and for the scrapyards.

Cars are in fact sold by door-to-door salesmen who, like traffic wardens, are allocated a beat, maybe six streets for each salesman. It is said that if you are washing your car in a Tokyo street on a Sunday (which the Japanese are forever doing) the car salesman with a briefcase bulging with catalogues will suddenly pop up like the vicar to remind you that your car is already three years old and it's time to change it. In the customer's home, in an encounter reminiscent of the traditional Japanese tea ceremony, the family will carefully select their new car from the salesman's brochures. Test runs are rare. Because of stringent compulsory safety checks and the high expense of garage repairs, cars are changed every two or three years, so it is little wonder so many cars on the Japanese scrap heap still look in showroom condition. Once the new car has been delivered, its progress will be carefully monitored by the solicitous salesman, until it is time for the next purchase. In this tranquil, but effective way, Japanese salesmen sell 3 million new cars a year in a market which grows annually.

In Nagoya, Japanese car salesmen at a Toyota dealership limber up for a hard day's selling with group calisthenics. They will shortly be off, trudging from door to door, clutching brochures and wearing a fixed smile. Even in Japan, where all work is considered honourable, the profession of car salesman rates low in public esteem.

In Russia they say that owning a car brings joy twice in an owner's life – when it is bought and when it is sold. In between there is only torture. Nevertheless at least 2 million people languish on a waiting list for new cars. Full payment is demanded in advance and delivery takes at least four years. It is hardly surprising that there is a flourishing second-hand car market, run largely by central Asians and Georgians, and subject to periodic crack-downs by the authorities. These same car dealers also control the illegal money market determining the 'black' rate of the rouble against hard foreign currencies. But even from these backstreet 'wheeler-dealers' a low mileage, late-model Volga family saloon will cost at least $25,000, and comes with no guarantee.

Buying a car in Brazil is a much happier, not to say festive, affair, despite the fact few people can qualify for credit with bank interest rates at a crippling 180 per cent. To overcome this hurdle, the majority of cars are purchased through a *consorcio*. In this ingenious scheme dealers gather together a hundred potential customers who pay a monthly fixed proportion of the latest car price over a period of fifty months. Who gets the cars first is decided in a monthly lottery held at the local dealer's showroom in a party atmosphere of samba and celebratory drinks. Even marriages have resulted from these lively social gatherings over which the car dealer presides like a jolly master of ceremonies . . . None the less, his unsavoury image around the world persists. More Americans consistently complain about their cars than any other device they own and year after year the car salesman is the object of more complaints to Better Business Bureaux than any other retailer. 'Would you buy a second-hand car from this man?' a question originally applied with such devastation to former President Richard Nixon, has become an international term of disparagement.

The car dealer's horsetrading image, however, may soon be irrelevant. Although car sales in the United States still make up one third of the world's total, and constitute 17 per cent of all domestic retail sales, car-making is no longer a growth industry. During the last twenty-five years more than half the businesses devoted to the sale of American-built cars, approximately 25,000, have gone out of business, and as owners hold on to their cars longer, the number of dealers in the second-hand business is shrinking even further. The American car dealer, like his British counterpart, is in fact a disappearing species, and in his passing goes one of the more extraordinary and least loved manifestations of the car revolution.

Lowering the Cost and Raising the Price

Motorists have compelled one hundred thousand people to withdraw their horses and carriages from the public roads. It is estimated that one hundred thousand men have been thrown out of work as a consequence . . .

So warned a handbill circulated on the streets of London in 1908 calling upon the Men of England to rise up against the motorist and his destructive vehicle. Many charges have been laid against the car but rarely in its history has it been accused of taking away a man's livelihood for the good reason that the phenomenal increase in the production and use of cars over the last fifty years has created wealth and employment on the grandest scale. Today the economies of many countries rely heavily on motor transport, notably the United States which in recent years has spent around $200 billion dollars annually, 10 per cent of gross national product (GNP), on road transportation. But even this calculation fails to take account of the indirect impact of the car on industries like tourism, where road transport plays a key role. Western Europe and Japan are also heavily dependent on the car. As the world's leading exporter the Japanese economy is particularly reliant on car markets in other countries; and even in western Europe cars represent 10 per cent of exports.

When it comes to jobs and to personal incomes, the economic role of the car looms almost frighteningly large. According to a UN-funded study it has been estimated that 30 million people around the world depend on automobiles or trucks for jobs. Close to half of these are in the United States, where one out of every six jobs is in the automobile sector. In western Europe, 5 million jobs are dependent on the automobile. However, cars *take* as well as provide an individual's earnings. A recent study indicated that Americans spend 22 per cent of their personal income on automobile transportation.

As we have seen, although developing nations are not yet so economically reliant on the car, they are moving in that direction. Some, like South Korea, have taken the decision to build up this apparently glamorous indigenous industry and have set their sights on increasing their car population from under a million to 3.5 million by 1991. Although uncertainty about oil prices and supplies has caused some hesitation, there is still a widespread belief that building up a nation's motor industry offers the surest road to industrialization and prosperity. They have seen it work spectacularly for others, so why not for them?

The earliest cars, were, of course, hand-made; they were 'horseless carriages' and employed the traditional skills of the carriage makers, many of whom easily made the transition from building horse-drawn vehicles to making car bodies. Perhaps the most striking example of the continuity of tradition from the age of the horse through the horseless age to the age of the computer can be seen at the Aston Martin Lagonda works at Newport Pagnell. The factory occupies the site where Salmon and Sons Ltd, Coachmakers to the Nobility, started business in 1820. Salmon's flourished as carriage builders and then became famous before World War I for their distinctive fabric-bodied designs on many of the famous English and Continental cars of the day. After the war the company became Tickford Motor Bodies which in turn was purchased by Aston Martin Lagonda. Today, cars are still hand-built in Newport Pagnell, using the same kind of craftsmanship

New 'Pony' cars outside the Hyundai works in South Korea. As one of the developing countries with ambitions to share in the wealth created by the car, South Korea is hoping to establish the kind of dynamic home market that did much to bring about the Japanese car miracle.

Mobile Auto Factory with a row of Mobile Steamers ready for delivery. This is the only American turn-of-the-century car plant still in production today. In 1900 the upholstery shop had an air of tranquillity that did not survive far into the twentieth century.

right] Craftsmen who built horse-drawn carriages easily adapted their skills to the needs of the motor car industry. In 1912 the Rauch and Lang Carriage Co. in Cleveland, Ohio was making bodies for electric cars.

At the Aston Martin works, Newport Pagnell, they have been coachbuilding since 1820. Although the product has changed, the craftsmanship is in the safe hands of some of the great, great, great grandchildren of the original workers.

and skills that the coachbuilders employed 150 years ago; and much of the work is done by men who can trace their coachbuilding ancestry back four or five generations. In car-building terms Aston Martin is not just exceptional, it is unique. To build one Lagonda takes 1750 man-hours spread over three or four months, whereas most cars today are built by robots and automated production lines in a matter of hours. To see the craftsmen at Newport Pagnell patiently banging a body panel into shape, and then to watch the new army of robots swing into action just up the road at Longbridge, is to see just how far manufacturing methods have come in one hundred years. The car itself is old technology, but the method of making it takes us almost into the realms of science fiction.

Henry Ford in his 1896 Quadricycle. He drove it for the first time on 6 June 1896 through the streets of Detroit.

Charles Duryea. Although they have always been obscured by the giant shadow of Henry Ford, Frank and Charles Duryea produced the first all-American petrol-driven vehicle in 1893 and should rightly be regarded as the fathers of the American automobile.

In the introduction of new technology and new management techniques, the car industry can claim many of the important advances of the past century; but for some of its alleged achievements the credit rightly belongs elsewhere. American children are brought up believing that Henry Ford was the first to introduce the assembly line, the standardization of parts and that he even invented the car. He did none of those things. What he did achieve was economy of scale: he turned out cars so efficiently and in such numbers that he was able to bring them within range of the mass market. The Ford Motor Company was founded in 1903 with the objective of bringing down the price of a car from over $2,000 to less than $500, and within ten years that target had been reached. The mass production methods incorporated in the Ford factory at Highland Park in Detroit had been borrowed and adapted from many other industries; from a railway wagon works, from the fire-arms industry, from brewing and milling systems and even from the Chicago slaughterhouses. By applying the same principles to the manufacture of the Model T, Ford was able to reduce man-hours for assembling the vehicle from more than twelve to an astonishing one and a half. By 1917, a car rolled off the production lines every two minutes, an average of more than 1500 every working day.

But even more astounding, in less than a decade, Ford had brought the 'toy of the rich' within the reach of the wage earner. By 1914, a Ford worker could buy a Model T for less than four months' wages. In Britain, William Morris also attempted to build a people's car but he found it difficult to achieve the economies of scale he needed. On his new assembly line in Oxford, he was able to turn out only 1550 cars in the whole of 1920, 1000 fewer than Ford was turning out in a day in Detroit three years earlier. What is more, it was another thirty years before wages in Britain grew sufficiently to make a working-class mass market a practicable goal.

As we have already seen, in the very early days of the car industry literally thousands of entrepreneurs were tempted to try their hand. However, early on, volume production of cars in the United States became concentrated in the hands of a few giant corporations and that process of amalgamation, of the stronger swallowing the weaker, has continued as a worldwide trend to the present day. In order to bring prices down and remain competitive, all factories had to adopt high speed assembly line working; and in order to cut costs and maximize profits there was always the temptation to speed up that assembly line and to squeeze more production out of fewer workers.

Assembly line work was endlessly repetitive; tasks were broken down into ever simpler and more easily repeatable functions so that the production line could be speeded up even more, so that the monotonous task came round even faster. Added to the feeling of being part of a mindless machine that took no account of everyday human needs like stretching one's legs or going to the lavatory, was the sense of guilt that arose from the knowledge that fellow workers would lose time and money if one failed to keep up the relentless pace.

It was this violence done to human freedom that Chaplin attacked so savagely in the opening scenes of *Modern Times*. Those who have seen the film will recall that Charlie is a worker on the moving belt where his job is to tighten bolts. Above him, watching every part of the factory on a TV screen, sits the evil figure of the factory manager. Even when Charlie goes to the washroom he's under constant scrutiny. At lunch time, in order to shorten

By 1913, Austin's Longbridge works was beginning to look more like a car factory and less like a coachbuilder's, but there was still no moving production line.

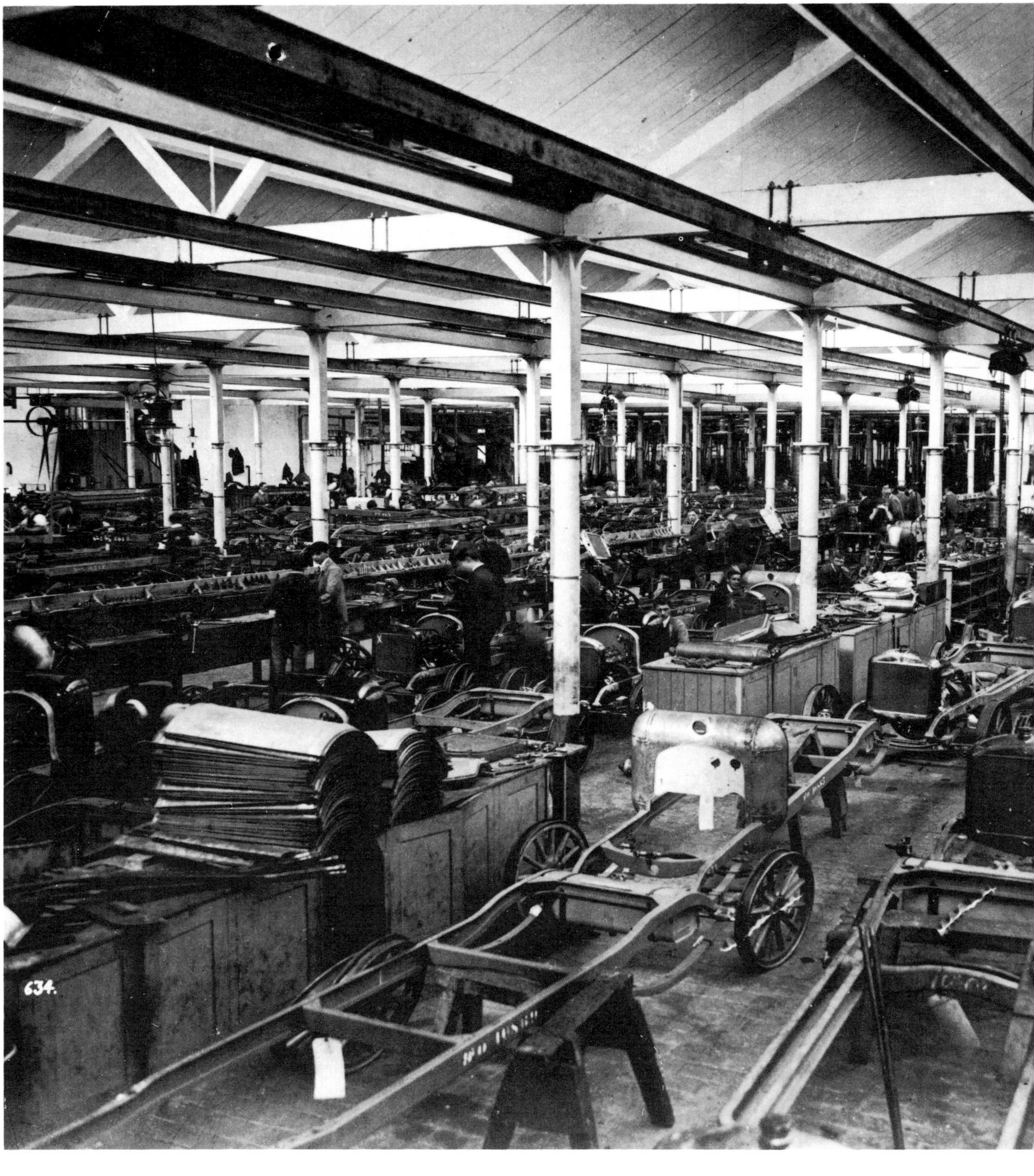

right] By 1928 these Singer Saloons were being built on a primitive sliding production line. The cars were pushed from hand to hand on wooden sleds.

the break, the management has decided to experiment with mechanical feeding. Charlie, of course, is the guinea pig; when the machine serving him corn-on-the-cob goes wrong the scene becomes ever more nightmarish and threatening. Finally, unable to keep up with his task on the assembly line, Charlie is dragged into the machinery where he revolves between gigantic cog wheels, still automatically tightening bolts. The sequence ends with the wretched Charlie being taken away for psychiatric treatment.

Modern Times was not of course supposed to be a realistic portrayal of working conditions but it must have struck a responsive chord with those who had worked in the car factories of the 1920s and 1930s. As far as pay was concerned, they were the aristocracy of industrial workers; yet not even high wages and high unemployment could do much to prevent a high turnover in the workforce. This was not only because men grew sick of the interminable drudgery of their jobs but because of the way they were regarded by the management as items on the inventory that could be replaced as easily as other rather simple bits of machinery. Henry Ford expressed this attitude, without any trace of shame, in a description of factory life: 'A business is men and machines united in the production of a commodity and both the men and the machines need repairs and replacement . . . Machinery wears out and needs to be restored. Men grow uppish, lazy or careless . . .'

This unattractive aspect of 'Fordism' came to permeate, to a greater or lesser degree, the whole of the motor car industry and it must carry much of the blame for the high rate of industrial disputes that have plagued carmakers – not least in Britain and the United States – and that in both countries have contributed to the industry's decline. Attempts by management to 'buy off' trouble with high wages have now made traditional manufacturers desperately uncompetitive with the formidable newcomers from Japan.

above left] One week's production of Lanchester cars at the Daimler works in Coventry in 1932. The Daimler Motor Company which was registered in 1896 established the motor industry in Britain and became one of its most respected names. Today cars are still being made here on the site of the original Daimler works at Drapers' Field and Sandy Lane.

left] A car for the millions, 1920. A batch of Graham White cyclecars outside the works in north London. Cheap cyclecars had a shortlived spell of popularity in the 1920s and 1930s and went a little way towards democratizing car ownership in Britain. On the whole they were poor machines and their demise was hastened by the slump.

above right] Hitler displayed many manic symptoms, including automania. From 1934 on, he urged the German car makers to produce a vehicle for the masses, a 'Volks Wagen'. Here Ferdinand Porsche shows the Führer his revolutionary design.

right] Today much vehicle testing is done in the laboratory. Using the highest of high technology, ten years of wear and tear can be simulated in three weeks. In 1928, there was no subsitute for the real thing and this Vauxhall seems to have survived its 'roll-over' test in good shape.

It was recently remarked that visitors from outer space might be forgiven for believing that the Japanese invented the industrial revolution; those same little green men could equally well be forgiven for assuming that Mr Honda or Mr Toyota invented the car. As the world's leading producer and exporter of motor vehicles, Japan has not only overtaken the United States by as much as 4 million units annually, she is beginning to share with Europe the distinction of setting car trends and fashions that the rest of the world follows. No longer can Japanese design be dismissed as merely imitative, and the tag 'made in Japan' that used to suggest a knob that comes off in your hand is now a trusted guide to reliability and quality. How the Japanese auto industry has done this is the subject of much analysis and heart-searching, particularly in the United States; and in the process there has been a good deal of mystification: a suggestion that success has been achieved because the Japanese possess some unique national characteristics that place the rest of the world at a disadvantage. The truth is probably much simpler. If you draw a graph of motor vehicle production in Japan between 1950 and 1975 and compare it with American production between 1905 and 1930, you find that the two lines shoot upwards in almost identical curves. Both countries had very large potential domestic markets on which both were able to build profitable industries because both were able to achieve that all-important economy of scale. A further irony is that Japan's infant car industry was put on the road to success by an American industrial specialist. Dr W. Edwards Deming was one of the advisers who helped in the industrial reconstruction programme after World War II. His contribution to that economic miracle was to persuade the carmakers that their future lay in the improvement of the production line and in the most rigorous quality control. Today, Japan acknowledges the debt it owes to Dr Deming by naming its highest industrial award for excellence the Deming Prize.

One of the most widespread assumptions made about Japan's car industry – and one that the Japanese are at pains to foster – is that they have overcome the 'problem of the production line'. Not only are we encouraged to believe that they lead the rest of the world in robotics, inventory control, labour relations, quality control and every other area of management but that they have somehow been able to make the production line a paradise. The image projected is of smiling assembly workers in spotless overalls happily and dextrously performing their tasks, stopping only for brief meal breaks or for meetings to discuss further improvements in quality control or for the inevitable calisthenics. All the human problems relating to 'Fordism' – absenteeism, strikes, stress disease and general degradation – have somehow, we are led to believe, been overcome by the genius of Japanese management.

Workers at Toyota participate in the much vaunted quality-control circles and employee suggestion system that is said to have played a vital role in raising product quality and production efficiency. However, there have been reports that labour-management relations are not as rosy as they are made out to be.

It was not until 1982 that a shadow of suspicion fell across that sunlit scenario. Satoshi Kamata, a Japanese freelance journalist, decided to see for himself what life was really like in an auto factory. Responding to a 'jobs vacant' advertisement, he joined Toyota, the world's second largest carmaker, as a temporary assembly line worker on a six-month contract. His account of that spell with Toyota was later published (in English under the title of *Japan in the Passing Lane*) and revealed a very different side of the economic 'miracle' and the 'art' of Japanese management. Instead of the loyal workforce, the kindly, paternalistic bosses, the joyful company songs and the group exercises, Kamata portrays cowed and disgruntled workers

It's a battle for survival! So fiercely competitive are the car makers that vehicle testing has become extremely rigorous. When the new Jaguar saloon was sent off to Arizona for hot weather testing, it was dressed up in dreary camouflage panels to hide its sleek and secret lines. To achieve the maximum interest at the launch, everything is done to guard against 'leaks' that might dilute the impact.

ground down by enforced overtime, holidays denied and, worst of all, by the management's ruthless speeding up of the production line.

However much one feels for Kamata on account of the physical suffering and acute fatigue he endured as he learned to assemble his gear boxes in the allotted time of one minute and fourteen seconds, there are more disturbing aspects of life as he describes it at Toyota. Above all, there is the intrusion of the company into every part of the worker's life. Twenty-four hours a day he is watched, monitored and reported on. The object of this surveillance is, apparently, to root out even the slightest failure to conform to the established Toyota lifestyle. As Professor Ronald Dore points out in his introduction to Kamata's book: 'It is all like nothing so much as an army camp. And joining Toyota as a regular worker is indeed rather more like joining the army . . . than like going to work for General Motors.' It must be remembered that Kamata describes the state of affairs at Toyota in the early seventies and one might imagine that things have changed for the better in ten years. Not so, says Kamata. 'The only real difference is that the work situation is worse and the competitive power of Toyota stronger . . . If the production of cars – mere machines – demands such a sacrifice of human freedom, just what does this say about the "paradox of modern civilization"?'

In answer to that rhetorical question, one can suggest that we obviously set a high priority on the possession of these 'mere machines' and that we are prepared to accept the high social cost involved in making them. The automobile assembly line always has represented the extreme of those oppressive working conditions which a modern industrial society imposes on some of its members, and it seems that even the Japanese have not yet been able to change that. Robots have made a difference by taking over tasks – spot welding and painting, for example – that are among the most hazardous on the auto assembly line; but perhaps the only way finally to abolish big car factory blues is to return to the leisurely ways of Aston Martin; which would be fine if we could all afford £70,000 for a new Lagonda.

MOTO - FLIRT

The Car and Courtship

. . . it was the most beautiful car I'd ever seen. It was green – but a deep shimmering green that made you think of antique armour, or the carriages of European royalty. Its hood was long, outrageously long, its gleaming, angular, utterly distinctive radiator grille was like a ship's prow, an image heightened by the slender, vertical louvers and the rakish tilt of the two-panel windshield, which flashed and flashed in the sun. The fenders swept down and away magnificently, the twin side-mounted spares rode in the front-fender wheel wells like Viking shields; the tyres were six-inch whitewalls around hubcaps stamped with the scarlet hexagon of Packard . . . it was a royal dream of all convertibles ever made, and it had stopped at our entry.

That passage from Anton Myrers's best-selling romantic novel *The Last Convertible* is the kind of prose men seem to lavish on only two objects of affection: cars and women. In the case of *The Last Convertible*, the car (a 1938 Packard Super Eight) is the symbol of the youthful romantic entanglements of five Harvard men and women in the years before World War II. But the romantic role of the car has never been merely symbolic; from the very beginning its practical function in courtship was recognized and eagerly seized upon.

Before the auto age, lovers had sought to get together in horse-drawn vehicles and on that 'bicycle-made-for-two'; there are even records of relationships consummated in howdahs or sedan chairs, but all suffered from disadvantages that the car was able to overcome. First, once it was out of its infancy the automobile offered much greater comfort and protection from the elements; and from the very beginning it extended the possible range of lovers' activities far beyond the radius of the horse and carriage. That limit was imposed not just by the ordinary capabilities of the animal but by the fact that, except in very wealthy families, the horse used for recreational journeys also had to earn its keep; and after a hard day on the farm or drawing a delivery van it had to be fed and rested and groomed before making any evening excursions.

With the car, on the other hand, there was the opportunity for instant escape from the prying eyes of anxious mothers, choleric fathers, nosy neighbours and mischievous younger children. We have already noticed that by increasing the range of courtship in the remoter areas, the car was expected to eliminate in-breeding and enhance the human species. This may have been regarded with approval in scientific circles but it met with a much cooler response elsewhere, particularly from ministers of religion. The churches were deeply worried about the dangerous possibilities opened up by the car and by its apparent encouragement of immorality; it immediately brought the temptations of the wicked city within much easier reach of the supposedly innocent and unspoiled country folk; and beyond that, it provided a new and relatively safe venue for 'spooning', 'petting' or indeed for 'going all the way'. It is impossible to know how far the advent of the car contributed to changes in sexual morality; it could be that its coming simply coincided with a number of other influences, notably the cinema, that led to a much more open discussion of sexual topics. As one elderly farm labourer remarked when recalling his youthful adventures in an English village: 'Just because we didn't talk about it, it doesn't mean we didn't do it.'

In films and romantic fiction the car was cast as the faithful ally of all lovers. For the eloping couple it was invariably the chosen conveyance.

Whatever was *actually* going on in back seats in those shady lovers' lanes, it was widely assumed that a great deal was going on. From the very beginning the car became the focus for saucy innuendo, the subject of risqué music-hall jokes and naughty postcards. Chauffeurs were believed to be 'fast' and, because of the opportunities their job gave them to be intimately enclosed with ladies of higher social status, they became the heroes of a new range of romantic novels. Peter Richley, whose stated objective is to collect every car-related book ever written, has dozens of these pre-1914 romances in his magnificent motoring library; and he has managed to wade through enough turgid prose to discover that, where the chauffeur establishes a liaison with a lady of quality, the morality of the time demanded that he turns out to be an earl or a count or some other titled person in disguise. 'The chauffeurs were always good-looking men with leggings and knee-breeches and had an aura of romance, almost an underlying sexuality about them.' The Queen of the Romantic Novel, Barbara Cartland, remembers how, in the stories she read as a girl, lovesick young ladies always ran off with, or were seduced by, their riding or dancing master;but that with the increasing popularity of the car it was always the chauffeur they eloped with. Elopement in a car

Driving lessons in leafy lanes provided the opportunity for increased intimacy between the sexes and often led to propositions – proper and otherwise.

pursued by the enraged father was the subject of several early car films.

Behind all this improbable romantic fiction there was a surprisingly abundant and well-documented body of fact. The *New York American* of 16 January 1906 printed a double-page spread headlined 'Why Beautiful Heiresses Run Away with Humble Chauffeurs. The Hypnotism of High Speed, Which Levels All Ranks in the Feminine Mind and Stirs Up Primitive Emotions – (Next, Look Out for the Aeroplane Driver!)'. The editorial that follows seriously suggested that 'that increasingly popular vehicle the automobile is responsible for one of the most perplexing social problems of these times. Why do heiresses elope with their millionaire fathers' chauffeurs? What is to be done about it?' In good popular newspaper tradition the article goes on to provide column after column of titillating evidence of this 'social problem'. There is the stirring account of how the handsome young American chauffeur Charles Carver wormed himself into the affections of a fair member of the old French nobility, the Viscountess d'Arnouville. Then there is the tale of heiress Elsie Cheney who eloped with chauffeur James Dennison, 'a good-looking youth with plenty of ability and self esteem. His conversation relieved the tedium of uninteresting stretches of Connecticut roads and paved the way for propinquity to produce its traditional result.' And in another breathtaking scandal, 'it was an exhausted gasoline tank which brought William Osterman into the life of pretty Elsie Hoagland, daughter of a rich Pennsylvanian farmer'. The stranded pair spent the night in a farmhouse where 'they struck up an acquaintance that was mutually agreeable . . . and now the farmer's heiress is a Pittsburgh matron'. To give its article some intellectual respectability, the *New York American* commissioned a certain Professor Emil Dietrich (of Heidelberg) to examine this strange phenomenon and explain why American society ladies were falling into the arms of Daddy's motorman. With characteristic Germanic bluntness, the professor first pointed out to the great American public that: 'Your women are drawn by pets, by fox terriers, by monkeys, and some of your white women by the blacks . . . if your women are attracted by these strange beings, is it any wonder that they are attracted by the chauffeur . . . a picturesque, romantic figure to a girl satiated with the ordinary man?'

Despite all the sensational stories of the chauffeurs and their conquests, Barbara Cartland believes that it was the car itself that made the greatest difference to upper-class courtship. With the coming of the car and the independence it provided, the young were able to escape from formal parties with their 'carriages at eleven' and their eagle-eyed chaperones. Robert and Helen Lynd made similar observations about life among humbler folk in Muncie, Indiana:

In 1890 a well-brought-up boy and girl were commonly forbidden to sit together in the dark; but motion pictures and the automobile have lifted this taboo, and, once lifted, it is easy for the practise to become widely extended. Buggy-riding in the 1890s allowed only a narrow range of mobility; three to eight were generally accepted hours for riding, and being out after 8.30 without a chaperone was largely forbidden. In an auto, however, a party may go to a city halfway across the state in an afternoon or evening, and unchaperoned automobile parties as late as midnight, while subject to criticism, are not exceptional.

According to popular belief, the chauffeur's relationship with the mistress of the house was often equivocal. His job demanded that he be intimately enclosed with his mistress for long periods. In romantic fiction he was portrayed as a virile and mysterious figure.

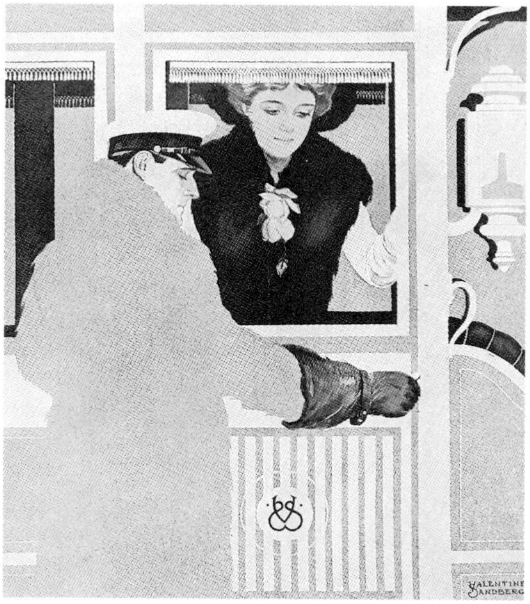

Two In the Car
The car accessory market provides all kinds of equipment to make car interiors more seductive. This 1914 mobile boudoir was a product of the classic age of automotive elegance.

It would be wrong to think that lovers were making enthusiastic use of their newfound opportunities without attempts by killjoys to stop them. There is a persistent tale concerning Henry Ford that may be more than a rumour, since it is even recounted by Professor David L. Lewis, one of Ford's biographers. It is alleged that the great carmaker tried to have passion-killing features designed into the Model T: namely that he limited the length of the seat to thirty-eight inches which had been calculated to be too small to allow lovemaking with any degree of comfort. If Ford was serious in this intention, then it must be recorded as one of his rare and resounding failures. Love always finds a way and has overcome far greater obstacles than that rectified by the simple step of removing the seat from the car and fulfilling its objective under the stars. Professor Lewis, who has made sex and the automobile an academic study and the subject of popular lectures at the University of Michigan, has also unearthed an extraordinary attempt by lawmakers to restrict even kissing in vehicles: 'Deerfield, Illinois, prohibits kissing within part of the dropoff zone at its commuter station, while sanctioning kissing within the other part. Signs which picture a kissing couple, one with a stripe drawn through, indicate which zone is which.'

English law legislates against 'committing an act of a lewd, obscene and disgusting nature and an outrage to public decency'. A celebrated case made the headlines in 1959 when Mr Gerald Selby and Miss Anne Rosa Firman were tried and acquitted on such a charge at the London Sessions. Subsequently the couple sued the police, claiming damages for assault, false imprisonment, malicious prosecution and conspiracy. The nature of the evidence in the Kiss in the Car Case, as the papers called it, ensured a high level of Press interest. The public was intrigued to learn that police suspicions of what might be happening in Mr Selby's vehicle were first aroused when they observed 'sideways movement of the car on its springs'. It was further revealed that PC Donald MacLennan had arrested ninety couples for the same offence in cars in the previous eighteen-month period; and in all but one of the cases, the accused had pleaded guilty. Not only had Mr Selby contested the charge, his defence claimed that he and his fiancée were simply kissing; and that in any case, the windows of their car were too misted up for any inside activity to be observed. The jury also heard expert evidence from a former chief engineer of the Automobile Association to the effect that there was insufficient space between the edge of the front seat and the footwell for Miss Firman to have adopted the kneeling position described by the prosecution. A similar Ford car was even brought to the Law Courts, so that the jury could make up their own minds on the matter. In the end they failed to agree on a verdict.

The law has never been a very effective means of regulating sexual activity in cars or anywhere else; but perhaps the award for the most notable failure in this area of law enforcement should go to the Paris Gendarmerie for their wholly unsuccessful attempts to stop the goings-on in the Bois de Boulogne. The reputation of the Bois as a trysting place goes back a long time, but the coming of the motor car vastly extended the possibilities for venery. In 1925 a certain Pol Prille published *Bois de Boulogne, Bois d'Amour*, a collection of allegedly true amorous adventures that confirm that the car was already, in the words of M. Prille, 'the rubberized chariot of love'. One chapter is headed 'Man Kidnapped by two Women in a Boudoir-car'. Another is the tale of the Parisian banker, unnamed, who was sexually im-

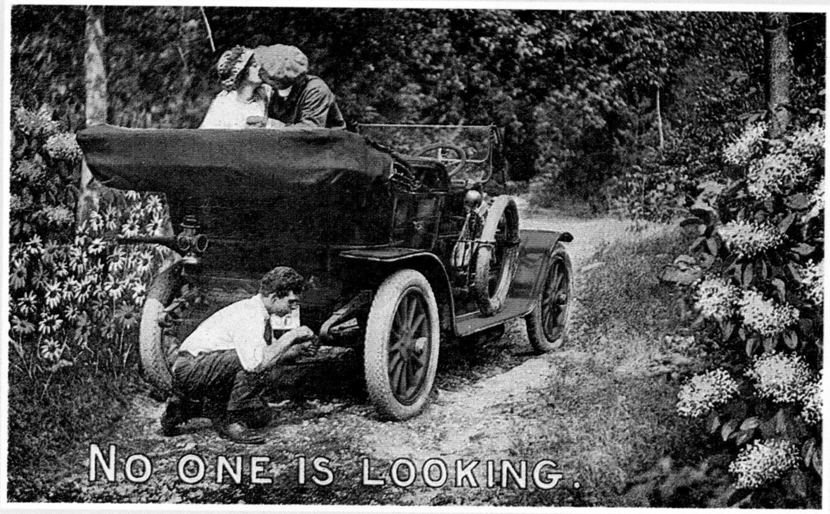

NO ONE IS LOOKING.

No time to waste! There are, these days,
No horses, but horse-power.
Our seat we take, and love we make
At sixty miles an hour!

5. With both her hands
upon the gear,
He kisses her and doesn't fear.

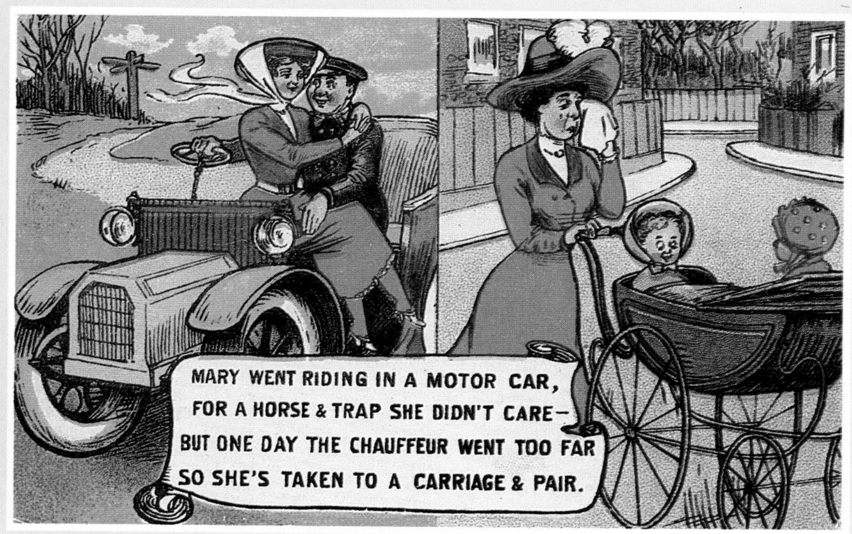

MARY WENT RIDING IN A MOTOR CAR,
FOR A HORSE & TRAP SHE DIDN'T CARE—
BUT ONE DAY THE CHAUFFEUR WENT TOO FAR
SO SHE'S TAKEN TO A CARRIAGE & PAIR.

Thousands of cartoons and postcards have been published featuring cars. In many of them the humour is sexually suggestive or entirely explicit.

LA VOITURE LA PLUS LÉGÈRE DU SALON 1931

TRES JOLI TAXI-REFUGE POUR AMOUREUX, DIT "TAX'CYTHÈRE"

potent except in his car and who thus became an habitué of the Bois – 'His car, with all its lights out, drives slowly up and down the alleyways, like a phantom machine.' His love for the shadows was the banker's downfall. His car was stopped by the police and he was discovered *in flagrante* with two companions 'so that there was three of them, an offence against public decency, for a trinity constitutes a crime in the eyes of the law'. But perhaps the most bizarre of M. Prille's revelations concerns the orgies organized by society people in the Bois which became highly fashionable in 1923. In order to guard these parties against disturbance by the police or by gate-crashers, it was the practice to dig a 'car trap' in the roadway. The 'car trap' was similar to those employed to catch wild animals: a ditch concealed by leaves and branches. On one occasion, a car loaded with society men and women on their way to an orgy fell into one of these traps and for days people attending the Paris Opera House wondered why a leading ballerina performed *Swan Lake* with a limp!

Even naturists are motorists and some motorists are presumably naturists. How the chauffeur was attired is not revealed.

Throughout this remarkable book there are references to the headlight code, the system of flashes that enabled motorists to identify each other's intentions and sexual preferences. It was happening in the 1920s and it's happening in the 1980s. Today we have a new authority on the Bois de Boulogne. After years of research Marc Charlan has published a guidebook and map for the benefit of the visiting motorist. M. Charlan has noticed great changes in the night life of the Bois – not least the huge increase in the number of transvestites, mostly Brazilian – but the most notable change is in the use of the automobile. It is now an essential part of the activities, first because the vehicle offers a sense of security in what can be a dangerous pursuit, but also because

If you went to the Bois on foot, and suddenly came face to face with your managing director, you'd have no excuse to give. It's obvious you do not come into the Bois at night to pick mushrooms or observe wild life. On the other hand, if you're in a car, you can always give the excuse that you're simply going from one point in Paris to another . . . in the Bois de Boulogne the car is your alibi and your Guardian Angel.

Not all drivers cruising the streets of the Bois are seeking prostitutes; some are looking for non-professional sexual partners, for *échangistes* or for companions to join them in a *partouse* and for these adventurers, the make of car they drive will have a great bearing on their degree of success. In M. Charlan's view, 'groups form in the first place, according to the type of car. It is to be expected that if you see a Rolls-Royce and you're driving a Jaguar, you'll be attracted to the Rolls rather than a 2 CV Citroën . . .' On the question of which car is the best sexual draw, M. Charlan has no doubts.

It's an English car, the Range Rover . . . which represents the 'macho' quality that women are looking for in the men they seek in the Bois. I believe that Range Rovers are the equivalent of John Wayne's horse; their drivers are the new cowboys . . . the 'Range' – as it is known in France – means you have money . . . that you love the wide open spaces and that you're physically strong. You must have a dog in the back because, of course, you're on the way to a shoot at your château. All these things the Range Rover says and they excite women very much.

opposite] This artist's impression of the perfect love-mobile appeared in *La Vie Parisienne* in 1931. Among its special accessories is a perfume atomizer, a drinks dispenser, and oval wheels for that sensational motion in the back seat! The chauffeur is a eunuch.

And which car, one was bound to ask, is the greatest sexual liability in the Bois de Boulogne? 'Driving Japanese isn't very sexy . . . but the least erotic car for my money is something like the little Simca 400; those are cars which lack personality.'

If we disagree with Marc Charlan's analysis of which car scores what in the sexual sweepstakes, even psychologists support him in the view that sexual symbolism is a powerful ingredient in our relationships with our cars. Dr James Hemming believes that the car plays at least as rich a part in the fantasy lives of women as it does of men. 'A man is very affectionate towards his car, he gets into his car, he switches on the power, he then has almost a passionate relationship and a passionate satisfaction out of controlling the power of the car. He admires its line, he admires its performance and all this immediately cross references to sex.' Women, on the other hand, up to this moment in history have been relatively powerless members of society and, according to Dr Hemming, 'it naturally gives them great satisfaction to feel that they have power under their control, which in a motor car they finally have'.

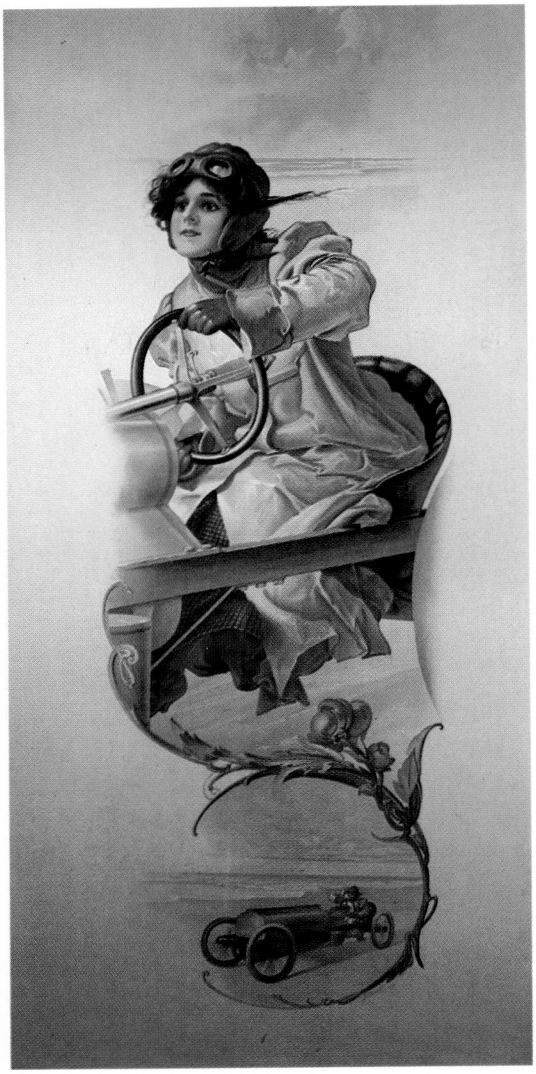

above] As this striking image suggests, the car was seen from its earliest days as the great liberator. In a social system that oppressed women in particular, its emancipating influence was profound, not least in the sexual field.

right] Young lady at the wheel of an Anhut motor, 1910. According to some psychologists, women responded instantly to the attractions of the car because, as members of the relatively powerless sex, it gave them great satisfaction finally to have power under their control.

far right] The gutsy sports car with a young man flooring it down the freeway squandering fuel with abandon was once the ultimate virile image. Now, with automatic transmission and power steering at her dainty fingertips, any woman can feel confident driving the most powerful supercar and saying with as much assurance as men once did: 'Come ride with me.'

left] Nothing is known about this photograph except that it dates from the 1930s. An informal competition among our friends to find a suitable caption produced not one suggestion that was printable.

right] The 1941 Nash sedan featured a full six-foot double bed. Judging from the advertising material, it was only ever occupied by two women.

below] Presumably the face at the window of the Nash Sedan is supposed to be expressing envy for the lady in the snug comfort of the 'World's First Car with a "Conditioned-Air System" for winter driving . . .' But is there something else in his eyes?

WAY BELOW ZERO
And No Wrap!
NO MORE FROZEN RIDES . . . OPEN WINDOWS FOR WINTER VENTILATION . . . CHILLING DRAFTS . . . FOGGED WINDOWS . . . DUSTY, GRIMY TRIPS . . . INSECTS . . . SMOKY AIR . . . OR STUFFY CARS
. . . the World's First Car with a "Conditioned-Air System" for winter driving is here! Always 70° comfort in zero weather. A revolutionary feature—exclusive with Nash!

Psychologist Dr Joyce Brothers agrees that the car is one of the most powerful of contemporary symbols and that our choice of model is highly significant: 'For some, it's a sexual extension. Their car says to others, "I'm a very successful sexual being. I've got lots of power and lots of drive." ' But, according to Dr Brothers, when a middle-aged man suddenly abandons his staid saloon to splash out on a sports car, 'although he thinks that he is saying "I'm still very interesting, look at me sexually", what he is really saying is, "Well maybe I am not at the crest, I may be starting on the down swing." ' Even the choice of manual over automatic transmission is seen to be significant: 'the physical symbol of a stick shift says male potency, male power, and that's exciting not only to men but to women as well'.

Dr Roy Manning, a Los Angeles psychiatrist, sees 'a very major change taking place in the way in which women relate to their cars. It has often been said that the way in which a woman relates to her house – viewing it perhaps as an extension of her body – is analagous to the way in which a man relates to his car . . . We see how women are becoming more conscious of their bodies through exercise and other forms of athletic endeavour and I think as a consequence they are going to respond to cars very differently. In my own practise, I hear women talking about cars in a way I have not seen in years past.'

Dr Manning's observation on the psychiatrist's couch is perhaps supported by the findings of market researchers in Detroit. It seems that the latest range of 'muscle cars', the Firebirds, Camaros and Sting Rays, that used to be the ultimate expression of aggressive masculinity, are now selling equally well to young women, who, if we are to believe Dr Manning, also find these powerful machines to be satisfying extensions of themselves.

As we have seen, those selling the car seem to be well aware of its complex symbolic significance. Car advertisements have made lavish use of sex, especially as related to dominant virility, to sell their product. But the question arises: have car stylists made a conscious effort to design a sexual content into their creations? Certainly they have sometimes provided useful features like fold-down seats that convert easily into beds; but they have always taken prudish care, in advertising these models, to show the whole family – or in one case, two women – preparing to bed down. It is a curious feature of early caravan and trailer advertisements that they usually include only female passengers. It was obviously considered improper to suggest that both sexes might co-habit in such intimate conditions.

On whether the designers intend the shape of their cars to be sexually suggestive, opinion is divided. Although its designer Sir William Lyons would be horrified to hear it, the suggestion has been made that the phallic shape of the E-type Jaguar contributed to its huge success. On the other hand, the likeness of the radiator grille of the Ford Edsel to the female genitalia – and the rude name that described that similarity – is thought to have been one of the many nails in the coffin of that commercial casualty. Lest one should be thought in the least sexist, it must quickly be said that bosomy, and curvaceously feminine, lines particularly in the cars of the fifties have proved to be commercially very successful.

Designers seem to be agreed that it is a mistake to attempt to create a car specifically directed at the women's market. They point to the miserable failure of La Femme, a special model that Dodge tricked out in pink and charcoal grey with matching pink umbrella and extra vanity mirrors in the hope of capturing the distaff trade. While La Femme was a total failure with women, it is said to have been a hit with pimps and gays.

There are numerous examples of cars failing to sell because they have been given the wrong sexual image. In Latin countries particularly, it is vital that the vehicle in no way suggests effeminacy or impotency. There was the curious case of the new VW with the sunshine roof. In Brazil, when a man has an unfaithful wife he is described as *cornuto*, or 'wearing the horns'; and when VW launched a Beetle with a sliding roof, the wags very quickly nicknamed it the CornoWagen: the VW with special accommodation for the horn; in other words, the cuckold's car. So damaging did the nickname prove to be that the option was quickly discontinued. Also in Brazil, the nickname 'Bel Antonio' proved to be the undoing of a particular Simca that was pretty to look at, but grossly underpowered. Bel Antonio was the name of a beautiful but impotent character, played by Marcello Mastroianni, in a popular film.

We cannot leave the subject of sex and car design without a word about the wildly extravagant vans, the mobile bordellos that appeared on the streets of southern California in the late sixties and early seventies and which must be the most sex-centred vehicles ever built. Perhaps the ultimate expression of the vanner's art are the creations of an unlikely Lothario, a 62-year-old disabled war veteran, Ken Jones, who has spent all his time, money and imagination over the past ten years creating three vans of ever increasing elaboration and eroticism. The first was called 'The Dark Room', then came 'The Massage Parlour', and now it is 'The Harem' that occupies his time. As the name suggests, The Harem is furnished like an Arabian Nights fantasy: with crystal chandeliers and mirrors, tasselled rugs and curtains, sexy lighting, cocktail bar, TV, refrigerator and, of course, with a large bed and dozens of velvet cushions. Whatever the vehicle suggests may be its purpose, the impression one gets from talking to Ken Jones is that the biggest thrill he gets from it is to take it down the freeway and bask in the admiration and the astonishment that inevitably come his way.

With the customized vans of the 1970s there is no sidestepping the fact that they were purpose-built for sex, and never was that purpose so unflinchingly stated as by Ken Jones with 'My Harem'. Inside and out, from ceiling to floor and from wall to wall, this van leaves nothing to the imagination – least of all its passengers.

There are, we have already noted, an enormous number of car-related popular songs and from the very beginning most of their lyrics combined motion with emotion in titles like 'In Our Little Love Mobile', 'Fifteen Kisses on a Gallon of Gas', 'When He Wanted to Love Her He'd Pop up the Cover' and of course, 'Get 'Em in a Rumble Seat'. The song writers of today show not the slightest sign of abandoning the theme of sex and the car. In Ry Cooda's delightful 'Crazy about an Automobile', the singer comments:

I used to be particular about the women I picked
Yeah, they used to be tender, lean and tall
But the way things been goin'
I take them knock-kneed and bow-legged
I will even take them bald . . . I'll tell you why
Every woman I know is crazy about an automobile
And here am I standing with nothing but rubber heels.

Later, the song explains that 'riding and love just can't be beaten' and that 'women in this town just don't pay any attention to you unless you are driving'.

This song, like some others, reflects the harsh fact of life that for the young male in the United States and other affluent societies, possession of or access to a car is an absolute essential for successful courtship. High school youngsters interviewed in Chicago had no doubt about it: 'the car is the second most important thing in a teenager's life. The first is getting the license to be able to drive it.' According to a girl: 'I'd rather be cruising with someone who's got this show-off type of car. My boy-friend drives this real nice sports car and it's part of the fun we have together . . . It's a bit materialistic I know, but the car is important to him and in that respect I regard it as part of his personality.'

For young people in Japan the coming of the car has been an even more basic means of sexual liberation. In a country where housing is scarce and expensive, the need was to find some privacy, some escape from oppressively crowded living conditions. According to Eigi Takanuma, a leading motoring journalist, 'There is a trend among young people to use their cars not simply as a means of transportation but as their own private rooms.' One of the reasons why the Japanese car market is so buoyant is that 'young men are prepared to spend lavishly on their cars and then to spend much more on accessories in order to personalize and enhance them'. 'In Japan today', says Mr Takanuma, 'the car is an essential tool for dating.' But it must be the right car: for the unfortunate owners of the Toyota Corolla and other ill-endowed vehicles, Japanese accessory shops provide a huge range of sex aids and cosmetic devices. With the help of a few stick-on signs proclaiming TURBO, TWIN CAM, GT or even Super GT, something as hopeless as the wretched Corolla can hope to gain a little sex appeal.

Even with the right car, the path of true love can be a difficult one for the Japanese male. In the larger cities, there is an acute shortage of parking space and desperately little that is not too well lighted and crowded to be a suitable site for lovemaking. So according to Mr Takanuma, 'usually it means driving to the seaside, the mountains or a lake, to places where there are no people and if all conditions are right, well . . .' There is no lack of guidance for young Japanese on how to proceed if the conditions *are* right. With characteristic pragmatism and lack of prudery, Japanese motoring magazines publish

In their choice of partners, young women in Japan place high priority on car ownership. In a country where houses are cramped and privacy hard to find the question of 'your place or mine?' hardly arises. The car is the only answer.

detailed instructions, fully illustrated, of the positions that can be adopted to achieve maximum satisfaction in the cramped confines of a car.

The most authoritative publication on that subject appeared however, in Europe, in 1971. *Harmonie Sexuelle dans une Automobile* must be the definitive car sex manual. It contains sixty-three photographs and the text is in three languages. Judging from the style, it was translated into English from the original German, giving us lines like: 'after which preliminaries, he can become bolder and seek to drink at new pastures [*sic*], the which can lead to the woman licking his thigh while he bites her elbow often erogenous'. Couples attempting to follow its instructions to the letter might well find themselves rendered helpless by laughter if they managed to avoid dislocating any limbs.

Terry Hayes, who wrote the scripts for the *Mad Max* car fantasy movies, says that the car has long been part of the Australian mating ritual: 'I would say that, were you to do a survey, you probably would find that an enormous

At Pop's Drive-in in São Paulo there are no films shown. The entertainment is provided by girls like Rosa. She prefers Pop's because, unlike motels, there is no time limit.

number of Australians had their first sexual experience in cars . . . to a lot of kids what would Saturday night be, without making out in the back of a car at the drive-in [cinema]?' Among Australian teenagers, according to Terry Hayes, drive-in theatres are known as 'finger bowls' – suggesting that it is not the film that is the main attraction.

In the United States, the drive-in enjoys the same reputation it earned in Australia, but its golden age is past. After the first drive-in theatres opened in 1933, their number rose rapidly, reaching a peak of about 4000 in the 1950s. The decline in their popularity since then is certainly related to changing habits of courtship. As Professor David Lewis points out: 'during the thirties, forties and fifties there were restrictions which prevented kids from getting into motels and making use of their homes and college dormitories as they do today; and at that time all the cars were big and roomy'. Inevitably, as more and more drive-ins opened their doors, the romantic possibilities presented by the front seat and the darkness became part of growing up.

The most curious manifestation of the drive-in emerged in Brazil, where there is not even a pretence at providing any on-screen entertainment. The Brazilian drive-in is simply a place where, for a modest payment, the motorist can park his car and remain undisturbed for a few hours. Maria Dos Anjos has spent several years running such an establishment in São Paulo called 'Pop's Drive In'. Behind its gates, in a respectable suburban street, are a score or so of parking slots or 'boxes', discreetly screened off. Apart from a limited bar service, privacy is all that Pop's provides. Although most couples come to make love, that is not always the case: 'There is a college near here and a group of students used to come in their car and study together, because it was safer and quieter.' Maria confirmed that in Brazil too, the drive-in is in decline. Lovers no longer wish to suffer the contortions and discomfort imposed by the cramped interior of a car when they can enjoy the comforts provided by the proliferating motels.

As we have seen, the motel was born in the United States where it has now become a thoroughly respectable institution; but that was not always the case; there was a time when 'we stopped the night in a motel' was likely to invite a snigger. One of the main attractions of the tourist cabin or motel was the privacy it offered to unmarried couples who wished to rendezvous in secrecy. No longer did shy young things have to run the gauntlet of the public lobby or go through the ordeal of the flinty-faced receptionist at the check-in desk. Instead, it was a short step from the privacy of the car to the privacy of the room, with no questions asked. James Belasco has shown that the hotel industry, which felt itself severely threatened by the popularity of the tourist camps and motels, launched a vicious public relations campaign against the new competition, claiming that it presented a threat to middle-class family life and that 'its "no questions asked" management policy attracted partying young people and unmarried couples'. Support for this campaign came from no less a quarter than the FBI. In 1940, its director, J. Edgar Hoover, who always saw himself as the guardian of American sexual morality, published a stinging attack on motels in the *American Magazine*, describing them as 'dens of vice and corruption'. It was difficult for the industry to live down the 'no-tell motel' image because they knew it *was* part of their trade and because it was constantly being dramatized and glamorized in magazines and Hollywood films. In the end, motels simply retaliated

Today's greeting cards where the traditional images of car and romance are as popular as ever. Even the elopement, which must be a rare contingency these days, is still part of four-wheeled folklore.

Brazilian motels are less flamboyant than Japan's love hotels. The invitation, however, to the middle-class, middle-aged car-owning executive is the same.

opposite] Japan's love hotels have tipped their hat at almost every architectural style man has devised since he left his cave. Even naval architecture has not been ignored. Whether Cunard would find such imitation flattering is another matter.

against their critics by making their establishments much more hotel-like and home-like, a process that perhaps reached its ultimate expression with Holiday Inns. Nothing, surely, could better embody American middle-class family values and virtues.

Whereas, in the United States, motels had to fight for respectability, in at least two other countries their prosperity depends on retaining a reputation for unrestrained licentiousness. In Brazil and Japan, the motel industry sets out to provide the motorist with one thing only: a setting for sexual encounters. In neither country is there such a thing as a 'respectable' motel; single guests or guests of the same sex are not admitted. The motel is the lavish alternative to the back seat of the car and in both countries its coming has transformed sexual mores.

The most striking characteristic shared by motels in Japan and Brazil is their fantastic architecture. No theme is too outrageous, no colour scheme too garish, no style too outlandish to be tried. The object is to design a building that will be recognizable from a speeding car for what it is; also perhaps to stimulate the fantasies of the potential customer. In Japan, where the motels – or Love Hotels, as they are called – seem to be concentrated near motorways on the outskirts of towns, the skyline will often resemble something from Disneyland: a crazy architectural tangle of French châteaux, Kremlin domes, Snow White's castle and Hollywood tat. Control of the Love Hotels is firmly in the hands of the 'yakuza', the Japanese equivalent of the Mafia. Their clientele, judging from the smart saloons pulling in and out of their gilded gateways at all hours, is a cross-section of Japanese affluent middle class: bosses and their secretaries and young executives with their girlfriends.

Although Brazil's motels are a shade more restrained than Japan's Love Hotels, they clearly proclaim themselves to be palaces of pleasure. Granted that their decorative motifs are different, in one architectural feature they are identical: they are constructed so that the car can vanish inside the structure and park discreetly, directly adjoining the accommodation. Lauro Cavalcanti, who has written a scholarly treatise on Brazil's motels, perceives in this act of penetration – the car entering the motel – a symbolic performance of the sexual act!

Perhaps there has been a little too much arcane theorizing about the car and Eros; but the facts themselves are impressive. Findings of a survey taken in the 1950s suggest that 38 per cent of American women born between 1900 and 1910 had their first sexual encounters on the back seat of automobiles. A strictly informal survey taken among friends and acquaintances suggests that that percentage would rise to a very high level indeed among those who were teenagers during the 1950s and 1960s. Since that time, the figure has probably been falling. Most people no longer need cars for sexual encounters. In households where frequently both parents are working, beds are readily available to ambitious youngsters; and hotels are no longer very concerned about the true identity of 'Mr and Mrs Brown'. Lovemaking in cars has passed its peak but it will still bring back many happy memories; and in much of the developing world it increasingly presents the answer to the question: 'Where shall we go?'

お食事24時間OK
CBCホテル
東へすぐ
オリンピア
新築オープン
24時間お食事OK
ホテル
ヒルトン
スグソコ

QUEEN ELIZABETH
60

The area of conflict between the motorist and the law proved to be a most fruitful ground for the humorist. As early as 1906, in addition to thousands of cartoons and postcards, books of car jokes were appearing like *The Automotive Joker: A Complete Garage of Jokes in Which is Depicted the Funny Side of Automobiling*.

Regulating the Car

'To my mind,' observed the Chairman of the Bench of Magistrates cheerfully, 'the only difficulty that presents itself in this otherwise very clear case is, how we can possibly make it sufficiently hot for the incorrigible rogue and hardened ruffian whom we see cowering in the dock before us. Let me see: he has been found guilty, on the clearest evidence, first of stealing a valuable motor car; secondly, of driving to the public danger; and, thirdly, of gross impertinence to the rural police. Mr Clerk, will you tell us, please, what is the very stiffest penalty we can impose for each of these offences? Without, of course, giving the prisoner the benefit of any doubt, because there isn't any.'
(Kenneth Grahame, *The Wind in the Willows*, 1908)

Of all social groups having cause to feel gratitude to the car, none, surely, can be more thankful than the lawyers. The vast corpus of law emanating from car ownership and the volume of litigation, civil and criminal, growing steadily year by year, no doubt goes some way to explain why so many lawyers are driving such expensive cars. As we have seen, from the moment of its birth the car was a controversial machine, and this continuing controversy has inevitably found its voice in the legislatures and in the law courts the world over. In Britain, the first major legal battle was won – or lost, according to your point of view, in 1896 when the motorist was released from the thralldom of the man with the red flag and the speed limit of 4 m.p.h.; but that was just the beginning of the endless and often acrimonious argument on the subject of speed. It was this matter of speed that obsessed both enemies and supporters of the car in the early days.

To take just one day in the deliberations of the House of Commons: on 11 June 1903, MP after MP rose to his feet to pronounce on the speed limit and on the proposal that all cars should be 'numbered for the purposes of identification', or in other words, that ownership should be registered and displayed. The views expressed were characteristically extreme. Mr Cathcart Watson railed against those who 'claimed the right to drive the public off the roads. Harmless men, women and children, dogs and cattle, had all got to fly for their lives at the bidding of one of these slaughtering, stinking engines of iniquity.' Mr Soares, the Member for Barnstaple, demanded much stricter regulations for motorists, pointing out that:

with motor driving there was only one brain to depend upon, but in horse driving there were two. In the case of two men who had dined not wisely but too well, the one who went home in a motor had to depend upon himself and the course he took in the circumstances might be of a very peculiar character; but the man who went home in the trap had the brain of his horse to depend on, and there were many steady old horses which could not be induced to run on the wrong side of the road . . . however hard the wrong rein was pulled.

However, the Member for Aberdeen, Mr Pirie, thought that cars should not only be licensed but that their drivers ought to be examined 'and obtain a certificate before being entrusted with the driving of a motor car'. It was to be more than thirty years before Mr Pirie's suggestion became law and the driving test was introduced, but it is clear that even in 1903 lawmakers had recognized the need for much of the regulation that would eventually follow. What they had to overcome in order to get the necessary legislation on the

left] 'What speed do you think you were doing, sir?' It's a question that has been asked thousands of times over the past hundred years – and has doubtless prompted some ingenious answers.

As cars became faster, the police were at a grave disadvantage and it took some years before they could catch up with the wealthy motorist in his speedy machine. The motorcycle cop proved to be a giant step forward in law enforcement.

statute books was the determined, articulate and well-financed opposition of the powerful car lobby. The principal objective of this lobby was to achieve the removal of all restrictions on speed, and it was suggested that as a quid pro quo motorists would raise no objective to the numbering and registration of vehicles; but to many leading members of the motoring community such a concession was unthinkable. In the words of a memorandum to the Automobile Club: 'There is no reason why a gentleman's private carriage should be disfigured by a label suitable for an omnibus or a hackney carriage or why a private individual should be subjected to the annoyance of being ticketed and labelled wherever he goes . . .'

Drivers of sports cars (in this case a Bugatti Type 13) have always found they attracted the special attention of the law. It's part of the price they pay for the sporting image.

San Francisco speeders stopped by mounted police, 1908. This imaginative impression of how traffic offenders were dealt with in the Wild West appeared in the French magazine, *Petit Journal*.

THE MOTE AND THE BEAM;
OR, THE PREOCCUPATIONS OF SCOTLAND YARD.

First Burglar. "WOT ABOUT THE COP, BILL?"
Second Ditto. "WE'RE ALL RIGHT; 'E'S TOO BUSY TICKIN' OFF THAT CAR TO NOTICE US."

There is an enduring belief among motorists that the police spend a disproportionate amount of time prosecuting driving offenders while *real* crime remains undetected.

One cannot help feeling sympathy for the pioneer motorist. Some of the laws enacted to control him were even more restrictive than Britain's Red Flag Acts. In Milan, where the Italian motor industry was to become so dominant, motorists were required by a city ordinance to apply in writing to the authorities every time they wanted to use their vehicle, giving precise details of their journey, the time of departure and the route they intended to take. Thanks to the efforts of the Italian Automobile Club, this bureaucratic absurdity was eventually repealed.

Almost everywhere, speed limits were fixed unrealistically low – the pace of a carriage and pair – and there was little or no consistency in the enforcement of the law. In some parts of Britain, police armed with stop-watches were out in force setting speed traps; and magistrates imposed hefty fines on those found guilty. It was at this time that a familiar grievance was first heard: that police spend far too much time prosecuting that honest citizen the motorist, rather than investigating serious crime and real criminals. Motorists felt justified in trying to evade what they considered to be unjust and discriminatory laws. They formed clubs in their own defence; they recruited scouts and provided them with bicycles, armbands and binoculars and sent them into the highways and hedges to flush out the police and warn the drivers. In what became a vicious little war of tit-for-tat, the police then prosecuted the drivers and their scouts for obstructing them in their duties. Not to be outdone, the Automobile Association devised an ingenious plan whereby its scouts were required to salute members' cars *except* when a speed trap lay ahead. Even the most carefully framed legislation could hardly prevent the motorist from stopping the scout to demand why he had failed to give a proper salute. At this distance in time it may all seem supremely petty but, eighty years on, the cat and mouse game continues, with the police investing in expensive and elaborate radar detection gear and the 'scorcher' countering with a whole range of patented devices to warn him of the radar speed trap.

If the laws of the road were capriciously enforced in the United Kingdom, the motorist had to be even more wary when touring in Europe, as we have seen in the case of Milan. Regulations and their enforcement varied widely from country to country and from town to town. Hugh Rochford Maxted, writing in 1905, warned:

Scorchers, desirous of making speed despite the laws and regulations should not go to Nice to do so. For the police here are very vigilant, and if they consider that the legal speed limit of 6 km is being exceeded, even though it be by 1 metre per hour, they are not slow to pounce on their prey and it is said that the fines inflicted in this way constitute one of the town's best revenues. Of course, it cannot be expected that the word of a foreigner should be taken against that of a native policeman togged up in all his regimentals and Be Ye Warned, he carries a sword with which to prick your tyres if you don't pull up when required to do so.

In the United States there were no special laws worth mentioning to cover the operation of motor cars until after 1900. But once the legislators got to work, not only did each one of the forty-five states introduce its own laws but, to add another dimension to the confusion, city and county governments often brought in their own by-laws to deal with what they regarded as special local problems. In some of the wilder parts of the West there were no laws at all until after 1910. By 1915 all the states had some kind of restrictions though it seems that they were usually flouted and infrequently enforced. According to one account:

the law was a joke. Nobody regarded it or pretended to. If the motorists of the day had received their legal dues, they would all have spent much of their time in gaol . . . They were all conscious of breaking the law, and the continued repetition of their offending against it stimulated the growth of a great disrespect for all law in the minds of many of them.

That final point – that motoring offences, lacking as they do much ethical support, have eroded respect for the law and have made offenders of normally law-abiding citizens – is one that has been more and more frequently made as motoring regulations have proliferated and become ever more technical.

The motorist has always regarded himself as a long-suffering Gulliver, tied down by a mesh of piffling Lilliputian regulations.

On the other hand, it is equally true that a minority of motorists have always resisted and flouted even the most rational and commonsensical measures to control traffic and keep death off the roads. Even the introduction of a driving test was successfully resisted in the United Kingdom until 1935. Those who wished to drive simply climbed behind the wheel and set off. What instruction there was, was provided by the manufacturers or their agents. As we know from George Roberts whose father sold Model Ts in the Australian outback, the salesman was expected to give basic driving instruction to the purchaser as part of the transaction. One over-confident buyer who turned down even the most elementary guidance had cause to regret it. 'The very next morning my father was called to his home and discovered that since the gentleman didn't know how to stop the Model T, when he went to garage it, he'd proceeded straight through the back of the building, through the fence beyond and came to rest in the neighbouring property. It was real Keystone Cops stuff.'

First Driving Lesson. It was frequently the duty of the chauffeur, who had been trained by the car maker, to teach his employer how to drive.

Driving instruction, Paris, 1898. This surely must have been one of the world's first driving schools. Over a 700-metre course at Aubervilliers, aspiring motorists were trained to negotiate a succession of obstacles including wooden cut-outs of women with prams, cyclists, dogs and children. Clearly, those most at risk from the motorist had already been identified.

In opposing the introduction of a compulsory test of driving competence – 'certificates' as they were called – motorists marshalled some curious arguments. In a long letter to *The Car* magazine in 1903, F. Strickland complained among other things that 'the police would have every car stopped every time it passed . . . for its driver's certificate to be examined. Jolly riding it would be on a cold, rainy day, with one's gloves to get off to reach into one's pocket every time, wouldn't it?' What would Mr Strickland think if he could see the pocketful of 'certificates' that motorists must carry today – The driver's licences (national and international), roadworthiness and insurance certificates, the parking permits, tax disc and vehicle registration documents? And what would he make of the driving test that is now mandatory almost everywhere in the world?

It is true that in many countries the testing is perfunctory and the only essential qualification for obtaining the driving licence is an adequate bribe for the official administering the test. However, even in developing countries that is not always the case. In the Republic of South Korea the car industry is in its infancy, the level of car ownership is relatively low and yet the standards demanded by the driving test are dauntingly high. First, aspiring drivers must pass a medical which requires minimum standards of eyesight and physical co-ordination. Next they must complete a one-hour written examination on their knowledge of traffic regulations and basic mechanical theory. Only if they achieve a 70 per cent mark in this theoretical exam can they set a date for the practical. If at any time during the test the smallest mistake is made – such as touching the kerb – the candidate is disqualified and must instantly vacate the car. It is like playing some cruel board game: the slightest error and the player must 'return to go'. The few who survive must then attend four hours of compulsory driver education before the precious licence is issued.

The introduction of compulsory driving tests brought booming business to driving schools the world over. The world's largest chain of driving schools, the British School of Motoring, was founded in 1910, to retrain coachmen who needed to drive the new 'horseless carriage'. In the absence of any official driving test the BSM developed its own, and in due course provided considerable assistance to the government when it introduced the driving test in 1935.

In Japan, where so many things are done differently, it has always been the driving schools that have been responsible for administering the official test; and it follows that to get a licence, every learner driver must buy professional tuition. Just in case any school might be tempted to undercut the competition and offer a bargain deal in instant driving licences, the school curriculum is laid down by law. Every pupil must complete a minimum thirty hours' instruction in basic theory and mechanics of the car. This must be followed by a minimum twenty-seven hours' driving instruction, seventeen hours in the controlled conditions of the school and ten hours on the open road. However, it is clearly in the financial interest of the schools to keep the pupils as long as possible and it comes as no great surprise to learn that only 10 per cent are judged to be competent to take the test after the minimum twenty-seven hours. Forty hours is said to be the average. By the time the school issues its proficiency certificate – which is taken to the police and exchanged for the licence – most pupils will have spent in excess of £400 on lessons. Every year about 1,200,000 Japanese reach the age of

4
3
2

eighteen and that is just about the number of men and women entering the country's 1300 driving schools each year. At £400 a time, it becomes clear why a permit to run a driving school is regarded as a permit to print money.

Although the Japanese driving test is unusually rigorous, wherever any kind of test is required one of the trickiest obstacles to negotiate is the knowledge of the Highway Code. Who can put his hand on his heart and swear that he knows the precise meaning of every road sign and signal and the correct procedure in every circumstance on the highway? Pioneer motorists found no such problem; for them, confusion arose not from a profusion of rules or signs but from the total lack of them. They knew which side of the road they should drive on but even then the British insisted on keeping to the left while most European countries chose to drive on the right. In Italy they could drive on the left or the right depending on where they happened to be. The basic rule was 'keep to the right'; but larger cities were permitted to adopt a 'keep left' rule if they so desired. Not until 1923 was this anomalous situation sorted out and the whole of Italy adopted a 'keep right' rule.

Passing the driving test is sometimes seen as a twentieth-century rite of passage taking the initiate from childhood into the adult world. Certainly by administering the test in a crowded amphitheatre as they do in Seoul, South Korea, the ceremonial aspect is greatly enhanced.

Learning road safety is included in Japan's school curriculum as part of an across-the-board campaign that has substantially reduced casualties on the road.

This era of blessed anarchy was short-lived. Before long, poles began to sprout beside the highway bearing every kind of direction, instruction, warning and threat. In the development of this traffic system one of the great forgotten figures of the past is William Phelps Eno who spent most of his long working life and his considerable fortune trying to create order out of chaos on the roads.

Eno was born in New York City in 1858. As a young man he travelled widely and was dismayed by the traffic conditions he saw everywhere; except in London where it seemed to him that traffic flowed more easily because drivers exercised a measure of courtesy and common sense. When his father died in 1898, Eno used his inherited fortune to set up the first ever scientific traffic study. His findings and proposals he published in *Rules for Driving*, a pamphlet that was used by the city of New York when it introduced, in 1903, the first comprehensive system of traffic regulation in the world. Eno's code laid down basic rules for passing, stopping, crossing and turning as well as the use of hand signals and the right of way. He also proposed the use of pedestrian crossings and safety islands, standard street signs and designated bus and tram stops.

Having done his best with New York, Eno then set about tackling the problems of Paris where the Système Eno was adopted in 1912. Among his other achievements, Eno foresaw the dangers of noise pollution and persuaded the authorities to ban the use of motor horns in the city centre. But perhaps his most notable contribution to the Parisian driving experience was his introduction of the one-way traffic circulation at the Arc de Triomphe. For strangers to Paris, this intersection is an intimidating experience even today. What it was like before it became one-way is beyond imagining. Some years later when Eno's one-way system was brought into operation at London's Hyde Park Corner, it met with adverse comment. According to the *Illustrated London News*, 'The experiment in a gyratory system of traffic at Hyde Park Corner . . . was not altogether a success. There was considerable congestion . . . and confusion among drivers, resulting in seven minor collisions.'

Although the name of William Phelps Eno has sunk into obscurity, he was highly regarded in his day. James Rood Doolittle wrote in 1916:

In the United States the first restricted-access, purpose-built roads were the metropolitan parkways. The most ambitious of these parkway systems built by the Long Island Motor Parkway Company was planned astonishingly early, in 1906, and became a model for express highways everywhere. By excluding commercial vehicles, the parkways provided fast and enjoyable travelling conditions.

Detroit asserts that this electric stop sign, erected in 1914, was the first of its kind. However it seems that Cleveland, Ohio, installed similar traffic signals earlier the same year.

'The Système Eno' is now in force in nearly every capital city of the world . . . It is estimated that under it, the volume of traffic can be, and often is, from three times to five times as heavy as it could possibly be without traffic rules. The automobile industry is distinctly appreciative of Eno's broad service as it added immensely to the possibilities of the car.

One final footnote on the man they called The Father of Traffic Regulation: he never drove a car. Eno was a lifelong lover of the horse and a talented equestrian, and when the automobile first appeared he regarded it as a passing fad. Finally, when car ownership became a necessity, he acquired the service of a chauffeur.

For many years in Britain, traffic signs did more to confuse than to elucidate. The very first ones were erected by cycling clubs in the 1880s to warn cyclists of particularly steep and dangerous hills. Having regard to the braking capabilities of early cars, these signs will have spared motorists from some unexpected thrills. The Motor Car Act of 1903 first gave local government the powers to erect traffic signs but not until the Road Traffic Act of 1930 was standardization introduced, something that the French had enjoyed since 1903. Britain also paid a heavy price for failing to keep in step with Europe on internationally standardized signs. Having ignored the steps that were taken towards a unified system in 1909 and again in 1929, when the final changeover to the European standard was made in 1964, some $1\frac{1}{2}$ million obsolete signs had to be replaced.

Every motorist has had the experience of entering a strange town with an unfamiliar one-way traffic system. He knows the location of his hotel from the map but the one-way system does not allow him to get there. Whatever he does, he arrives back at the point of entry. Finally, in desperation, he hails a taxi and begs to be guided to his destination. It may be some small consolation to learn that the one-way street was not devised for the torment of motorists. More than 350 years ago in London, an Act of Common Council set out to cure 'the disorder and rude behaviour of Carmen, Draymen and others usinge Cartes' by introducing one-way traffic into a maze of narrow streets in the City.

As the numbers of vehicles on city streets grew, more and increasingly elaborate means were sought to control the direction and flow of the traffic. The American Traffic Signal Co. claims to have erected the first electric traffic lights in Cleveland, Ohio, in August 1914. The system was well ahead of its time for as well as the red and green lights for stop and go, a strident buzzer alerted vehicles and pedestrians of an imminent signal change. This feature was also incorporated in the traffic lights erected in Paris in 1923, though it appears to have been a more primitive system with a manually operated stop-light and a gong that was struck by the operator as he controlled the traffic flow. Automatic traffic lights made their appearance in Britain in 1927 but long before, in 1868, a single manually operated signal lamp, lighted by gas and with revolving red and green lanterns, was used in London to stop traffic in Parliament Square for the benefit of MPs and peers wishing to attend or to leave the Houses of Parliament. Operating this contraption cannot have been a popular task. In 1869, it blew up and wounded the duty constable. Shortly afterwards it was dismantled and Londoners were freed from the frustrations of traffic lights for a further half-century.

STOP
LUNCH

Is the parking space big enough? Tokyo residents may not purchase a car until police have sized up their off-street parking space, judged it adequate and issued the permit.

At a very early stage, traffic engineers and police discovered that it was not just the movement of traffic that had to be regulated, but the very presence of vehicles on the streets of the cities. In the United States, even in a small town like Muncie, the Lynds discovered that parking was already becoming a problem in the 1920s; if they could return to Muncie today, they would find that in 'formerly deserted residential streets', cars are parked bumper to bumper; and in the business district, despite knocking down whole blocks to provide parking and despite regiments of parking meters, the problem of accommodating the car has not been solved. While for small towns like Muncie all this amounts to little more than a routine difficulty, in many larger cities it is a problem of crisis proportions. Some traffic authorities are now introducing laws that not only regulate traffic flow and parking but which actually restrict the use and the ownership of cars. In Tokyo, no resident may purchase a car until he can prove to the city police that he has adequate off-street parking. Some of the spaces for which parking permits have been granted are so awkward and unlikely that getting the vehicle in and out is a major manoeuvre. It is little wonder that some vehicles appear to be rarely used, shrouded in protective sheets and dusty with disuse. Because of Tokyo's stringent parking rules, car ownership in the capital is significantly lower than in Japan's rural areas.

Hong Kong and Singapore have gone even further to discourage the use and ownership of private cars. In Singapore a solution has been sought by making car ownership prohibitively expensive in terms of increased duties and taxes and by charging heavily for the privilege of bringing cars into the business district in peak hours. In Hong Kong a similar course is being pursued but with an ingenious twist. The object of the new regulation has been to bring the old concept of road tolls up to date and thus to deter motorists from using the most congested roads at peak hours. Hong Kong has 350,000 vehicles on only 762 miles of road – if they all attempted to go for a spin at once there would not be enough road to go around. To avoid

On Japan's highways, police do intensive spot-checks on cars' roadworthiness. Owners of defective vehicles are not prosecuted, just given a time limit to make repairs.

Hong Kong where, if all the cars ventured out together, some would fall into the sea. Using the latest technology, the colony is experimenting with a revolutionary system of 'electronic road pricing' to bring the car population under control.

LEYLAND
BR 3145

In New York City, the sanitation department has to collect over a thousand abandoned cars a week from the streets and cart them off to the scrapyard.

such a catastrophe, in future every one of the territory's private cars will be fitted with a device known as the electronic number plate which, when it interacts with wire loops set in the road will send a signal to a central computer which registers the toll. There will be varying tolls for different stretches of road, depending on the degree of congestion and the time of day. At the end of the month, the computer will issue a bill to each car owner, just like the telephone bill. 'Charging for the use of the road', says Alan Scott, Hong Kong's Secretary for Transport, 'does not prevent an individual from owning a vehicle, nor from using it. It leaves him to choose when and where to use it, on a financial basis and by comparison with the alternatives.' That may be, but it is rather like saying that having to employ a man with a red flag to walk ahead of your car as you proceed at 4 m.p.h. does not prevent you owning a car, nor from using it. Indeed it does not, but it certainly takes away the fun. If we use the red flag as a metaphor for regulation, then there is no doubt that the motorist has come full circle and that he is returning to the age of the red flag. It is significant that it is the British government's

Department of Transport that has been awarded the contract for the Hong Kong experiment and, if it is successful, it is hard to imagine that the same principle will not be applied to solve the problems of Britain's congested cities. Hong Kong firmly believes that once it has perfected the technology, as well as keeping its own traffic moving, it may have hit the jackpot in terms of worldwide sales of the ERP (Electronic Road Pricing) system.

With regulations now entering the age of the computer it is worth reminding ourselves that any law is only as effective as enforcement can make it; and that compliance with the law is a very patchy affair; it is also undoubtedly a matter of national characteristics and national traditions. Despite all the chauvinistic jokes about Irish, Italian or French behind the wheel, drivers do seem to share some national behavioural characteristics. Visitors to the United States are amazed that in a country where speed and aggression play such a powerful part in popular culture, motorists have for so long accepted – and largely complied with – a 55 m.p.h. speed limit. The fact is that on the whole Americans are careful and considerate drivers and the United States remains the safest country in the world in which to drive. Australians on the other hand are aggressive drivers and appear to take a pride in being so. It has been suggested that the competitive spirit that serves them so well in their sporting endeavours serves them less well when they climb into their cars. Bill Tuckey, one of Australia's leading motoring writers, believes that a love of powerful cars and a passion for driving fast and aggressively is part of the Australian male tradition. He points out that until recently Australia

Congestion on London's South Circular. Attempts to build urban motorways through London have encountered stubborn resistance. One day this may mean that motor traffic will have only limited access to parts of the city.

On this Australian mini-car circuit, primary school children start early to learn how to be safe drivers and sensible pedestrians. Road hogs are banished from the vehicles with engines and relegated to pedal-powered 'Mad Mate'.

was building the fastest production sedans in the world: 'straight off the showroom floor they'd do about 145 miles an hour, and they're still very popular with the kids . . . they still want "bulk grunt" in their motor cars'. Along with this passion for speed and for fleet machines goes something less attractive, described by Tuckey as 'the chip-on-the-shoulder attitude . . . When this attitude is translated into driving behaviour even innocent, little suburban matrons will risk T-boning you to get into a parking space before you and will abuse you for even daring to suggest you might have been there before them.'

Philip Gold, an Englishman who has been employed by the City of São Paulo to try to suggest means of reducing road casualties, has carefully studied Brazilian driving behaviour. He finds that it is characterized by a supreme indifference to all restrictions and regulations. 'Most Brazilian drivers have never seen the Highway Code and those that have seen it forget it very quickly because there is absolutely no enforcement of the Code in Brazil.' In his six years in the country, Gold has seen the situation deteriorate to the point that motorists now ignore red traffic signals and totally disregard the rights of pedestrians. Those who break traffic rules, he says, are rarely caught and even more rarely punished. Even for the most serious offences, the likelihood of an offender losing his licence is negligible. Gold believes that driver behaviour can be changed and that by simply enforcing the law accidents could immediately be reduced by 50 per cent. In attempting to establish why motorists failed to stop at red traffic lights Philip Gold chanced on some unexpected information. It seems that a resourceful group of criminals had been using the enforced vehicle halt to attack and rob motorists. These offences had occurred at night, and to reduce the risk of mugging the police suggested that motorists should ignore traffic lights after dark. The habit soon caught on and without much discouragement from the police was extended to the hours of daylight.

How far driving behaviour can be changed by regulation and how far national characteristics influence the way we drive is something that can never be precisely measured; but the difference between men and women at the wheel has been the subject of several scientific studies. Women are undoubtedly safer and less aggressive drivers but it seems that there is some basis in fact for all those male-chauvinist jokes about female driving incompetence. Tests in Australia have shown that under identical conditions women are less successful than men in making correct assessments of distance; they therefore find it more difficult than men to perform certain functions in cars such as parallel parking or negotiating tight turns – and that is something that no amount of regulation can ever improve.

Abandoned cars along the roadside in Hawaii. Even in this Polynesian paradise the illegal disposal of cars has become a major headache for police and environmentalists.

Σ Π
82

The Car and Death

The initial automobile death [in the United States] occurred in 1900 and the victim was Hieronymus Mueller. While filling the gasoline tank of his automobile, he came too close to a match which ignited the gasoline and set his clothes on fire. Said the insurance adjuster with some premonition: 'Mr Mueller was so badly burned that he died in a few hours. This is the first fatal case of this kind which has come to our notice. There are undoubtedly more to follow although the manner of accident may differ.'
(Horace Sutton, *Travelers*)

The price of world automobility in terms of the toll it has taken in human life and suffering is one almost beyond calculation, let alone comprehension. In the United States it has been estimated, following the unfortunate example of Mr Mueller, that *twice* the number of people have been killed by the automobile on the nation's highways in a little over eighty years than in all the wars (including the Civil War) ever fought by Americans. Somewhere between 15 and 20 million people worldwide have died in road accidents since the motor car's invention and *hundreds* of millions become permanent victims of their injuries, often terribly mutilated and disfigured. It is an epidemic which, with heart disease and cancer, forms the three biggest killers of our society. Gordon Trinca, chairman of the Royal Australasian College of Surgeons Road Trauma Committee, and a spirited campaigner in the fight to reduce car accidents, calls it: 'the disease of road trauma . . . a dirty disease, a savage disease. It thrives in a situation of high speed and intoxication, unroadworthy vehicles, fatigue, poor visibility, high traffic density, inexperience, indifference and lack of road sense. This disease kills sometimes suddenly, sometimes slowly and agonizingly.'

One of the least pleasant aspects of police work around the world is dealing with the mechanical and human debris of the car smash. In both these bizarre American examples, the cops concerned have cause for reflection . . .

There is no immunity to the disease. The one significant difference between road trauma, and the other two great killers, is that the former destroys the young. In western society for those aged one to fifteen, highway accidents are the most frequent type of accident, and the disease can claim to be the biggest killer in the under-35-year-olds. The threat to the child born today is that one in four will be killed or injured in a road crash during their driving life. There is more than a hundred times better chance of being killed in a road crash than in an air crash. Highways, and not wars, have become the largest arenas of violence in the world.

How ironic it is, that so many members of the medical profession initially welcomed the arrival of the motor car and the demise of the horse, since it is doctors today who are in the very front line of coping with the epidemic. Typical was James J. Walsh, Ph.D., MD, writing in *The Automobile Magazine* at the turn of the century. Under the title of 'The Automobile and Public Health', he declared that:

The automobile should meet with a hearty welcome from the professional sanitarian and from all those who are sincerely interested in municipal health. Whatever can be done to advance the day that will usher in the horseless era for our city streets, will be just so much done in a great humanitarian cause. It will lead to a distinct lessening of human suffering . . .

Only a few years later the greater realities of life with the car had descended. Under the title of 'Get After the Chauffeurs', in 1906 *Life* magazine declared, *right and below*] Mayhem on the roads even in 1907. With its splendid *routes nationales*, high-powered cars and few speed restraints, France experienced some of the earliest and most spectacular crashes. Even allowing for artistic licence, the devastation caused by such smashes is confirmed by photographs of the time.

opposite above] Caught at the moment of impact, this somersaulting car has plunged off the road in the American countryside and, with steam pouring from its burst radiator, teeters on the edge of an abyss.

opposite below] In 1907, even with a speed limit in Quarry Street, Guildford of 10 m.p.h. (at a time when the general speed limit was 20 m.p.h.) this early automobilist has managed to career off the road and demolish a fence.

L'ACCIDENT DE POMPIGNAC

4496-191
509

SPEED LIMIT
10
MILES PER HOUR
FOR MOTORS

POPULAR SCIENCE
APR. 1946
25 CENTS
MONTHLY
How To Drive And Stay Alive
pp. 66—75

The suggestion was lately made in convention that it would help very much to make human life safer in New York if a suitable apparatus could be put up in Madison Square and a dozen reckless chauffeurs (drivers) could be hanged on it. Their reply was: 'A dozen? There are two or three hundred of those fellows that need hanging.'

The article concludes: 'Is homicide by automobile so much less culpable than homicide with a gun?'

It is a debate that has continued to this day. How to control the demon behind the wheel? The various theories explaining driver behaviour tend to fall into two categories. On the one hand man's instinct, and on the other his learned behaviour. Under the first category, the car is represented as an important piece of territory to be defended. Meyer Parry found in his detailed study of driving behaviour in the borough of Hornsey, London, that all drivers accused other types of causing all the problems. For example, 18- to 30-year-olds accused older people of being inconsiderate, and often of dithering. Over-35s accused the young of being reckless and incompetent. Various attempts have been made to explain and isolate the part played by male aggression in the driving process, even to the extent that one research study in the United States on the Ute Indians discovered that their car

accident rate exceeded that of any other racial group. As they were formerly known for their outstanding fighting qualities, subsequently curbed, it was concluded that the civilized Ute's lack of outlet for his aggressive drive since laying down the tomahawk and taking up the steering wheel was being compensated for on the open highway. In the category of learned behaviour, it is suggested that people drive as they would like to live (their behaviour based on social and cultural influences) and that bad driving is reinforced by most people's lack of proper training in the first place and because for much of the time their excesses go unchecked anyway.

If driving behaviour and attitude remains a major preoccupation of researchers and legislators, it has largely given way in the last twenty years to a concentration on making the car itself safer and also improving the vehicle environment. The catalyst was Ralph Nader and his book *Unsafe at Any Speed*, published in December 1965, which exposed Detroit's unlimited power at the expense of public safety and their cynical neglect in failing to

above left] At the end of World War II there were 26 million cars registered in the United States, but over half of them were more than ten years old and ready for the scrapheap. Road accidents soared as returning GIs, celebrating the pleasures of peacetime and the return to Mom and apple pie, climbed into these 'clunkers' and took to the highways. *Popular Science Monthly*, in an April 1946 issue, devoted ten pages to defensive driving techniques.

below left] For one hundred years we have carefully insulated ourselves from the full horror of death on the roads. The cinema has unfailingly presented a sanitized view. In the pre-war German cinema it was said that every road accident had to feature 'a noble carriage' as the aggressor (in this case a Mercedes-Benz), and a 'dramatically postured beauty' as the victim.

A most unusual car for people
who enjoy the unusual
'66 Corvair Monza Convertible—with outside rear-view mirror and back-up lights among the safety assists that are now standard equipment.
If you perked up when you turned to this page, our research computer says you're probably well informed, earn above average income and have more or less "in" type tastes. That's the kind of person who usually drives a Corvair. But then you can't always go by research. The fellow who turned all this up on our computer, for instance, was a frugal soul who read nothing but technical stuff and drove the same black sedan for 15 years. Then one day he showed up in a Corvair convertible a shade redder than the one above. How did he square this with his research? He didn't. That was the same day he asked to be transferred to a job that would get him out on the road more...driving his new Corvair.
'66 Corvair by Chevrolet
Chevrolet Division of General Motors, Detroit, Michigan

right] 'A most unusual car . . .' boasts the General Motors ad. for their 1966 Chevrolet Corvair. 'Unsafe at Any Speed,' replied consumer advocate Ralph Nader, prompting a safety revolution around the world and the introduction in the United States of compulsory government safety standards on all vehicles. Through their vigorous campaigning Nader's Raiders brought a major unregulated industry under the law, created a new safety awareness and lowered the American road toll, although in the six years after *Unsafe at Any Speed*, 330,000 Americans died on the highways and another 25 million were injured.

Rapacious monster, small child . . . and near accident, dramatically depicted by French illustrator George Ham in the late 1930s. As many as 100,000 young people around the world die in road accidents annually.

make cars more crashworthy. Although his particular *bête noire* was the Chevrolet Corvair, his book was a general indictment of the carmakers' poor safety practices and he urged the passing of federal and state legislation to bring them to task. An apoplectic General Motors responded by clandestinely hiring detectives to investigate Nader's private life in the hope of discrediting him. It was a gigantic blunder. Perhaps no other action was singly more responsible for the passing of the National Traffic and Motor Vehicle Safety Act, or for influencing the greater concentration on automobile safety throughout the world. Public Law 89-563, bearing President Lyndon Johnson's signature in 1966, provided for the establishment of improved safety standards for all motor vehicles and a co-ordinated national safety programme to reduce accidents involving motor vehicles. Henceforth, Detroit was to have its federal policeman in the form of NHTSA (the National Highway Traffic Safety Administration).

In a sense, it was surprising that it had been such a long time in coming. John Keats, as far back as 1958, had worked out in *The Insolent Chariots* that:

each year more than 4,320,000 cubic feet of American earth is excavated to make graves of what the newspapers call our traffic victims . . . because Detroit sees itself as selling nothing but dreams of speed, sex, luxury and horsepower. It would no more occur to Detroit to try to sell safety at the same time than it would occur to a fashionable restaurant to provide sodium bicarbonate and a stomach pump with every place setting.

While Detroit consistently defended its product, blaming the 'nut behind the wheel', a Cornell University research team, working with the Indiana State Police, had estimated that of 600 fatal accidents studied, only 16 per cent were non-survivable, and that the remaining 84 per cent of lives lost *could* have been saved by proper interior design.

By the mid 1960s, death by car had become the nation's single greatest cause of violent demise, with an appalling 16 million accidents a year. It would be wrong to cite Ralph Nader, the leading consumer advocate of the time, as being the sole mover in the onslaught upon Detroit. Kenneth Roberts, a congressman from Alabama, a group of concerned doctors called Physicians for Automotive Safety, and Jeffrey O'Connell, a professor of law who had written *Safety Last – An Indictment of the Auto Industry* (which was published shortly after *Unsafe at Any Speed*), by their various efforts had all helped to lay the foundations of the consumer revolt which Nader so articulately and prominently led.

Eighteen years on from those heady days when the president of mighty General Motors, James M. Roche, had to apologize before a Senate Sub-Committee for persecuting a private citizen, Ralph Nader can now assess the improvements brought about by his spectacular campaign:

They've improved to the level of saving about ten thousand lives a year and reducing the severity or presence of hundreds of thousands of injuries – principally by the availability and use of shoulder strap seat belts, stronger door latches, padded dash panels, breakaway rear-view mirrors, head restraints, collapsible steering columns and stronger side protection. But since 1970 the government, first under Nixon, then Ford and now Reagan, have done nothing to push the auto companies to meet higher levels of safety which conventional engineering would have permitted them.

As early as 1903 the motor car was being portrayed as a death trap by Otto Seitz in the German magazine *Jugend*. More than 15 million people have been killed by the motor car since.

In fact, from 1966 to 1979 the traffic death rate in the United States decreased by 39 per cent. A driver today can motor more than 1600 miles with the same degree of risk as someone who drove 1000 in 1966. None the less an average of 50,000 people still die each year on the roads of America, some 4 million are seriously injured, and the cost to society in terms of lost work time, insurance payments and medical costs is in the region of $50 billion.

'We have a saying', says B. A. Boaz of NHTSA in Washington, 'that the greatest killer of young Americans is other young Americans who drive and

The problem of the drinking driver has been with us from the beginning. *Life* magazine in 1906 was particularly outraged at the way in which wealthy and inebriated motorists placed themselves above the law. 'One of them came racing down Central Park at midnight with a convivial party of his friends, ran into another machine, broke his own neck and killed two or three of his companions. That one got his dues. We read every day of innocent people killed or hurt by automobiles, but we never read that any adequate degree of inconvenience has been incurred by the chauffeur who did the killing . . .'

have accidents. They represent about 22 per cent of the driving population, but about 40 per cent of fatalities in the country.' The sad thing, as Boaz points out, is there are three simple things – all of which require changes in human behaviour – that could reduce these figures even more dramatically. One is keeping to the 55 m.p.h. speed limit. The second is wearing seat belts, which only about 11 per cent of Americans do. The third factor, and the most crucial of all, is drinking and driving. Alcohol is involved in 55 per cent of fatal accidents, and in most major cities of America, after 6 p.m. or 8 p.m. (depending on which metropolitan area) it is estimated that about one out of every ten drivers are legally too drunk to drive.

'If we could really succeed in controlling the drinking and driving problem we would probably reduce our deaths by 25,000 a year,' says Boaz. 'If we could get 70 per cent usage of seat belts in this country we would save another 9 to 10,000 lives a year, so by those two things alone you are talking of 35,000 lives out of 50,000.'

One country where tough and perhaps unexpected legislation on the drinking and driving issue has brought about dramatic results is Australia. The year 1970 was a vintage year in relation to the mayhem on Australian roads – 3798 dead and 100,000 people injured, at least a third of them so seriously that they were admitted to hospital. The state of Victoria, which in 1966 had pioneered stricter drinking and driving laws, under increasing pressure from the medical profession introduced in 1976 random breath testing. Other important initiatives adopted by Victoria were: compulsory wearing of seat belts for *all* vehicle occupants; compulsory blood alcohol testing of all those aged 15 years or more who attend hospital for treatment of injuries received in a road accident; and *mandatory* cancellation of licence and disqualification from holding a licence to drive for certain minimum graduated periods for exceeding a blood alcohol level of 0.05.

The results of the legislation were remarkable. In the period 1970 to 1980 Victoria achieved a record 38 per cent decrease in road deaths – down a massive 404 from 1061 in 1970 to 657 in 1980. Where Victoria led, the other states have followed. As Sergeant Roy Beverstock of the New South Wales Police Breath Analysis Unit observed to us: 'Look! I've been thirty-one years in this game. I've pulled bodies out of wrecks. I've pulled children out of the arms of dead women in cars. I've seen people incinerated by vehicles and when you see these sort of things, nothing is too severe.'

Even if Australians are achieving remarkable improvements in dealing with their road trauma, the overall figures still make up a depressing litany. As in the United States, it is the young people who are massively over-represented in the statistics, and seem least touched by attempts to curb their behaviour in the areas of drink–driving and excessive speed. This worries Gordon Trinca, surgeon and national chairman of the Road Trauma Committee:

Today the only mechanism in which the young can express their irresponsibility, their taking of risks, against authority, leaving the nest, overcoming their inferiority complex as they get out into the big bad world – is the motor car. Now there are no mountains to climb, no lands to discover, there's no alternative but the motor car and that is what disturbs me . . .

In a country where young people of thirteen or fourteen are often drinking to excess, experts believe a change in attitudes must lie in early education.

"OF COURSH I'M GONNA DRIVE HOME, OFFISHUH--I'M IN NO CONDISHUN T'WALK!"
HIC
210

Society has traditionally viewed the drunk driver with either tolerance or amusement, as this postcard shows. The realities are far more sobering. On average, three Americans are killed and eighty injured by drunk drivers every hour of every day, and drunk driving accounts for half of all automobile fatalities in the United States.

Following the Jesuit principle of 'Give us the child and we will give you the man', the dangers of drinking and driving are now being taught in many Australian classrooms to ten- and eleven-year-olds with detailed discussions and explicit visual material. The purpose is not just to inform and educate but, it is hoped, to bring about a basic change in future society's attitude towards the drunken driver. He has been traditionally and universally viewed with sympathy by judges, juries, prosecutors and legislators, most of whom drink socially and drive. In Australia it is now felt the most important element of all in the fight against road trauma is public condemnation of the road user who puts himself and others at risk.

In the United States, where three people are killed and eighty injured by drunk drivers every hour of every day, a grass-roots rebellion with nationwide repercussions against the unacceptable epidemic suddenly began one spring afternoon in 1980, when thirteen-year-old Cari Lightner of Fair Oaks, California, was struck from behind and killed by a hit-and-run driver as she walked to a church festival. Cari's grief-stricken mother was appalled to learn that the driver, 47-year-old Clarence Busch, who had two previous drunk-driving convictions and was out on $100 bail after a third arrest, had spent only two days in jail previously and was unlikely to wind up there for killing Cari (in fact he was paroled after spending nineteen months in gaol). Candy Lightner left her job and launched an organization called Mothers Against Drunk Drivers (MADD), giving the increasing public outcry against drunk driving the constituency it had always needed– the victims.

'It is the only socially acceptable form of homicide that we have in the United States today,' says Candy Lightner with passion. 'You hear the attitude, "there but for the grace of God go I", everyone seems to identify with the drunk driver and not with the victim. The judges in this country are very lenient . . . Drunk driving is the most often committed crime in this country and it costs the tax payer more money than all the crimes combined. You are talking anywhere from 24 to 40 billion dollars a year.'

Aggressive, self-righteous and punitive, MADD – and other grass-roots organizations like it (AIM – Alliance against Intoxicated Motorists, SADD – Students Against Drunk Drivers, RID – Remove Intoxicated Drivers) are swiftly changing both official and public attitudes towards the drunken driver. 'We don't want to think that we're capable of killing and yet we are,' adds Candy Lightner. 'Each and every one of us who drinks and gets behind the wheel of a car is capable of killing. That's a horrible thing to have to admit to yourself.' In 1983 alone 358 new pieces of legislation were introduced on drunk driving, and twenty-five states adopted new and tougher drinking/driving standards. While legislation varies from state to state, 0.10 blood alcohol content (double the Australian standard) has been set by most as the legal limit. It is generally recognized that driving impairment occurs at below that level, but 0.10 is the kind of compromise that recognizes, as one reformer pointed out, that the United States is both a drinking society and a society which undertakes most of its journeys in the automobile. Many of the new laws make prison mandatory – if not for the first offence, certainly for the second. The state of Maine, which in 1981 began mandatory gaol sentences for the first-time offenders, experienced a 47 per cent reduction in alcohol-related fatalities. At the same time it rather sensibly introduced a new tax on liquor for the treatment and prevention of alcohol problems.

In the early 1970s Japan had one of the worst road accident records in the world and it now has one of the best. Whether the practice of taking the new family car to the local shrine for a temple blessing was a factor in this transformation has not been established.

One country where attitudes towards the drunk driver and persistent traffic offender are predictably severe is Japan. In a unique approach to the problem, twelve special prisons exclusively for road offenders have been established, where speedsters, inebriated motorists and other car convicts are held for periods of three to twelve months, partly in solitary confinement. Behind the barbed wire at Ichihara Prison, on the outskirts of Tokyo, hardened traffic offenders file out of the Dormitory of Hope. Dressed in white pyjamas and with shaven heads, they parade at dawn each day to recite a prayer of penitence in front of the Monument of Atonement, a memorial to road victims. At the time of their offence, 43 per cent of them were driving under the influence of alcohol and 45 per cent without a driving licence, and 34 per cent of them were convicted of 'Homicide, Negligent'. Common personality features of the inmates we learn are 'egocentricity, emotional instability and over-confidence in their driving skills'. In addition to spending time reflecting upon their traffic misdemeanours, they attend classes to analyse car accidents and their own particular offences. There is, within the prison confines, an actual driver training circuit, where inmates are taught how to improve their driving skills. They are even allowed to do maintenance and tuning work on the warders' cars.

Tough laws make a dramatic difference. Between 1971 and 1982 traffic deaths in Tokyo plunged from 1200 a year to 300. On the drinking and driving issue police do not settle just for motorists. Each year they round up nearly 600 bartenders, hostesses and publicans for providing too much liquor to customers they know will be driving later.

above] Morning parade at the Ichihara Prison, Tokyo – an institution exclusively for traffic offenders. Drunk driving is a particular hazard for the Japanese, who are especially susceptible to the effects of liquor. Researchers at Tokyo University have shown that the average Japanese lacks an enzyme which prevents his bloodstream from absorbing large amounts of alcohol. This means there are few alcoholics in Japan compared with America and Europe, but many more drunks. Two or three drinks, and the Japanese driver is insensible . . .

The Monument of Atonement before which prisoners at Ichihara confess their driving misdemeanours and beg the forgiveness of their victims.

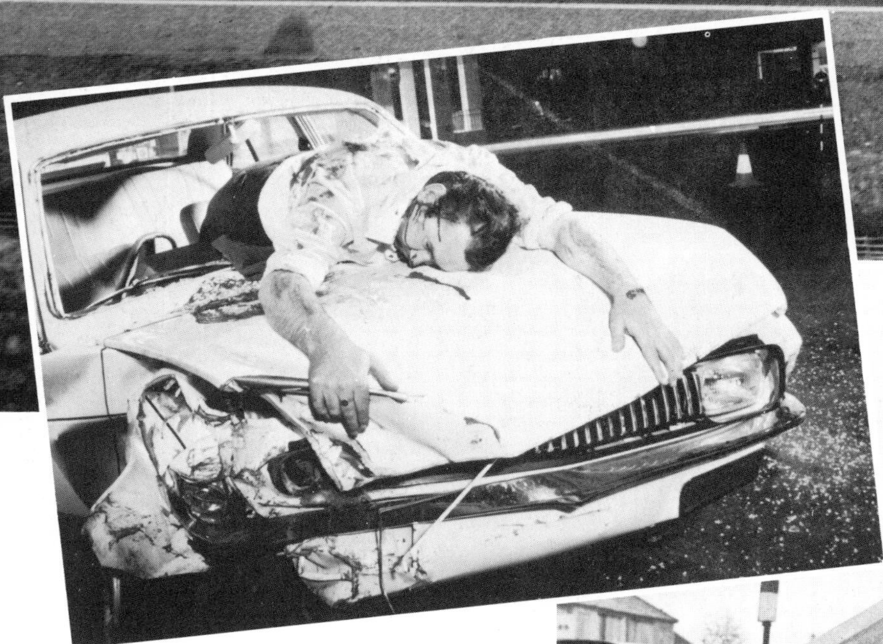

above] The tragedy of death behind the wheel in all its stark horror.

above] Motorway madness in England, March 1972. The dead and dying lie in the wreckage of their cars in a multiple pile-up on the M1 motorway caused by heavy fog and high speeds. In the isolation of our mobile, metal boxes we are easily lulled into a sense of security that can prove all too fragile . . . especially when we impact with today's juggernauts of the road.

right and left] Death on the roads is especially shocking because it brings violence into our familiar, everyday surroundings. Moreover, it is a well-established fact that over 50 per cent of car crash victims die in accidents that occur at less than 30 m.p.h. and within five miles of home.

SAFETY FIRST
CROSS THE STREET AT REGULAR CROSSING
NOT IN THE MIDDLE OF THE BLOCK
AVOID ACCIDENTS
EDUCATIONAL CAMPAIGN SAFETY FIRST SOCIETY OF NEW YORK
5TH AVE. SECRETARIAL SCHOOL
PETTUS CURTIS
ENTIRE FLOOR AND OFFICES FOR RENT

left] Safety campaigns to protect those on foot from the car – in this instance, on Fifth Avenue in New York City – began at the beginning of the century. In many countries today, especially in the Third World, pedestrians make up half the road fatalities.

Horrendous though it is that a quarter to a third of a million people die each year because some part of a car hits them, there are, at least in the western world, strong indications that accident growth rates are levelling off and that the epidemic is beginning to be mastered. In Britain in 1931, for example, 6700 people were killed by the 2 million vehicles on the road. By 1982 the number of vehicles had risen to 20 million, but the fatalities had fallen to 5800, and the introduction of compulsory front seat belt-wearing in 1983 resulted in an immediate 25 per cent reduction in the casualty rate.

The new area for massive road trauma, however, is the Third World, where over the last decade growth in the car population has been phenomenal. In some countries, particularly those that have oil, the number of cars has been doubling in periods of four to five years, and with it their road casualties and death rates at an equal if not greater rate. Accidents on the roads are costing the developing countries more than £15 billion a year, and most Third World nations suffer a greater financial loss from these accidents than they receive in foreign aid. Africa has been the worst hit. In a survey of thirty-three Third World countries, the eleven with the highest fatal accident rates were all African. Nigeria, oil-rich and in love with the car, tops the league. It suffers 234 people killed in a year for every 10,000 vehicles on the roads, compared to *three* fatalities per 10,000 vehicles in Britain. Of those who die in the Third World between the ages of 5 and 44, 10 per cent are killed in road accidents, a higher proportion than from any disease listed in the World Health Organization's statistics. In many countries, pedestrians make up half the road fatalities. In most African countries it is estimated that virtually any car before it is scrapped will injure a pedestrian seriously enough to put that pedestrian in hospital for treatment.

Experts generally agree there are three ways in which road accidents can be reduced: first, by trying to modify people's behaviour; secondly, by making the road environment safer; thirdly, by improving vehicle safety and crashworthiness. Dr Murray McKay, of the Accident Research Unit at Birmingham University is pessimistic about the first two in relation to the developing world, but optimistic about the latter category:

right] Devices to make cars safer have sometimes been overly simplistic, if not comic. Epping, no doubt with winding English country lanes in mind, promoted a car carrying a flag that could be seen over a high hedge, thereby giving warning of the car's presence at blind corners. The urging to 'Fly the flag' met with a cool response.

More than a quarter of a million people die every year in road accidents in the Third World and the figure is climbing rapidly. These three posters issued by the Royal Papua New Guinea Constabulary spell out in pidgin English their universal warnings: Don't Speed, Don't Drink and Drive . . . and Wear Your Seatbelt.

If you look at the behavioural side, in my view things are pretty gloomy, particularly in the Third World. It's very much a generation problem. The time scale is something like thirty years before you can expect to produce sensible and measurable improvements in road user behaviour. If you look at the road environment, the problem there is much more of money. You need an absolutely enormous investment in good roads. The whole infrastructure does not exist and that's a sort of fifty to a hundred years kind of change, so those two areas are pretty hopeless.

He believes the solution lies in the third area – that of the vehicle: 'The potential of crash performance is enormous. We can probably save half at least of all the people who now die, with the current technology that we know to be available if that was applied in cars over the next ten years . . . It might increase the price of cars by 20 per cent in real terms and that's not a great deal.'

But would the consumer pay the difference? 'Safety does not sell', said Henry Ford II in one of his less fortunate statements twenty years ago. Since then several manufacturers – Volvo, Saab, Mercedes-Benz and Rover in particular – have proved the opposite by making a demonstrable success of selling safety as a feature of their cars. Even so Ford's director of car sales in Britain, following a detailed survey of consumer preferences in 1983, concluded that: 'people are not prepared to pay for safety . . . In the survey rear seat belts came out high, but you know that in the real world it's the radio cassette they want . . .'

In the eighteen years since *Unsafe at Any Speed*, the chances of individual survival have been greatly enhanced by the production of vehicles that are infinitely more crashworthy. Gone are those cynical days when Ford of America, with their Pinto model, deliberately fitted, on a cost benefit calculation, a fuel tank that was highly exposed to rear collision rupture and subsequent incineration of the occupants of the car. They had coldly calculated they would save more money fitting the sub-standard fuel tank than they would have to pay out to the injured and bereaved claiming damages in court. Even the Japanese are finally making safety a greater priority on their vehicles, although as late as 1982 Japanese small cars were markedly less crashworthy than American-made cars of comparable size.

Regulations have made cars far safer than those even of ten years ago. Even though the American maxim that the bigger the car the better your chance of survival still holds true (there is more deformable metal to soak up the energy of a collision), careful detail design can put sheet metal to striking use even in small cars. Such is the improvement that any car designed from the mid 1970s onwards, even relatively small ones like the Austin Metro or Renault 9, will have the energy-absorbing ability of a 1971 car twice its weight.

Paul Gikas, a pathologist and professor at the University of Michigan in Ann Arbor, believes manufacturers have much further to go in making their cars safer – even if their only motivation is to guarantee that they have more customers to buy them. 'When you kill 44,000 people – and that was the toll in 1982 in the United States – you have 44,000 fewer potential customers. Many of those are young people and they would be buying several cars throughout their lifetime.' He believes cars should be sold on the basis of their crashworthiness, and that manufacturers should make the safety attributes of their vehicles a positive selling point in advertisements. Such a view perhaps underestimates the strength of man's love affair with the dream machine and all the escapist imagery that goes into the marketing of the car. Just as airline advertisements never mention safety records or fears of flying, one wonders if the day will ever dawn when a prospective car purchaser can wander into his local showroom, to discuss not so much performance, colour, style or even m.p.g., but rather a particular model's roll-over capabilities, or his chances of survival in a front end collision.

What angers Paul Gikas, and pathologists like him, is that so much of the human tragedy that pours into their autopsy rooms could be prevented. Ben Kelly of the Insurance Institute for Highway Safety is equally angry:

It's as if we were holding penicillin from the market twenty years after it had been invented. There is no car being sold in the world today that is other than obsolete from the standpoint of protecting people in crashes . . . A human body can survive impacts of well up to 300 m.p.h. if it is properly packaged. If it is not, it can be killed as low as 5 m.p.h. We are not doing the job that we could be doing for literally pennies, of getting people through these crashes.

He points to the RSV (Research Safety Vehicle), a government-funded research project during the Carter era that came up with a remarkable little vehicle that was intended to illustrate what improvements could be made in automobile safety using existing technology. With a unique foam-filled sheet metal structure and plastic exterior, and with air bags in both the driver and passenger positions, its Californian inventor, Don Friedman, was able to show in tests that the car provided total protection for its occupants hitting a wall at 50 m.p.h., or another car at 100 m.p.h. It would have required $200 million to put the car into production, with each car selling for about $10,000. There were no takers, and perhaps the safest car in the world and one of the more inspired solutions to America's road deaths now lies forlornly under dust covers in the basement of the Department of Transportation building in Washington.

Air bags that automatically inflate in the passenger compartment to cushion you in an impact could save an estimated 9000 lives a year in the United States, but have suffered the same neglect. They were offered to the public in the mid 1970s as an optional extra by one manufacturer, General Motors, with (as Ben Kelly puts it): 'no advertising and with no marketing or promotion whatsoever . . . fleetingly and very insincerely. The manufacturer clearly had already decided that it did not want people to buy the safety equipment and it did not want to have to sell it in the future.'

Ironically, it will probably be an importer of cars into the United States, Mercedes-Benz, who will give the air bag concept a new lease of life, although there is strenuous opposition from American manufacturers who believe seat belts can do the same job and cost less. It is also whispered they fear the avalanche of litigation and claims that could follow the introduction of passive, rather than active, restraint systems into their cars, since the success of such systems in crashes clearly places greater onus on the manufacturer.

However, even the air bag might have difficulty in counteracting one of the most bizarre and undocumented kinds of motor vehicle fatality: the suicide. The use of the motor car as an instrument of self-annihilation – whether by a driver or a pedestrian – is as old as the invention itself. The first academic work on the possibility of car suicides was published by a Dr Beikowsky in Vienna as early as 1914, but more recent researches in Germany and California have revealed extraordinary data on this tragic subject. Professor Werner Weber of the Institute of Legal Medicine at the Technical High School of Aachen thinks that road suicide is growing dramatically. His researches suggest at least a threefold increase over the last ten years based on a minute examination of 146 dead motorists and their cars. As he points

The safety car, which many Americans feel could have halved the death toll on their roads, stands outside the Department of Transportation building, Washington. The RSV (Research Safety Vehcile), which got government backing under the Carter Administration, never went into production – but several of its design features have since been adopted by the Detroit manufacturers.

out: ‘Suicide, even attempted suicide, brings a stigma not only upon the individual concerned but also upon the family. This is one of the reasons why people contemplating suicide try to discuise the fact, at least in its execution, and the motor car seems to them to provide the perfect solution.’

Even more troubling are the findings of David P. Philips at the University of California at San Diego. He has found that automobile fatalities ‘go up very briefly and very sharply after a heavily publicized suicide story, and the more publicity given to the suicide story, the more automobile accidents go up’. He found, in particular, that on the *third* day after the suicide story appeared in California, there was a 31 per cent increase in automobile fatalities throughout the state. To convince the doubters he later replicated the study in Detroit and discovered that automobile accidents rose by *35* per cent on the third day after the suicide story appeared. Even more disturbing, he found in another study on the effects of television ‘soap opera’ suicides that real-life suicides and single automobile accidents went up significantly for a brief period of time. He pointed out: ‘Females seem to die at a much greater rate after these stories than males do – presumably because they are more likely to watch these programmes.’

For whatever reason, death in the automobile is tragic and in the western world increasingly avoidable. At least in the second century of its life the car has a greater opportunity to bestow its manifest benefits on society without the unacceptable human toll.

A roadside plea from the Los Angeles Police Department. In a society where more than 87 per cent of all trips are made in private passenger cars, it is young drivers and passengers who are most at risk.

LE PETIT POUCET MONTAIT UNE PEUGEOT
PIERRE SIMMAR
AUTOMOBILES
PEUGEOT

The Car and Popular Culture

I think that cars today are almost the exact equivalent of the great Gothic cathedrals: I mean the supreme creation of an era, conceived with passion by unknown artists, and consumed in image if not in usage by a whole population which appropriates them as a purely magical object.
(Roland Barthes, *Mythologies*, 1957)

It is hardly surprising that an object as dynamic in its physical and symbolic presence as the motor car should become an immediate source of inspiration for artists and writers, musicians and film-makers who almost from the moment of the car's creation were reflecting the complexity and diversity of man's relationship with his 'transport of delight'. It is those varied and changing cultural outpourings that over the last hundred years have played no small role in influencing people's conscious and unconscious perceptions of life with the automobile.

In art the pace was set by the Italian Futurists, who were the first major art movement to adopt the automobile as a key image in 1909. F. T. Marinetti, poet and propagandist for the movement declared in that year: 'We affirm that the world's magnificence has been enriched by a new beauty: . . . a beauty of speed. A racing car, its frame adorned with great pipes, like snakes with explosive breath – a roaring motor car that seems to run on shrapnel – is more beautiful than the Victory of Samothrace.' One artist in particular, Giacomo Balla, who did more than a hundred auto-related pieces, was indicative of the movement. He emphasized not just the beauty of speed and motion, but focused on the car as an escapist, almost fantasy, vehicle. The car as an object is not concentrated upon, but rather the sensations that are experienced speeding along in a car – in particular, the exhilaration and feeling of near intoxication. Drivers are portrayed as huddled, windswept figures, almost demonic in appearance, wrestling with huge steering wheels against the whirling elements, like classical heroes involved in some deeply symbolic confrontation with invisible spiritual forces. Abstract motifs were used to convey these dynamic sensations – what the Futurists called 'force lines' – coiling, eddying and whirlpooling around the hurtling car. These gave not only a sense of speed and forward movement, but were in themselves representative of the car's cataclysmic effect on society. Gerald Silk, the American art historian, sees the automobile for the Futurists as a kind of cultural, political, social and economic 'getaway' vehicle:

Inspired by the turn-of-the-century technological revolution, the Futurists regarded the automobile as a paradigmatic innovation . . . a rejection of the past in favour of the ideas and objects of the modern world. The selection of the automobile was based on the belief that it best expressed 'the beauty of speed' and the concept of dynamism, and that these twin conquerors of space and time not only were the unique characteristics of the twentieth century but also . . . the underlying forces of nature.

If serious artists prior to the Futurists were curiously unaffected by the car, there were notable exceptions. In what was perhaps the world's first motoring portrait, Toulouse-Lautrec in 1896 portrayed his car-enthusiast cousin Dr Gabriel Tapié de Celeyran, in goggles, motoring cap and *peau de bique* motoring coat, grimly clutching the wheel of his Panhard, enshrouded

The influence of the Italian Futurists is seen at work on this dramatic advertisement for Peugeot by Pierre Simmer in 1907.

The influential artist Ernest Montaut, who invented or popularized almost every visual device for conveying the thrill and drama of the speeding car, demonstrates his skills in this hand-coloured lithograph of 1906 entitled 'Circuit des Ardennes Belges'. It was such works by artists like Montaut that reinforced the romance of the high-powered car in the popular imagination.

René Vincent was at his best amongst the young and fashionable, when the beautiful car – in this case a Hispano-Suiza – was perfectly complimented by the equally beautiful people surrounding it.

in dust and exhaust fumes, while the epitome of a nineteenth-century lady with a small dog and parasol passes serenely, almost mysteriously, in the background – the contrast, as it were, between the pre- and post-auto age.

It was, however, largely the early poster and commercial artists of Paris such as Ernest Montaut, Bellery Desfontaines, Abel Faivre, A. E. Marty and René Vincent that established popular motor car art and many of the images of the car that still survive in contemporary culture. Ernest Montaut, in particular, who died in August 1909 aged a mere 31, was the most influential of them all, inventing or popularizing nearly all the artistic tricks for rendering speed. Montaut was a master of visual distortion; borrowing from photographic techniques, he blurred foregrounds and backgrounds as if out of focus; he conveyed impressions of speed by bending his cars, employing 'speed lines' sparingly, distorting wheels, making the front wheels larger than the rear, using dust and smoke strategically.

'Montaut's spirited designs must have decorated more showroom walls, private garages and enthusiasts' studies than any other productions of his time', D. B. Tubbs has written in *Art and the Automobile*. 'His big coloured lithographs were decorative, dramatic and very much in the spirit of the age. The *Belle Époque* was a time of heroes and hero worship and invention. People took pride in, identified with and took credit for new inventions like telephones, phonographs, airships, aeroplanes and motor cars.'

René Vincent was the other French artist who, like Montaut, but over a much longer period (he was born in the same year as Montaut but did not die until 1936), exerted tremendous influence over the European public's perception of the automobile. Vincent loved cars, fashionable women and society life, and as an illustrator for *La Vie Parisienne* for motor car manufacturers Berliet, Citroën and Peugeot and for *L'Illustration*, the Frenchman's window on the world, he was responsible for creating some of the most delicate and lasting dream images associated with the motor car. He became the prime interpreter of the car in social settings, as accoutrements of the wealthy. In his *Ambusqué* gouaches in 1915 (*ambusqué* meaning someone well protected from the firing line), a languid young officer heads off to an easy war with all the comforts of home in his elegant Peugeot; in 'Eve and her Car' a check-coated, fur-collared beauty stands next to her massive Delage, disingenuously clutching oil-can and spanner, a picture of both allurement and cool independence.

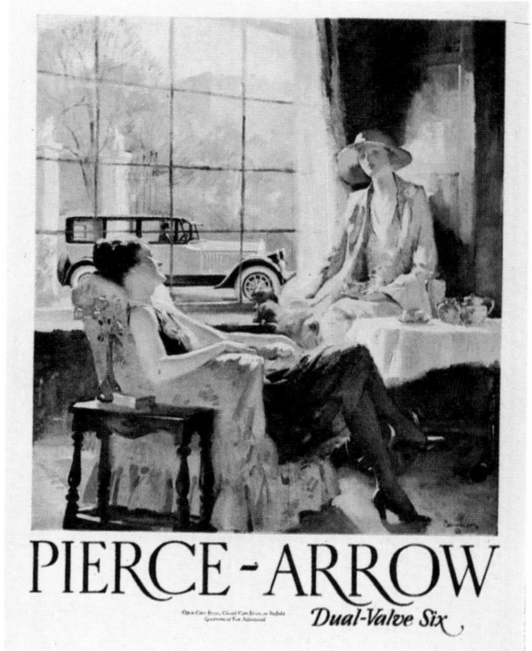

above] Certain cars were only used by certain people. Pierce-Arrow brilliantly reinforced the marque image with their understated soft sell in 1925.

The elegant but tough Teutonic goddess sits behind the wheel of her all-conquering machine – cool, confident and contemptuous of those around her. This arresting oil painting entitled 'Autoportrait', by Tamara de Lempicka, was commissioned as a front cover by the German magazine *Die Dame* in the 1920s and gives us one of the strongest images we have of woman and the motor car for that period.

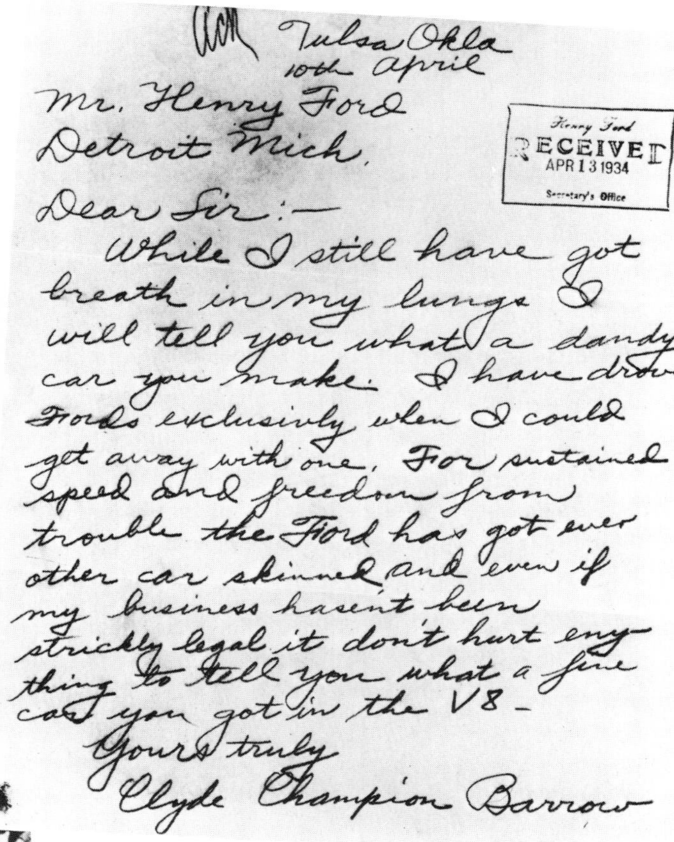

Tulsa Okla
10th April

Mr. Henry Ford
Detroit Mich.

Henry Ford
RECEIVED
APR 13 1934
Secretary's Office

Dear Sir:—

While I still have got breath in my lungs I will tell you what a dandy car you make. I have drove Fords exclusively when I could get away with one. For sustained speed and freedom from trouble the Ford has got ever other car skinned and even if my business hasen't been strickly legal it don't hurt enything to tell you what a fine car you got in the V8 -

Yours truly
Clyde Champion Barrow

Gangster Clyde Barrow poses menacingly with arsenal and getaway car (a Ford V-8 convertible sedan) in this photograph taken by fellow criminal Bonnie Parker and found in Joplin, Missouri in April 1933.

Both Bonnie and Clyde loved their Ford and are reputed to have penned this appreciative note to Henry Ford from a hideout in Tulsa, Oklahoma – a commendation which one suspects the Ford Motor Company could hardly have welcomed.

On the other side of the Atlantic, the image of automobiling was similarly establishing its clichés in the American consciousness through the work of artists commissioned by the manufacturers, newspapers, magazines and advertising agencies. The first decade of the twentieth century was the golden age of American illustration and commissioned work enjoyed wide circulation promoting and reflecting the public's interest in the new device. As in Europe, there was that triple concentration on the thrill of speed, the elegance of motoring and its participants, and the constant juxtaposition of woman and machine. Edward Penfield was perhaps the most prolific of all American automobile artists. In his work the motorists are always 'well garbed and well born', motoring still being strictly, at least until 1910, the sport only of the wealthy. In his cover for *Colliers* magazine in 1907, the elegant automobile family, with a chauffeur at the wheel, ride high and secure through the streets of Manhattan, surrounded on all sides by seething humanity, restrained from their path by a respectful policeman. Possession of a car means power, privilege and wealth – a theme pursued with such outstanding success even up to the time of the Depression by artists commissioned by the Pierce-Arrow Company. Cars are seen from the perspective of sophisticated ladies taking tea in large drawing-rooms, or a company president dictating final notes to a seated secretary in a baronial office, while the ship of state, glimpsed through the window – a Pierce-Arrow of course! – waits dutifully at the kerbside.

Perhaps the most American car picture of all time, and certainly the most widely distributed, was that done by William Harmden Foster in 1910 for Oldsmobile, in which an Oldsmobile Limited is portrayed racing against, and successfully outpacing, New York Central Railroad's crack Twentieth Century Limited. One wonders how many young Americans' first automanic fantasies in small towns across the continent were first fuelled by it.

Perhaps not as many as were being affected by the car as it appeared on the silver screen in movie houses around the world. For no other medium has been more responsible for influencing our attitude towards the automobile or reflecting its role in our culture than the moving picture. Hollywood and Detroit were born at the same time. Automobiles and movies shared cultural origins and grew in popularity together. Cecil B. De Mille, that archdeacon of the movie epic and avid car enthusiast, once pointed out that both auto and movie industries reflected 'the love of motion and speed, the restless urge towards improvement and expansion, the kinetic energy of a young, vigorous nation'. Both industries also quickly discovered a use for each other's products – the film industry in terms of the versatility of the

The Chicago Police took no chances in bringing back gangster Frank Zimmerman from Washington on 6 August 1933 in their Chrysler Imperial. The men in the photograph are all policemen and the car is armoured with bullet-proof glass and gun slots. Car chases in gangster films and photographs such as this have coloured, however unfairly, our perceptions of the city of Chicago ever since.

In Warner Bros.' "GOLD DIGGERS OF 1935," Buick is featured with Dick Powell and the Berkeley Girls. Warner Bros. consistently choose Buick for shots of lavish musical revue display, and for those depicting people in the modern manner. Today's Buick is exquisitely styled. It harmonizes perfectly with the advanced and newly created styles which Warner Bros. productions display.
Hollywood – Creator of Style – Chooses BUICK for Its Own
Buick
In brilliant Hollywood—where picture directors and stars create the styles for a nation—Buick plays the star style part. A world once ruled by Paris now looks to Hollywood; and there Buick is the featured car. In production after production, for the hit pictures of the year, Buick is chosen . . . just as it is favored by those who value the prestige of modish, modern design. ¶ All you have ever known or heard of Buick size and roominess . . . of Buick quality and dependability . . . luxury, performance and economy . . . is now surpassed. To see Buick today is to feast your eyes upon aristocratic, sparkling style. To drive it is to gratify your enthusiasm for unsurpassed performance and to enjoy the unprecedented ease and simplicity of the newest automatic operating features. To ride is to know the finest of all fine motoring. ¶ Twenty-five beautiful models, in four series. Four popular price groups, $795 to $2175, list prices at Flint, Mich. Prices subject to change without notice. Special equipment extra. Favorable G.M.A.C. terms.
$795
and up, list prices at Flint.
BODY BY FISHER . . . A GENERAL MOTORS PRODUCT
WHEN BETTER AUTOMOBILES ARE BUILT—BUICK WILL BUILD THEM

That symbiotic relationship between Detroit and Hollywood, with each exploiting the other's products, is perfectly expressed in this 1935 ad. for Buick.

Exoticars continue to massage Hollywood egos. But this car, like so much in 'tinsel town', is not entirely what it seems. With a clear nod to the legendary 1929 Mercedes-Benz SSK, the Excalibur – which established the replicar business in southern California – has a truck engine, a fibreglass body and uses scavenged components. Nonetheless, it still turns heads and looks a million dollars in a town where nothing is ever too outrageous.

below] Films used automobiles, automobiles used films. But not even the promotional efforts of these Warner Brothers' starlets could save the streamlined Chrysler Airflow, which was years ahead of its time. The public hated its looks. Made between 1934 and 1937, less than 30,000 were sold.

Director, actors and Hollywood film crew on location in the 1920s. The car had become the industry's most versatile prop and work tool, a role which only diminished with the coming of sound, when filming moved largely into the studios.

car as a cinematic prop and as a working tool, in addition to its not inconsiderable image-building possibilities for its stars, both on and off the screen. The automobile industry, in turn, quickly seized the vast opportunities for promotion of its products offered by this new and influential form of mass entertainment. Julian Smith, Professor of Film Studies at the University of Florida, has undertaken a major study of the relationship between Hollywood and Detroit, and cites Biograph's *Runaway Match* (1903) as the first true auto-centred narrative film:

Not only did the automobile supply film-makers with a natural subject for romance, comedy and adventure, but the narrative conventions that soon sprang up around movie automobiles helped intensify popular interest in the automobile itself . . . America fell in love with both movies and cars, while Hollywood and Detroit fell in love with each other. The star-in-the-car soon became a staple of publicity within both industries . . .

Runaway Match is the story of an elopement. A young man has been refused permission to marry the daughter of a rich man, so he rents a car (thus demonstrating he is a *really* smart young man) and elopes with her. The rich father pursues them in *his* chauffeur-driven car, but arrives too late to stop the marriage. There is a grand reconciliation with the father, no longer angry, inviting the wedding party to board his big touring car, and they all drive off happily together. Julian Smith calls these early films 'transports of delight' because the main themes associated with cars in the early films tend to have to do with elopement and with courtship. He also makes the point that from the beginning:

Automobility has been consciously marketed and both consciously and subconsciously embraced by the American public as a form of emotional transport, *the state or condition of being transported by ecstasy, of being enraptured. As Hollywood and Detroit came of age, they both learned how to supply dream vehicles that would carry us away from danger or boredom, transport us to better times and bigger adventures.*

Time and again in early films, young men demonstrate their adaptability, virility, even superiority, by utilizing the motor car – the new technology – to capture the heart of beautiful heroines, or to pluck them from the evil attentions of the villain. One of the greatest problems facing early film-makers, however, was that of managing to tell a romantic story built around a handsome young man who could represent the egalitarian values considered appealing to the mass audience. Democratic young men could not afford cars. Neither was it considered heroic to place the young man in the back seat urging on a chauffeur in the hot pursuit or, indeed, even to put him in the driver's seat as the chauffeur. Either role would have made him a menial hero. Hollywood's solution, again and again, was to feature the carless young man somehow taking over the rich man's car, knocking out his chauffeur, jumping from a horse or a train, or a tree into a car and taking control – which also invariably meant taking control of the future of the rescued girl. He who adapted to the new technology inherited the riches of the earth, in the shape of the gorgeous heroine.

A lunchtime break for film star Mary Pickford, with brother Jack, while on location for the United Artists film *Through the Back Door*. Behind is the indispensable accoutrement of stardom . . . the Pickford Rolls-Royce, described in the overblown prose of the studio press hand-out, as 'the most expensive car ever made'.

above left] Even superstar Clark Gable looks dwarfed by the vastness of his 1935–6 Duesenberg SJ short chassis Roadster. In Hollywood a 'Duesie' became the ultimate symbol of success.

left] Guess who . . . ? Still a long drive from the Oval Office, but with his Buick Electra firing on all eight cylinders, actor and now President Ronald Reagan gives a Detroit product the Hollywood smile.

above] Actress Jean Harlow displays all the trappings of success with her impressive 1932 Packard Dual Cowl, Dual Windshield Sport Phaeton.

right] 'Get 'Em in a Rumble Seat' said the chart topping song of 1927. In 1931 a young James Cagney did exactly that with co-stars Joan Blondell and Mae Murray.

Another solution to the chauffeur problem, demonstrated in at least twenty films made between 1913 and 1920, was for the rich young hero to masquerade as a humble chauffeur (or in some other car-related role), in order to place himself in suitable proximity to the heroine. The car is invariably the means of bringing about happiness – only villains career fatally over cliff edges (as in Edisons's *Dashed to Death* in 1909) or excaping convicts plunge to their doom in a stolen car (as in Vitagraph's *Wheels of Justice* in 1915).

Perhaps the most persuasive and frequent cinematic image relating to the car in early films is that which Julian Smith calls the 'happy accident'. Out of the 500 films that made significant use of the automobile between 1900 and 1920 in terms of theme or characterization, almost a third feature car mishaps (accidents, breakdowns and other misadventures) that 'lead almost invariably to happy outcomes: rich motorists stranded in the country, fall in love with beautiful farm girls, villains are punished in last-minute crashes . . . inconvenient spouses die so that love can triumph'. Thus while there was an early recognition that cars could be dangerous, in films they only killed off people who needed killing! Cars and what happened in them were extremely moral, and they were invariably part of a narrative system that resulted in happiness.

The first negative images of the car did not appear until 1942, in Orson Welles's *The Magnificent Ambersons*, based on the Booth Tarkington bestseller and Pulitzer Prize winner of 1918. Eugene Morgan, Tarkington's fictional pioneer automobile magnate, already senses that the effects of the automobile on society may be a step backward in 'spiritual civilization': 'Automobiles have come, and they bring a greater change in our life than most of us suspect . . . you can't have the immense outward changes that they will cause without some inward ones, and it may be that George is right, and that the spiritual alteration will be bad for us.'

Also two years previously John Ford had directed Steinbeck's *The Grapes of Wrath* and highlighted the inflated importance of the automobile in Depression society. The Joads hock everything and buy a used car, 'a jalopy' or 'rolling junk' and head 'west to California . . . where there's work and it never grows cold'. But their instrument of salvation, the automobile, in effect becomes their prison, transporting them from one transient community to another, their vision being gradually reduced to the narrow concrete miles: 'They were not farm men any more, but migrant men . . . eyes watched the tyres, ears listened to the clattering motors, and minds struggled with oil, with gasoline, with the thinning rubber between air and road. Then a broken gear was tragedy.'

However, until these latter-day reassessments, for cinema audiences around the world in the early years the car was seen as an object without criticism. It created happiness, brought success, excitement and fulfilment. It delighted audiences with its antics. For the majority, perhaps the most influential and lasting celluloid image of the automobile has been the car chase and the inevitable crash. The comic pursuit began with Mack Sennett who, it is said, was inspired to see the comic potential of the car in films by the Book of Ezekiel, 10:10: 'As if a wheel had been in the midst of a wheel.' In the hands of the Keystone Cops – and Harold Lloyd, Buster Keaton, Laurel and Hardy, and even Charlie Chaplin – the car became invested with an immutable life of its own, liable to collapse in pieces around its driver or

A despondent Oklahoma sharecropper, broken down near Indio, California, while the relentless black top stretches to the horizon. For many migrant workers the car could quickly turn from a symbol of escape, as it was for the Joads in *The Grapes of Wrath*, into an equally powerful symbol of hopeless frustration.

All the familiar frustrations of a Los Angeles traffic jam for Stan and Oliver Hardy and passengers. In their films they made some of the most inventive uses of the motor car as a comic prop.

career along the road out of control – yet in the end to miraculously survive these mishaps or collisions.

With the coming of sound, the development of wonderful images of the automobile slowed down, as film-makers moved indoors. Audiences could now, at least, hear the roar of the engine and the screech of brakes (bringing greater authenticity to many a chase sequence), and screen characters could talk about what cars meant to them, but the automobile essentially became a prop amongst others in the film-makers' repertoire. As Werner Adrian has pointed out in *Speed-Cinema of Motion*:

In the films of the great directors such as Godard or Hitchcock, the car has resonances beyond its appearance. It is fascism in Made in the USA, *it is conspiracy and disaster in* Pierrot Le Fou, *it is the total savagery and inanity of bourgeois values in* Week-End. *For Hitchcock the car can be both the vehicle of suspense and retribution. Who can ever forget the night-driving sequence in the rain in* Psycho *and the police car stopping the girl with the stolen notes, only to check her licence? Ingmar Bergman . . . can make even a Volkswagen appear to be a deathwatch beetle in* Wild Strawberries. *To the brilliant camera eye, a car is more than a car.*

In the late 1960s and early 1970s, however, the car chase and 'crash and bash' movies suddenly took on a life of their own. Films like *Vanishing Point* and *Bonnie and Clyde*, the acrobatic Minis in *The Italian Job* and Steve McQueen's frequently airborne Mustang in *Bullitt* displayed new levels of cinematic ingenuity in the use of the automobile. They also revealed a changing attitude towards the car – an ambivalence, even a disenchantment. As Julian Smith pointed out to us: 'Again and again the heroes in these

The car as star. One of the best loved car films of all time was *Genevieve*, made in 1953 with Kay Kendall and Kenneth More. The story was built around the London-to-Brighton Veteran Run. 'Genevieve' was a 1905 Darracq.

Kids, cars and cruising. One of the strongest American cultural images of the 1950s, re-created in the film *American Grafitti* in 1973.

movies are outlaws, rebels, people who use the car aggressively. I think these characters represent something that we wish we could be but know we should not be. And our whole love/hate relationship with these heroes is really a projection of how we feel about ourselves and our cars.' The mid 1970s were, after all, the last period – for Americans at least – of free and easy access to the road, with the introduction of the 55 m.p.h. speed limit, recurring fuel crises and the downsizing of the Detroit dream product to more workaday proportions.

The car has increasingly been viewed in negative terms. In *Breaking Away* (1979) the father of Dave, the film's hero, owns a used-car lot and as such is part of a system of values in which the car represents heavy, oppressive qualities, and is a symbol of the 'old' way of doing things. Even in *American Graffiti* (1973), very much a car culture film where young people's lives revolve around their automobiles, it is significant that the characters who are most fascinated with cars are the least successful. The boy who parks his car at the start (Dreyfuss) is the one who breaks away to college.

Even more explicit are those films where the car is predator and even killer as in *The Cars that Ate Paris*, *The Car* (in which James Brolin is pursued by a possessed killer car with no discernible driver) and, most recently, *Christine*. In the latter, a truly terrifying horror film, a sadly unattractive high-school student buys and restores a junk car with a mysterious history – it is one of those tailfinned monsters of the late 1950s – to find it possesses an uncontrollable killer instinct all of its own – a far cry from the gentler adventures of Kenneth More and Kay Kendall in *Genevieve* or the innocent delights of

The Love Bug, Disney's humanized 1963 Volkswagen Beetle, which becomes a person with feelings, miraculous powers and the ability to control the lives of the people around it. (In its first three films, featuring the chases and stunts that have become a trademark of the series, it brought in more than $200 million.)

Beginning with the James Bond *Goldfinger* Aston Martin in 1965 (even in its toy form it was the best-selling model car of all time), with its spitting machine guns, hot oil sprayer, hydraulic battering rams, bullet-proof shield and ejector seat, the cinema added a whole new dimension to the term 'dream machine'. The car at its most fantastic seems universally irresistible. 'Chitty Chitty Bang Bang', named after Count Zborowski's British racers of the 1920s, was in the musical film based on Ian Fleming's writings able to transform itself magically into a flying machine and a sea-going hovercraft . . .

Even if the youthful dream of the 1980s is now to take trips with computers rather than in automobiles, the car as star has none the less shown remarkable staying power with the mass audience. The very latest addition to the ranks of the wonder car is a product straight from the computer age. *Knight Rider*, proving itself to be one of the most popular American television series in recent years, features a car called KITT, a kind of avenging angel that can talk to its driver and make James Bond's Aston Martin seem positively archaic. Amongst its more than forty unique attributes are a rapid thought analyser, a microwave jammer, an infra-red tracking scope, an electronic field disrupter and a trajectory guide (able to launch KITT at any

The world's most desirable pedal car must surely be James Bond's Aston Martin DB5. Two one-third scale working models of the car were built at the factory – one was presented to Prince Andrew and survives; the other went to Prince Reza, son of the late Shah of Iran. Undaunted by the pistol-packing son of the Managing Director of Aston Martin, the Shah takes delivery in 1966. Where, one wonders, is the car now?

angle within a ninety-degree arc). It can even deflate and reinflate other automobile tyres! From Australia within the last few years have come the highly successful *Mad Max* films, and with their reworking of old stunt routines they have brought a new vigour and panache to traditional chase and crash sequences.

However, Kenneth Hay, Associate Professor of Film Studies at Brooklyn College, on the matter of the resilience of the car as an image in the cinema, admits that with the *Star Wars* genre, film-makers 'have been able to come up with a way to perfect even faster, more thrilling movement'. He believes:

cars have a kind of tactile, real working-class past, against a middle-class technological present and future. The cars did the things that are shown in films. They jumped other cars, they ran into other cars, someone drove them, someone there – even though they were stunt people – did the trick. No one does the trick in Star Wars. *It's all done with pencil and paper, with graphics, with computers. It's a non-experience experience. That may replace cars, but nothing else.*

One part of popular culture where the influence of the car is growing rather than diminishing is in the area of auto myths and legends. It was perhaps inevitable that an object as powerful in its attractions – especially to the young – and as mysterious in its workings, should become a rich source of folkloric stories rapidly replacing tales told by older generations about haunted houses, hunting adventures and witchcraft. There are three essential elements in all such legends: strong basic story appeal, a foundation in actual belief, and a meaningful message or moral. And they are of course, all communicated by word of mouth. Professor Jan Brunvand at the University of Utah in Salt Lake City has made a study of such auto legends, isolating several common themes. One of the most durable of such stories is the cheap car, the fantasy idea that somebody can get a wonderful car for a ridiculously low price. In one version known as 'The Philanderer's Porsche', somebody sees a newspaper advertisement for a fifty-dollar Porsche, answers the ad and immediately buys the immaculate vehicle from the woman who has been advertising it. Before departing with his bargain, the purchaser cannot resist asking her, 'Why have you sold this car for a mere fifty dollars?' She smiles and says, 'My husband ran off with his secretary and just wrote home saying sell the car and send me the money!'

'The Boy-friend's Death', a legend which has emerged since the 1950s, is part of a growing number of references in urban legends to the social effects of living in a youth-oriented, mobile, car-loving society. As Professor Brunvand explains:

The boy-friend's car stops in an isolated place. He goes walking off to get petrol or to get help to start the car and leaves the girl behind in the car. She locks the doors and windows and stays there. Increasingly terrified, she hears strange sounds or sees strange shadows and finally she is rescued in the morning by the police who tell her not to look back at the car. When of course she does (the rule in folklore is that taboos are always broken!), there is her boy-friend hanging upside down above the car decapitated by some maniac and his finger nails have been scratching the roof . . .

In such tales ('The Hook' and 'The Killer in the Backseat' are others), there are always incorporated the themes of young driver, defenceless female,

Millionaire Ray Holland in Allenstown, Pennsylvania, possesses one of the finest private collections of art and automobilia in the world. Housed in a single room, it provides evidence of the vast number of items made in the image of the automobile during the last hundred years. Formerly a poor boy from North Carolina, Mr Holland explains his love affair with the car: 'I've always been fascinated by it. The motor car brought colour into our lives but above all it was the means of taking us away to something better.'

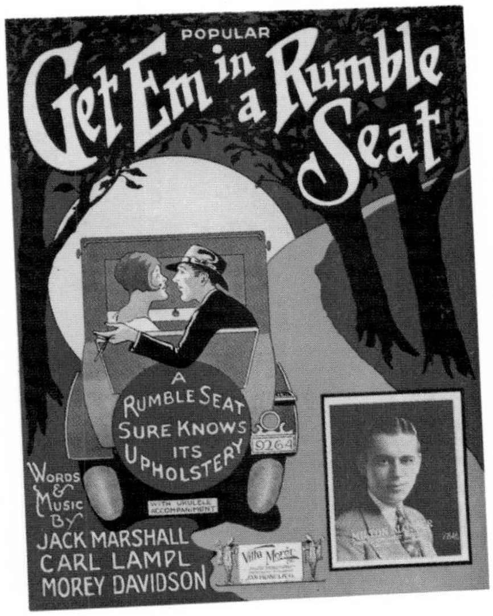

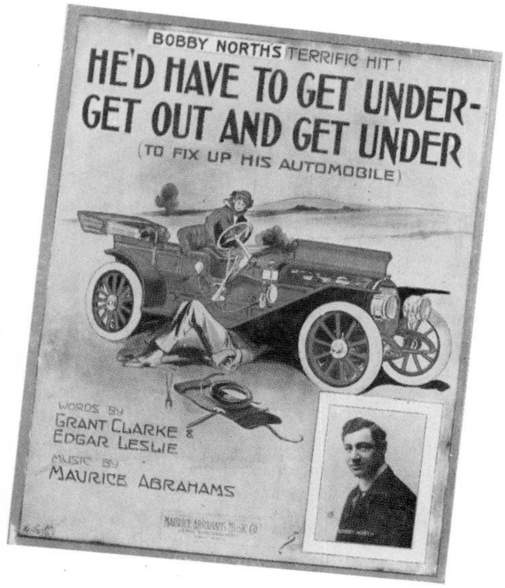

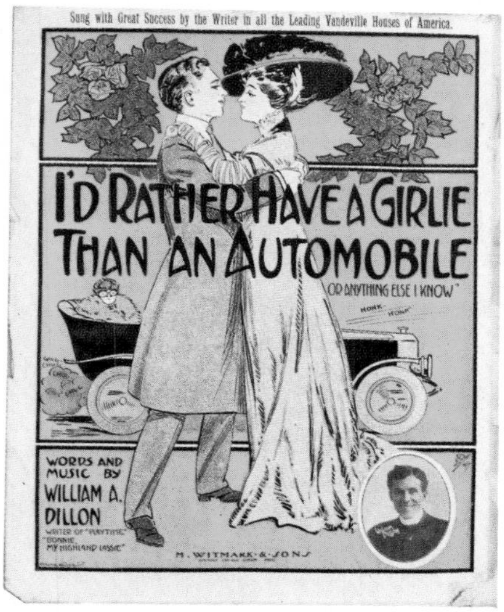

Of the six hundred songs written about the motor car, 'Love in an Automobile' by Alfred R. Dixon was the first to make the romantic connection in 1899. However it was in 1905, with 'In My Merry Oldsmobile' – music by Gus Edwards and words by Vincent Bryan – that the car song really caught hold of the public imagination. Marches, waltzes, two-steps and polkas poured from the pens of composers. Through to World War II the car song remained a staple item in Tin Pan Alley's output with such titles as: 'I'm Wild about Horns on Automobiles that go Ta-ta-ta-ta', 'I Love to Bumpity Bump', and the never-to-be forgotten 'Toot your Horn Kid, You're in a Fog!'

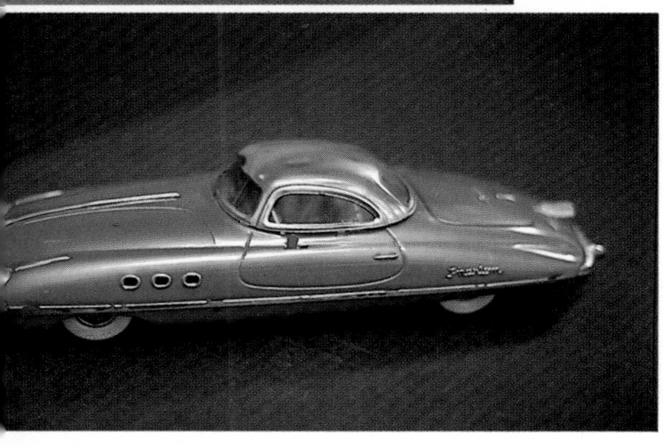

Tin toys are now highly collectable. British toy enthusiast David Presland, who also loves real cars, has several hundred tin toy cars in his collection. He says, 'What they really say about our relationship with the car is that although we are not able to drive in this country until we are seventeen, from a much earlier age we are being geared to be totally used to cars.'

opposite] Car books for children reflect all the adult images associated with automobile ownership . . . including the occasional encounter with the law. For the most part, however, the prevailing image is a happy one, with all the pleasures of the open road unfolding.

fearsome stranger, all of which highlight that the car – that most intimate of places – is not always a totally safe cocoon and indeed, by the nature of its mobility may be the means of placing us in extreme danger.

If the car has attracted its fair share of legend-making since the 1950s, nothing in the same period can have been more responsible for fuelling teenage fantasies about the car than popular music. As we have already seen, the car song has always been with us, at its strongest in the early days of automobiling with all those saucy numbers linking the car with romance, but it seems almost as if 'rock and roll' and 'cruisin'' were born for each other. From Bo Diddley, Chuck Berry, Jan and Dean and the Beach Boys through to the more recent prolific car-related compositions of Bruce Springsteen, every nuance of emotion in our complex love/hate relationship with the motor car has been explored. From love at first sight:

I remember the day
When I chose her over all those other junkers,
Thought I could tell
Under the coat of rust she was gold
No clunker . . .
The Beach Boys

to arrogance of ownership:

I got me a car and I
got me some gas
Told everybody they could
kiss my ass . . .
Glen Frey

even to confessions of eternal love:

Eldorado fins, whitewalls and skirts
Rides just like a little of heaven here on earth
Well buddy when I die throw my body in the back
And drive me to the junkyard in my Cadillac.
Bruce Springsteen

Also it is very clear that to be carless in an automobile world is painful:

O Lord, won't you buy me a Mercedes-Benz?
My friends all drive Porsches
I must make amends . . .
Janis Joplin

One final area of popular culture where our automanic fantasies have found their finest flowering has been in the extraordinary variety of items devoted to, or made in the image of, the automobile. Motoring ephemera in the form of bronzes, paintings, postcards, porcelain, mascots, silverware, to name but a few, can now realize huge sums of money. There are even clubs catering for those who collect hubcaps and sparking plugs! Model car collecting, in particular, has moved from being the casual pastime of a few people into a worldwide hobby of such proportions that it supports an industry.

It was once estimated that over an identical period of months, 2½ million real Citroëns were sold and 2,109,177 miniature models of the same car.

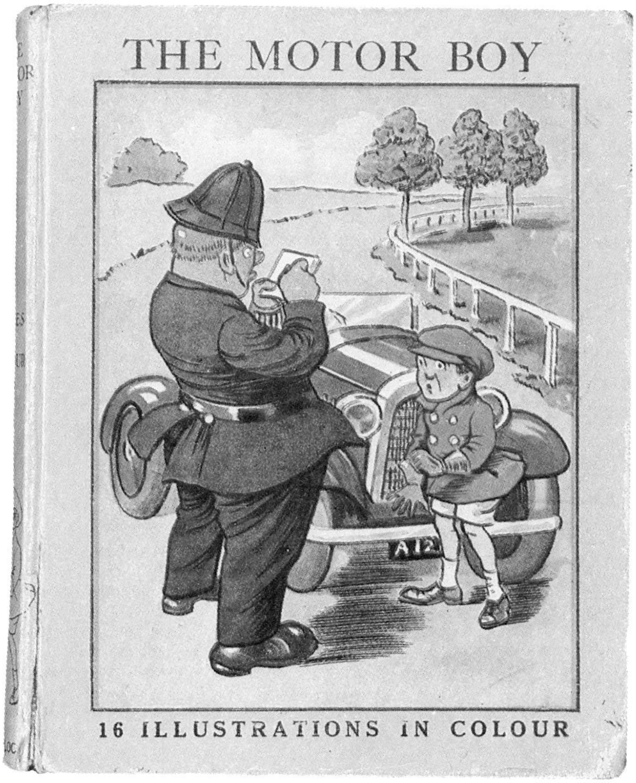
THE MOTOR BOY
A 12
16 ILLUSTRATIONS IN COLOUR

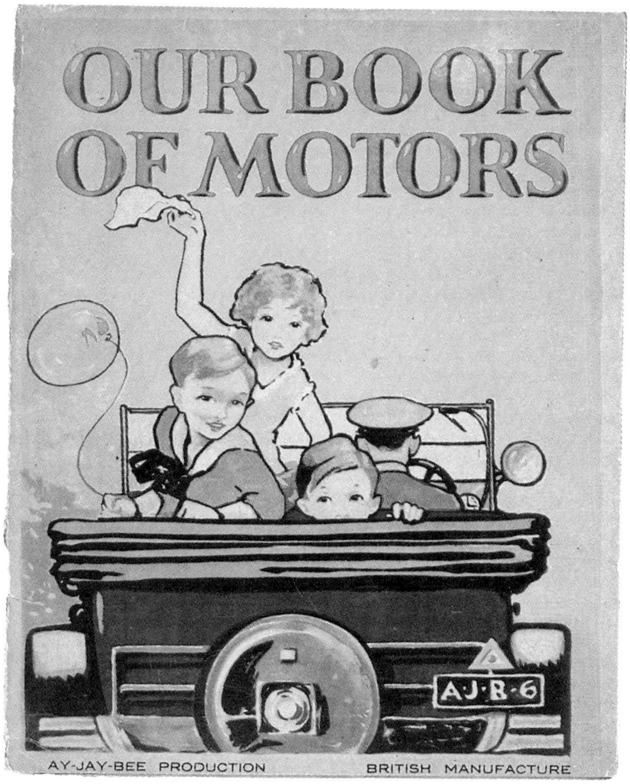
OUR BOOK OF MOTORS
AJ·B·6
AY-JAY-BEE PRODUCTION
BRITISH MANUFACTURE

Our Motor Car
EN-99
ERNEST NISTER LONDON
E.P. DUTTON & Co NEW YORK

top] Much modern car art suggests the affair is over. The shape and form of this car is still lovingly dwelt upon as it sits on its pedestal but, bereft of wheels in the lonely canyons of the city, it has ceased to be a transport of delight and is simply a junk object.

above] Bill Harding of Kansas City and his Grass Car – a 1966 Buick Le Sabre with a verdant covering of Manhattan perennial rye . . . He believes it symbolizes the delicate balance between nature and machines: 'You can't have perfect technology or pure nature; it has to be a balance of those two things for the world to work.'

right] At Jouy-en-Josas, south of Paris, an extraordinary car sculpture – a multi-storey memorial to the international obsession with the motor car – reaches for the sky. Dozens of cars embedded in a concrete column are polished daily with loving care.

right] A celestial chariot of blue and silver is carried through the streets of Hong Kong. For the status-conscious Chinese the car has become a highly treasured object. So much so, that when a rich man dies it is not uncommon for a large wood and paper model of his car to be made, complete with chauffeur and lucky number plate, which is then burnt by the mourners. Through this fiery offering the Oriental automaniac is guaranteed his favourite transport on the Other Side.

below] Man's continuing re-interpretation of the four-wheeled machine has shown limitless artistic ingenuity. This bizarre road monster, made in Norway by Ivo Caprino and called Il Tempo Gigante, seems to bear everything but the proverbial kitchen sink.

RB 1

GKD 2

The talented Gerald Wingrove, master model maker, with one of his Duesenbergs. He has built only 150 cars over a period of fifteen years. 'I consider the original is the work of art, and I try to miniaturize it,' he states.

André Citroën, the founder of the car manufacturing concern, once said that the first three words any French child could utter should be, 'Mama, Papa and Citroën'. Children should not say 'my car', but 'my Citroën', and to further this goal from 1923 to 1940 he produced 200,000 pedal car versions of Citroëns every year. Perhaps the world's finest model-maker of today is Englishman Gerald Wingrove whose specially commissioned metal models (he has a penchant for Duesenbergs of the late 1920s and early 1930s) are exquisite works of craftsmanship, if not art. His total output over a period of fifteen years has not numbered more than 150 models. He sums up, perhaps best of all, why the car has played such a dominant role in popular culture:

I think the car is the twentieth-century sculpture. You see these lumps of stone with big holes in them and people think this is art. I think in a thousand years' time people will wonder what on earth they are. I think the artist of the twentieth century is the engineer and to me this is the nearest man has ever got to nature, to produce something which is an extension of himself and to make it beautiful as well. I don't think anything really compares with the car for this.

above left] Just like Daddy's! Made by the Austin Car Company between 1949 and 1971, 32,000 of these J-40 pedal cars (known appropriately as 'joy cars') adorned Austin showrooms and became every schoolboy's dream. Modelled on the Austin A40 (background), they were designed and manufactured on actual car principles at a factory in Wales.

left] Toy pedal cars of exquisite workmanship are still being made for young automaniacs with rich fathers. This reproduction of the Citroen '5CV' of the 1920s is handcrafted by Lely Small Cars in England.

Future Car

Probably the genius and practical sense of the British engineer will lead him to seek a solution of the problem with the aid of steam, for I think it highly improbable that motor cars working with highly inflammable or explosive oils will ever take hold in England to any great extent owing to the danger of handling the stuff; while electricity is still more, at present, out of the question owing to the cost of its production and the weight of storage batteries required.
(*Newcastle Daily Chronicle*, 1895)

At every stage of its development, from its infancy to the present day, there have been those who claimed that the motor car had no future. History has proved them to be profoundly wrong. Equally, there have always been those who forecast a more exciting and extravagant future for the car than it has ever been able to achieve. Fifty years ago, designers and dreamers were prophesying that by the 1980s we should be transported by a wondrous fleet of flying cars, amphibians, rocket and nuclear powered machines of a kind that inhabit the pages of Dan Dare. Typical of this advanced thinking was the wonder car created by the late philosopher–scientist R. Buckminster Fuller. His eleven-passenger, 120 m.p.h. Dymaxion, a streamlined three-wheeler with the rotary manoeuvrability of a pirouetting dancer, was conceived in 1927 as 'omnimedium, wingless transport' for ground, air and water travel. It made a successful debut in July 1933, but crashed at 70 m.p.h. on a Chicago road later that year when its driver rashly became involved in a high speed race with another car. Even another Dymaxion, completed in 1934, could not counter the unfavourable publicity and the project died. More recently a Canadian, Dr Paul Moller, while working as Professor of Aerodynamics at the University of California, developed a series of two-seater Flying Saucers in his search for a low-cost sky-car. In 1971 Dr Moller said: 'What I've tried to do is simplify the machine to the point where it can be mass produced at the price of an automobile, and build in the safety factor necessary so that a housewife can fly to the local market.' Production never commenced.

opposite above] In the days before futurologists were inhibited by the realities of space travel, this is how artist Syd Mead saw the Ford cars of the space age. By that time we should all be running a fleet of special cars, including luxury vehicles like this one – capable of space travel as well as short intercontinental commuter trips on Planet Earth.

opposite below] The Moller Flying Saucer or 'Sky Car', 1971. Lift and propulsion were provided by the outer ring which spun at high speed to provide a gyroscopic effect sufficient to enable the craft to cruise at 240 k.m. per hour, carrying ten times its own weight.

In reality, we are still driving around in vehicles based on that same nineteenth-century technology employed by Daimler and Benz one hundred years ago. As the car enters its second century it seems that in the foreseeable future what we shall be getting from the carmakers is more of the same. Although designers and engineers speak of exciting changes in the pipeline, not one of them forecasts the imminent disappearance of the power unit descended from the Otto engine or the two-box profile. On two developments they are all agreed: the car of the future will be made of different materials, and electronics will play an increasingly prominent role in its engineering. According to Professor David Cole of the University of Michigan, the cost of the vehicle represented by electronic systems will rise rapidly from about 5 per cent to at least 15 per cent in 1990. By that time, he believes that microprocessors will be standard in almost all vehicles and that at least one computer will provide the motorist with instant information on the state of tune and maintenance needs of the vehicle. As to whether we are approaching the age of the 'driverless' car, there is much less unanimity. Professor Cole certainly expects to see navigational aids such as an electronic display on the dash that gives the driver his pinpoint location from a satellite signal:

'I think the application of this electronic technology is going to be dramatic and it is ultimately going to lead to the so-called "driverless car".'

Professor Hubertus Christ, Head of Vehicle Research at Daimler-Benz, has collaborated on the project 'Auto 2000' funded by the West German government to develop and test passenger cars which are to exceed the state of the art in all essential criteria. His findings so far lead him to be much more sceptical than the Americans about the increased application of electronics. As for the 'driverless' car which steers, brakes and accelerates automatically and which looks ahead using radar, Professor Christ reports gloomily that the systems developed for 'Auto 2000' proved to occupy more space, to be heavier and much more expensive than estimated: 'The idea that the tiny microchip would revolutionize the motor vehicle quickly proved to be a Utopian dream.' There is also the crucial question whether the motorist wants all these additional electronics. Even Professor Cole admits, 'It would take one of the most important elements of the car away from us: the fun of driving. I'm not sure we are yet ready to accept that. I'm not.'

Vehicle safety experts hope that the information systems of the future car will help the drivers avoid accidents by giving them warning of changes in road and traffic conditions. However, they are concerned by the forecast that, in the never-ending efforts to reduce vehicle weight and improve fuel consumption, steel content will be considerably reduced and replaced by plastic in all its forms.

As long as the world does not experience another major oil crisis, it seems that the internal combustion engine and the diesel will be with us for a while yet. Engineers point out that enormous improvements have been made in its performance and some believe that there is still a lot further to go. The Japanese, who have done so much to make our cars more fuel-efficient, believe that it is still possible to go on improving fuel consumption by about 1 per cent a year.

As far as appearance goes, it is likely that our cars are at last going to start *looking* more like those futuristic vehicles of science fiction. In their efforts to make their cars slip through the air more easily, all designers are turning for help to the wind tunnel and it is the resulting 'slippery' look that will dominate the motor shows of the future. Does that mean that the present trend of all marques of car – particularly small cars – tending to look alike, will continue? Here opinion is again divided. Mr Akira Hosono, engineering chief of Toyota, believes it is unavoidable. 'When you are restricted by size, striving to be cost effective and produce the best and most efficient car for the money, similarities will inevitably arise. It is something that gives us a headache.' All design studies show the car of the future becoming increasingly ovoid. Chuck Jordan of General Motors and Sergio Pininfarina reject this boring vision of the future. Both stylists insist that even within the constraints imposed by the wind tunnel, safety regulations and cost, it will still be possible to create car designs as stirring and as individual as anything we have seen in the last hundred years: 'In the pell-mell to build smaller, more fuel-efficient vehicles, some of us seem to have forgotten an important ingredient – simple attractiveness and excitement,' says Chuck Jordan. 'The love affair with the automobile is alive and well. All it takes is an exciting car to kindle to flame.'

Gordon Buehrig, who as chief designer for Duesenberg created in the thirties some of the most timelessly elegant automobiles ever built, reminds

When in 1976 Farina was asked by the Italian National Research Council (CNR) to produce the ideal aerodynamic shape, this was what he came up with. Some critics unkindly called it the 'banana car'.

Despite today's modish talk about drag coefficients and wind tunnel testing, this Dixi experimental electric car, with its aerodynamic styling, dates from 1925.

us that there is nothing new about aerodynamics, that the wind tunnel was invented early in the century, and that it doesn't necessarily sell cars. 'When the salesman says to the customer, "Look, this has a drag coefficient of 0.32," and the customer says, "I don't care, I don't like it", it is evident that it is a great fallacy for the designer to become a slave to the wind tunnel and to the computer.'

What will fuel the car of the future? Following the Arab oil embargo of 1973 and the subsequent surge in the price of fuel, the Automobile Association reported that British motorists would be prepared to pay as much as £1.00 a gallon before considering other means of transport. Today they are paying almost double that price and show no sign of abandoning their cars. Nevertheless, an absolute shortage of oil could undoubtedly render the present generation of cars functionally obsolete, unless of course we can find alternative fuels. As we have seen, Brazil has already moved towards fuel independence by stepping up production of ethanol, and South Africa has gone even further by investing hugely in a new plant for producing methanol from coal. These are undoubtedly the two fuels that could most readily provide the alternative to gasoline. In 1979, however, Saab-Finland introduced a multi-fuel engine capable of running on fuel distilled from timber, so that the nation could aim towards self-sufficiency, and in the continuing quest for other means of filling the tank researchers around the

Cars have already been propelled by fish oil and orange peel so there is nothing too outlandish about a future when they will run on solar cells or biomass, as the German visions suggest.

The search for alternative fuels predated the OPEC energy crisis by many years. This experimental German vehicle crossed the Alps in 1936 using only wood as a fuel. Then, as now, the objective was to free the car from dependence on imported oil. During the trial, the car crossed twelve Alpine passes in eight days and gave no trouble. How much wood was consumed is not recorded.

Judging by this drawing, dating from forty years ago, it was assumed that by now our motorways would have highly banked corners and would be flanked by massive searchlights, loudspeakers and mirrors.

world have come up with some exotic possibilities. Cars have been built that run on sardine oil, extract of orange peel and chicken manure. None of these would seem to present a long-term solution.

On a more realistic tack, biochemists have been looking with interest at a whole range of plants which produce not carbohydrates like sugar, but hydrocarbons that resemble the chemical structure of fossil petroleum. The most remarkable is an Amazonian forest tree, *Copaiba langsdorfii*, which is said to yield a sap so similar in make-up to diesel that it can be used straight from the tree to fuel a diesel truck. In the Philippines, the National Oil Corporation has planted several hundred hectares of Hanga, the petroleum nut tree, which has already proved to be a valuable source of fuel for household use and which the Japanese exploited to run tanks during World War II. Although these hydrocarbon plants offer interesting possibilities, their large-scale cultivation arouses the same concern that surrounds the production of alcohol from sugar cane in Brazil: that the diversion of land creates competition between growing food for people and fuel for automobiles. Even the production of synthetic fuels from coal and from oil and tar sands does not escape this criticism. All the industrial processes involved consume huge quantities of water and inevitably, where supplies are limited, it would be a question of whether to give priority to the needs of the car or of agriculture.

below left] Forty years before the opening of the M1 in 1959 Lord Montagu (father of Lord Edward Montagu) envisaged this trunk road from London to Birmingham.

below] From time to time, planners have moved in the direction of a multi-level solution to the problem of congested city centres. We can be grateful that this 1920s view of the future metropolis has been realized only in the artist's sketchbook.

In 1948, the American Sports Car Company looked into its crystal ball and saw the sports car of the future looking like their custom-built Tasco.

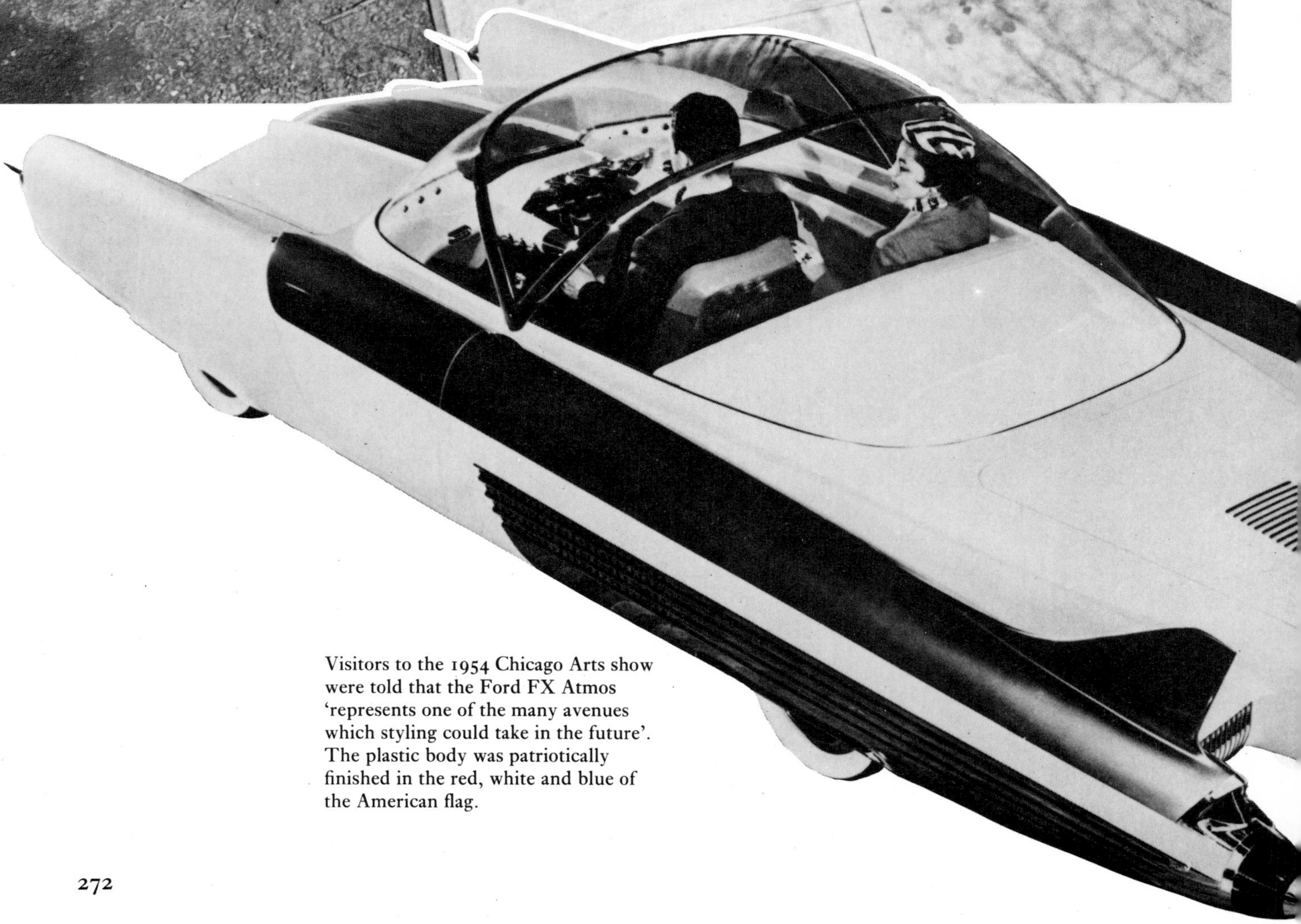

Visitors to the 1954 Chicago Arts show were told that the Ford FX Atmos 'represents one of the many avenues which styling could take in the future'. The plastic body was patriotically finished in the red, white and blue of the American flag.

1979 Ford Probe 1. The idea for this fascia panel for the Maserati Boomerang was conceived by Giorgio Guigaro and then elaborated by Ford engineers at Dearborn, who added the illuminated digital displays and the keyboard controls for a pair of computers.

Once again the influence of aircraft design is seen in this 1967 research vehicle, the Chrysler 300X, described as 'mobile proof of what's ahead of you in safety, style and comfort'. Not too many of its features are yet with us. We do not steer with retractable handles and employ a TV camera and screen to replace the rear-view mirror, nor do we feel a strong need for a front passenger seat which swivels 180°, or ashtrays that empty by vacuum action at the touch of a button.

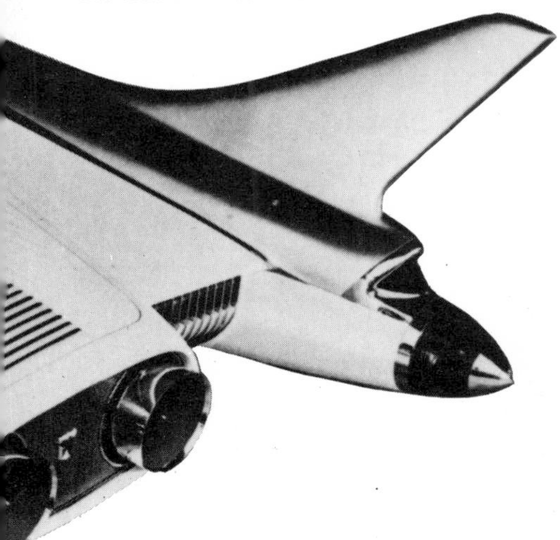

A vehicle of the future-"The Autohydrogyro".
The Autocar

Flying cars have long haunted the imagination of designers. This 'Auto hydro gyro' of 1936 goes one step further and proposes a flying amphibian. Even the extreme demands of a world war never made it a practical proposition.

With these rather dismal prospects of finding alternative fuels that are economically and socially acceptable, the possibility of developing engines that do not require liquid fuels clearly merits attention. The shortcomings of the electric vehicle are well known, and until there is a great leap forward in battery technology its potential use is limited. According to one view, the best long-term solution lies with a power unit fuelled by hydrogen. Roger Billings, one of America's most dynamic young engineers and entrepreneurs, believes passionately that hydrogen is the supreme energy source of the future. His hydrogen powered vehicles are already on the road and he states confidently that 'the day will come, in my lifetime, when all cars will run on hydrogen'. Among the advantages the hydrogen car offers, Billings numbers 'the fact that hydrogen is pollution free . . . but the real driving factor is that hydrogen can be produced on a limitless basis from many natural resources and it's going to be the sheer economics of it that will encourage the world to convert in the future.' However, in order to produce substantial quantities of hydrogen from water, a 'clean' energy source, such as electricity produced by nuclear energy, would have to be available. After testing more than 1200 vehicles using methanol, hydrogen and electric power units, Auto 2000 researchers concluded that 'there is no comparably suitable fuel for the road as gasoline or diesel fuel produced from crude oil'.

1951 Aerocar. This was a creditable attempt by Molt Taylor, an American aviation enthusiast, to produce a flying car. He designed and flew this machine which could be driven normally to an airport, towing its wings and fuselage in the form of a compact trailer. Taylor built a dozen or so such machines over a period of twenty years, but he never managed to achieve his ambition of mass production.

Shorn of its wings the Aerocar became a little runabout that would go almost unnoticed outside the supermarket.

If the internal combustion engine is to remain the principal technology for the next few decades, how efficient could it ultimately be made? Experimental vehicles have achieved astounding mileages, in excess of 2000 m.p.g., and there are many pressures, beside uncertain oil supplies, nudging the auto industry in the direction of still smaller, lighter and more efficient cars. It is above all the plight of the cities that demands it. At a World Congress on Housing and Planning in Paris as far back as September 1962, it was moved by delegates still in the grip of automania that maximum city populations in future should be held to 700,000 people, as in cities of that size it would still be possible to arrive at reasonable automobile traffic arrangements. Robert Bradbury, the then director of housing in Liverpool, England, was even able to remark: 'Traffic is the life stream of the twentieth century. It is a sign of success and prosperity. After all, what is a pedestrian? He is a man who has two cars, one being driven by his wife, the other by one of his children.' Japanese manufacturers, responding to the needs of the especially congested Japanese cities, are now pushing ahead with a new generation of mini-cars, some electric and some gasoline powered, that are likely to become a familiar sight on our city streets in the future. In Europe too where twentieth-century growth has often been imposed on medieval street design, there will be increasing emphasis not just on scaling down cars but on excluding them entirely. During the 1960s and 1970s, dozens of European cities found that the introduction of pedestrian precincts greatly improved mobility and increased the attraction of city centres. In Tokyo's Ginza and several other popular shopping areas, motor traffic is banned on Sundays, and once people regain possession of the streets an extraordinary air of carnival prevails. Much to the delight of shopkeepers, business has generally been improved by these schemes and it seems certain that we shall see them greatly extended in the years to come.

In Denmark, the use of the car is already severely limited in metropolitan areas, not just by cost and by regulations but by public attitudes, which according to one view may soon render the ownership of automobiles both socially and economically unacceptable. An official Swedish 'think-tank' has recommended that the use of private cars should be phased out entirely in urban areas. Resources should be diverted, it says, to expanding public transport systems. These would be backed up by fleets of hire cars for out-of-town excursions and recreational use.

Despite the alleged strength of Scandinavian public opinion against the car, one cannot help wondering whether the motorists elsewhere are ready to be deprived of their personal transport, meekly to return to buses and trains. In the United States, only if the love affair with the car has drastically cooled could one expect such an eventuality; and that is precisely what one researcher claims has happened. Dr Richard Michaels, working in Chicago, has found that attitudes towards the car have become increasingly negative. Only among very young drivers does he find the familiar symptoms of automania; those over twenty-five are displaying distinct signs of autophobia. Dr Michaels puts forward an intriguing thesis. He points out that as we grow older, we become psychologically and physiologically more economical in our ways. Older people travel less; furthermore their attitudes towards travel change. They become increasingly aware that the demands of the car run quite contrary to their inclination towards greater economy. Twenty years ago the automobile consumed about 15 per cent of disposable income

Long before the present obsession with 'slippery' shapes, the maverick designer Luigi Colani was insisting that body contours should undergo fundamental changes for aerodynamic reasons. These two proposals, dating from the late 1960s and 1970s, are in sharp contrast to the box-like and razor-edged shapes coming from most stylists during that period.

Sports car - 1978 スポーツカー

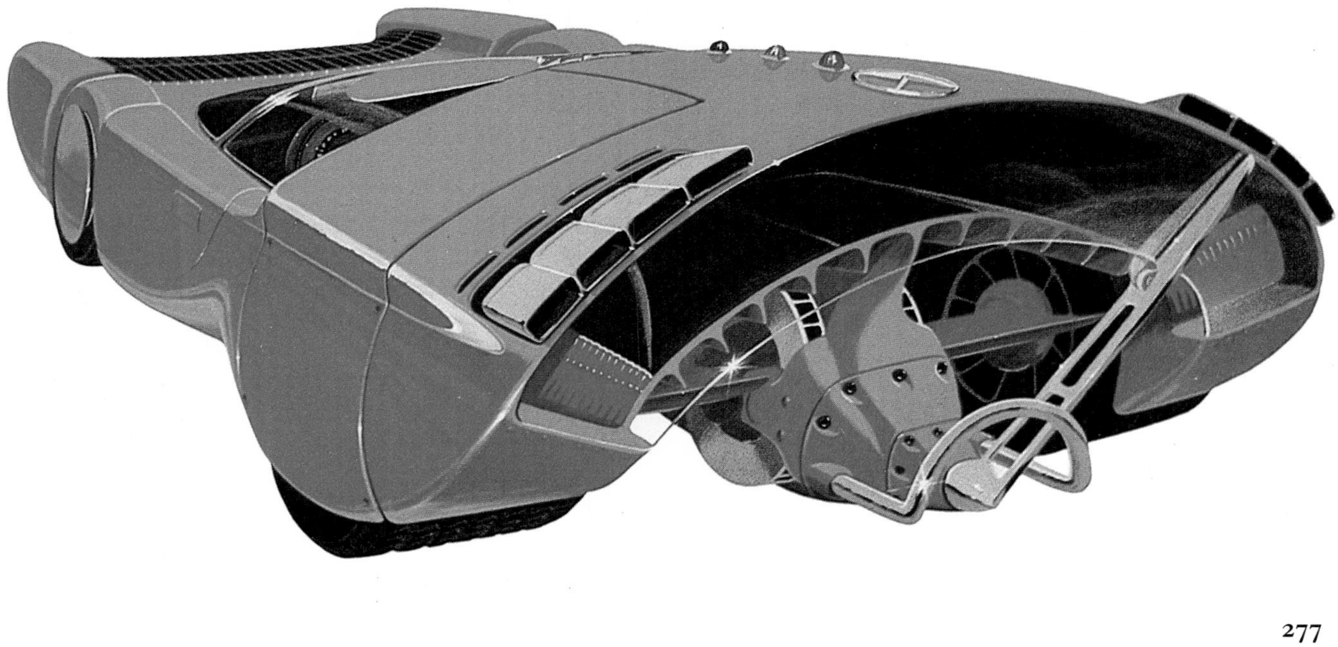

How some of the top stylists have seen the car of the future.

above] The Lamborghini Athon by Bertone, 1981.

opposite below] The Megastar advanced concept model by Ghia. This design, done for Ford of Europe, used glass for 80 per cent of the total area of the front doors and 60 per cent of the rear doors.

opposite above] The Spa. Another idea from Ford. This time a sports car, also by Ghia.

to own and operate; now it is more than 20 per cent. But above all, Dr Michaels says, driving a car has become an increasingly stressful occupation and, as older people strive to conserve their energies, they seek to avoid this stress and find some alternatives to the car. What one of these alternatives might be is now emerging. The scenario sees a future where the need to travel has largely been removed by electronic communication and by computers. We shall shop and work from our own homes and when we do wish to travel, we shall use some form of public transport. Road vehicles would still be needed but largely to convey goods and services. 'As I see these changes occurring', says Dr Michaels, 'the automobile is going to become unnecessary. We shall look back at it as an anachronism that lived for a short time in history and we shall wonder why it lived that way at all.'

Even those who confidently expect to see the car banished from the cities concede that it will continue to have a role in rural areas. Only a highway transportation system can satisfy the needs of a very diffused, low-density population; and in the United States, in these circumstances, the car would be returning to its original mission, defined by Henry Ford as 'getting the farmer out of the mud'.

While North America is still the largest single automobile market in the world, the highly profitable 'growth' markets in the next decade and beyond will be those outside the United States. After all, between 1960 and 1980 American demand for motor cars grew by 39 per cent while demand in Europe for the same period increased by 188 per cent and in Latin America by 600 per cent. This trend is not likely to be reversed in the foreseeable future. There will also be fewer manufacturers. In the 1960s, for example, there were over 110 car manufacturers worldwide; today there are fewer than 30. With increasing internationalization of the industry and new alliances and amalgamations, by the beginning of the twenty-first century it is likely that number will be at least halved again.

ACTION

The future of the car will present governments and the auto industry with complex choices and individuals with difficult personal decisions. Although most governments outside the Communist bloc have encouraged and tolerated the movement towards motor car-centred transport systems – and still do – there are signs that this is changing. Although few communities have so far been able to summon the political will to take the most drastic measures, it seems certain that the freedom of the motorist will be more and more restricted in the years to come. The right to personal transportation will no longer be considered inalienable; it will be regarded more as a privilege that can be withdrawn, as it is in the centrally planned economies of eastern Europe and the Soviet Union. The Bulgarian magazine *Autoturism* recently reported that a man convicted of stealing hens from a state-owned poultry farm was sentenced to a gaol sentence and had his car confiscated. Loss of car rights is a sanction we all might face in the future.

With all this in mind, who can doubt that in the first hundred years the golden age of motoring is already past? Some would say that it is long past, that the few who were lucky enough to be at the wheel during the twenties and thirties enjoyed a style of motoring of which we shall never see the like again.

Today it is hard to rhapsodize about the wind in your hair, the sweet sound of a well-tuned engine and the ribbon of road unrolling ahead, when the car you are driving is nagging you in nannyish tones to moderate your speed or to fasten your seat belt; and when, at the end of the road, traffic wardens are licking their pencils and the clamp squad is preparing to put in the Denver Boot. The fun of driving has been very much a part of Automania and what will happen when the fun runs out is something we shall discover in the next hundred years.

Selected Bibliography

Bardou, Jean-Pierre; Chanaron, Jean-Jacques; Fridenson, Patrick and Laux, James M.
The Automobile Revolution.
The Impact of an Industry.
University of North Carolina Press, 1982.

Bayley, Stephen.
Harley Earl and the Dream Machine.
London: Weidenfeld and Nicolson, 1983.

Belasco, Warren James.
Americans on the Road. From Autocamp to Motel, 1910–1945.
Cambridge, Mass: The MIT Press, 1979.

Berger, Michael L.
The Devil Wagon in God's Country.
The Automobile and Social Change in Rural America, 1893–1929.
Hamden, Connecticut: Archon Books, 1979.

Bhaskar, Krish.
The Future of the World Motor Industry.
London: Kogan Page Ltd., 1980.

Brunvand, Jan Harold.
The Vanishing Hitchhiker.
New York: W. W. Norton & Co., 1981.

Cavalcanti, Lauro and Guimaraens, Dinah.
Arquitetura de Motéis Cariocas,
Espaço e Organização social.
Rio de Janeiro: Espaço, 1982.

Dettelbach, Cynthia Golomb.
In the Driver's Seat. The Automobile in American Literature and Popular Culture.
Westport, Connecticut: Greenwood Press, 1976.

Doolittle, James Rood.
The Romance of the Automobile Industry.
New York: Klebold Press, 1916.

Dorney, Muriel.
An Adventurous Honeymoon.
The first Motor Honeymoon around Australia.
Brisbane: The Read Press, 1927.

Dunn, James A. Jr.
Miles to Go. European and American Transportation Policies.
Cambridge, Mass: The MIT Press, 1981.

Flink, James J.
America Adopts the Automobile, 1895–1910.
Cambridge, Mass: The MIT Press, 1970.

Flink, James J.
The Car Culture.
Cambridge, Mass: The MIT Press, 1975.

Girard, Joe.
How to Sell Anything to Anybody.
New York: Warner Books Inc., 1981.

Heimann, Jim and Georges, Rip.
California Crazy: Roadside Vernacular Architecture.
San Fransisco: Chronicle Books, 1980.

Indigo, Elizabeth.
Harmonie sexuelle dans une automobile.
London: Fitzwilliam Publishers, 1971.

Jerome, John.
The Death of the Automobile.
New York: W. W. Norton & Co., 1972.

Kamata, Satoshi.
Japan in the Passing Lane.
New York: Pantheon Books, 1982.

Keats, John.
The Insolent Chariots.
New York: The Lippincott Co., 1958.

Lee, Raymond.
Fit for the Chase. Cars and the Movies.
Castle Books, 1969.

Levitt, Dorothy.
Woman and the Car.
London: John Lane, The Bodley Head, 1909.

Lewis, David L. (Ed.)
'The Automobile and American Culture.'
Michigan Quarterly Review,
University of Michigan, 1980.

Lynd, Robert S. and Helen Merrill.
Middletown: A Study in Contemporary American Culture.
New York: Harcourt Brace, 1929.
Middletown: A Study in Cultural Conflicts.
New York: Harcourt Brace, 1937.

Mandel, Leon.
Driven. The American Four-Wheeled Love Affair.
New York: Stein & Day, 1977.

Mitsukuni, Yoshida.
The Wheel. A Japanese History.
Tokyo: Cosmo Public Relations Corp., 1981.

Mumford, Lewis.
The City in History. Its Origins, Its Transformations and its Prospects.
New York: Harcourt Brace Jovanovich, 1961.

Nader, Ralph.
Unsafe at Any Speed: The Designed-In Dangers of the American Automobile.
New York: Grossman, 1965.

Piccard, Jean-Rodolphe.
The Automobile Year Book of Dream Cars. Their Design and Development.
Lausanne: Edita, 1981.

Plowden, William.
The Motor Car and Politics, 1896–1970.
London: The Bodley Head, 1971.

Prille, Pol.
Bois de Bologne, bois d'amour.
Paris: Editions Montaigne, 1925.

Rae, John B.
The Road and the Car in American Life.
Cambridge, Mass: The MIT Press, 1971.

Ramsey, Alice Huyler.
Veil, Duster and Tire Iron.
Privately printed, Covina, California, 1961.

Rothschild, Emma.
Paradise Lost. The Decline of the Auto-Industrial Age.
New York: Random House, 1973.

Sears, Stephen W.
The Automobile in America.
New York: American Heritage Publishing Co. Inc., 1977.

Stern, Jane and Michael.
Auto Ads.
New York: Random House, 1978.

Sturmey, Henry.
On an Autocar Through the Length and Breadth of the Land.
London: Iliffe Sons and Sturmey Ltd., 1897.

Sutton, Horace.
Travelers. The American Tourist From Stagecoach to Space Shuttle.
New York: William Morrow & Co., 1980.

Thompson, J. Michael.
Great Cities and Their Traffic.
London: Victor Gollancz, 1977.

Tubbs, D. B.
Art and the Automobile.
London: Lutterworth Press, 1978.

Warnock, C. Gayle.
The Edsel Affair.
Arizona: Pro West, 1980.

White, Jean (Ed.)
The Saturday Evening Post Automobile Book.
Indianapolis: The Curtis Publishing Co., 1977.

Wik, Reynold M.
Henry Ford and Grass-Roots America.
University of Michigan Press, 1972.

Wilson, Paul C.
Chrome Dreams. Automobile Styling since 1893.
Radnor, Pennsylvania: Chilton Book Co., 1976.

Yates, Brock.
The Decline and Fall of the American Automobile Industry.
New York: Empire Books, 1983.

Picture Credits

The contemporary material in this book was photographed by Nigel Turner. The authors are grateful for the photographic materials and generous help provided by the following individuals and organizations: The Academy of Motion Picture Arts and Sciences, Los Angeles; Alternative Car Magazine; Automobile Quarterly Publications, Princeton; Auto Zeitung, Cologne; Business Press International Ltd; Chrysler Motor Corporation, Detroit; Ford Motor Company, Detroit; General Motors Photographic, Detroit; Ray Holland Collection, Pennsylvania; Metropolitan Police, London; National Archives, Washington; Merle Norman Cosmetics, San Sylmar, California; Paper Moon Graphics and Carol Bouman, Los Angeles; Jean-Rodolphe Piccard, Lausanne; Perry E. Piper and the Edsel Owners Club; Press Association, London; Peter Blair Richley, Ashford, Kent; Dick Teague of American Motors; Verkerke and Jan Hunt, Holland; State Library of Victoria, Australia; Michael Woodward Associates and Mal Watson, Harrogate, Yorkshire.

The authors wish to thank and credit the following collections: BBC Hulton Picture Library, London: 17 middle, 52, 96, 233; The Bettmann Archive, New York: 48/49, 85 top; Bilderdienst, Süddeutscher Verlag, Munich: 23, 70 top, 158 top, 177 top, 206 bottom, 222 bottom, 265 bottom, 269 bottom; Henry Austin Clark Jr Collection, Glen Cove, NY: 18, 20, 39 top, 64–65, 86, 148, 152, 156 top left, 171 top, 203 bottom, 242–243, 248, 249 top, 251 bottom, 272 top; Culver Pictures, Inc., New York: 43, 82/83, 85 bottom, 94, 221 top, 232; Detroit Public Library: 44 bottom, 218 top; Mary Evans Picture Library, London: 13 top, 40, 71, 73 top right, 92 bottom, 93, 108 bottom, 184, 204 top, 224–225; Kobal Collection, London: 252–253; Library of Congress, Washington: 39 bottom, 127, 226; Loomis Dean, Life Magazine, Time Inc., New York: 100; Mansell Collection, London: 190 top, 240 bottom; Motor Vehicle Manufacturers Association, Detroit: 41 bottom, 44 top left, 50–51, 54–55, 62 bottom, 63, 66/67, 68, 70 bottom, 74, 87, 90/91, 97, 98, 101, 102–103, 149, 153, 156 bottom, 157, 159, 160 top, 172, 191, 203 top, 210–211, 249 bottom; Museum of the City of New York: 14, 73 bottom, 170; National Motor Museum, Beaulieu: 17 inset, 19 bottom, 22, 38, 42, 46 bottom, 110, 147, 150, 160/161, 174/175, 188 bottom, 218 bottom, 221 bottom, 270 bottom, 271, 278/279; New York Historical Society: 10; Punch Publications, London: 204 bottom; Smithsonian Institution, Washington DC: 182, 190 bottom, 202; Western History Collections, University of Oklahoma Library: 88 bottom, 155 bottom, 251 top.

Index

Index